A MUSICAL
CRITIC'S HOLIDAY

A MUSICAL CRITIC'S HOLIDAY

ERNEST NEWMAN

NEW YORK

ALFRED · A · KNOPF

MCMXXV

TO
VERA

THE ARGUMENT

The critic, distracted and puzzled by the clash of opinion in the world of music, withdraws a while from that world to think things over. Is there any possibility of reaching certitude in our judgments, seeing that music is always changing, always adding to its vocabulary and its technique?

Objective and subjective criticism in general. Anatole France's dictum. The theory that criticism is, and can only be, and ought to be subjective breaks down in the hands of the very people who profess it. In the act of denying that standards can be objective, they virtually claim to possess such standards themselves.

Can anything like a technical basis for criticism be discovered,—something roughly corresponding to the technical fundamentals of composition?

Why not make a study of a representative critic of the past, (as a scientist would study an organism), trying to see just how the critical faculty functioned in him, the principles, true or false, on which he worked, how far he succeeded or failed, and why?

Johann Christian Lobe taken for this purpose. His *Letters of a Well-known* (1852). Except for the differences in the names, it might be the music and musicians of our own day that he is discussing. His theoretical principles are admirable; but in spite of these his judgment of his contemporaries is sometimes at fault. What can we learn from his mistakes?

Necessity for the critic to stand apart from the cliques of his day, and see his own age—so far as this is possible—as if it were a remote historical period, to separate the vital composers of the day from the composers who will be forgotten in a generation or two. In every period of change, the minor artists and their partisans tend to deflect the judgment of the critic. The point illustrated from the early history of French romanticism.

But is it possible for the critic to know the vital from the secondary minds among the composers of his own day? Does not musical history abound in instances of great composers being neglected or abused by their contemporaries, and having to wait for posterity for recognition? Had not a Monteverdi to contend with an Artusi, a Mozart with a Sarti, a Wagner with a Hanslick? Detailed examination of these cases, as well as those of Bach, Gesualdo, Beethoven and Hugo Wolf. The conclusion reached that, contrary to the accepted legend, there is no case in musical history of a composer being so much in advance of his time that only a few chosen spirits were capable of appreciating and understanding him.

No need, then, for the critic of today to turn over to posterity the task of seeing contemporary music in its true focus. Our own age can be as sure as any other which are its first-rate and which its second-rate composers. The true reproach against past criticism in general is not that it has failed to welcome the great master but that it has been too generous in its welcome to many who were only minor masters.

Having studied in Lobe a complete critical type, and learned what we can from his successes and his failures, can we also study a complete period that resembles our own, and apply to the criticism of the music of our own day the lessons learned from the course of events during and after that period? Our own time is one of radical change, both in musical theory and musical practice. For purposes of comparison we want a similar period of radical change. There has been only one such in history—that of 1600.

The many resemblances between that epoch and this, the lessons we may learn from these, the laws we may formulate as being valid for all periods of violent change. No great composer uses all the theoretically possible resources of his time. "Progress" largely the work of men of the second or third rank. "Progress" a term without real meaning, for none of us can foresee the evolution of music for even a dozen years ahead. Innovators generally despise their "conservative" predecessors or contemporaries; but it is the work of these latter that survives, while the work of the innovators is mostly, for succeeding ages, only of antiquarian interest. Little or nothing durable comes from the movement of revolt until it is fertilised by some of the more stable forces of the past. Thus the Florentine "reform" remained largely theoretical, doctrinaire, and dilettantish in the hands of its first practitioners; it needed, to vitalise it, an admixture of the despised technique of the "conservatives." The future is veiled from us; all we can be sure of is that it will correspond only imperfectly with our forecast of it,—for two reasons.

In the first place, the vital changes in music come not

so much from a general and conscious movement in a direction that is clearly seen, as from the irruption of some original, incalculable, and highly dynamic mind. In the second place, the doctrinaire idea is always modified by pressure from a thousand other forces.   Thus the Florentine speculation ended, not as its originators thought it would, in a re-birth of the Greek drama with music, but in a very different thing—the Italian opera. All talk of "pioneers" among us today is thoroughly vain, for until the future has revealed itself no one can be sure whether the "pioneer" has led music into an inhabitable new territory or into a *cul de sac*.   Originality of itself counts for little, for there are two kinds of originality—one that matters and one that does not. The opener out of a new path may prove sterile, while a Bach, who originates nothing, may be a seminal force for all succeeding generations.

Resemblances between the experiments of our time and those of earlier days.   Our wilder polytonality anticipated by the improvised discant of the fourteenth century.   Evidence of Jean de Muris.

The critics of the late Wagnerian epoch faced by much the same problems as ourselves, especially that of distinguishing between the vital men of the period and the mere imitators and speculators.   Hirschfeld on de Muris and his own period—that of 1884.   The minor Wagnerians—Kistler, Ritter, etc.,—are now forgotten.   The critics of that time who saw that these men would soon be forgotten were no doubt charged with impeding the progress of the art; but they were merely seeing things as they were.   It is the task of the critic of today to see contemporary personalities in their true relative proportions.

The critic should look backward rather than forward. He cannot hope to deduce the future from the present; but he can read the present in the light of the past. "Back thought" more difficult than forward thought.

Is "Criticism of the Living" so difficult as is generally supposed? "Progress" and "reaction" in the past; Chorley, Rossini, Beethoven and others. No classic a classic to his own generation, which rightly calls a fault a fault in him when it sees it. Posterity too sentimental towards the classic to be ideally judicial with him.

Genuine criticism must always function in the past rather than the present. It is only from the past that our aesthetic standards can come, and these are valid for any new form of the art. Let the critic leave the future alone. We do not know which of the speculative theories of our own time will survive and be fruitful; but we can be pretty sure which of the music of our own time will live.

I

A MUSICAL CRITIC'S HOLIDAY

I HOPE some one will break it as gently as possible to London music, but however much it may be distressed at the news, London music will have to struggle on as best it can without me for a few weeks. I am going away to think things over. I would put it that I am going up into a high mountain to pray, but that a musical critic's troubles are not, as a rule, of the sort in which prayer is indicated. But at any rate I am going up into a high mountain, and if I cannot save my critical soul there by prayer, perhaps I can by quiet thought.

I often wonder if men in other professions ever grow as doubtful not only of themselves but of their work— and by "their work" I mean not so much their actual daily labour as the very principles upon which they labour—as the musical critic does. Perhaps the conscientious clergyman does at times. Charles Bradlaugh, I have read somewhere, used to receive letters from clergymen confessing that they had no longer any faith in the fundamentals of the religion they professed, but asking despairingly how, at their time of life, and with their domestic responsibilities, they could be expected to throw away their only means of livelihood. But a clergyman, though his faith be fled, can still find reasons that seem to him, and perhaps to others, valid for remaining in the ministry. He can still salve his conscience with the hope that he may have more opportunities for helping the sick and sorrowful of soul by remaining within the Church than he could outside it. The first principles of his theology may have been shattered; but a minister of religion is not wholly and essentially and exclusively a theologian, and there are other and greater first principles upon which he can still act.

The lawyer, I fancy, knows no such doubts and torments of conscience. He cannot and ought not to consider any first principle but that of his profession, which is to do the best he can for his client in a professional way, without making himself the judge of the moral aspects of his client's case. Nor does the doctor, I imagine, lie awake o' nights searching his soul to find whether he is or is not justified in continuing his practice. A good deal of his diagnosis and prescription must necessarily be guesswork; but at any rate there is some sort of a science of medicine, and certainly a very solid science of physiology. And if his practice must often be little more than a fumbling in the dark, at least he has certain unshakable first principles to hold to, and the hope to sustain him that every experiment he makes may bring him a step nearer to the truth.

But the musical critic has no established first principles to start from. He is far worse off in this respect than the practitioners of the other arts, for these remain fairly constant, not only in objects but in material, while the material of music is always changing, and with the changes come new forms and new ideals of expression. Roughly speaking, the vocabulary and the grammar of each nation's speech have remained unchanged for centuries, and, in the nature of things, can change very little in the future. But the grammar

and more especially the vocabulary of music have
changed enormously in the last three hundred years
alone, and, so far as we can see, new additions will
be made to them, new changes rung upon them, in
every century to come. Are standards of criticism,
that is to say, of judgment, possible under conditions
such as these? The very unchangeableness of the vocabulary and of the "genius" of a language are bound
to give a certain uniformity to the poetry of a nation
throughout its history; but the character of a nation's
music may alter greatly in the course of a few generations. A lyric of Heine has not travelled one-
thousandth part of the distance from a lyric of Wal-
ther von der Vogelweid, or from one of the German
folk-poems of the thirteenth century, as a song by
Hugo Wolf has from the German folk-melody of that
period; while there is no comparison between the distance that separates the first Elizabethan dramas, or
even the earlier mystery play, from the drama of
to-day, and the distance that separates the first Florentine operas from the music drama of Wagner. Music,
from age to age, has acquired new harmonies, new
techniques, new instrumental colours, and these, orig-
inating in new desires for expression, have themselves
awakened new visions in composers. So the process
has gone on from generation to generation, and so, we
may be sure, it will continue. But how can critical
standards pretend to any sort of fixity under conditions that are always changing? We can say that the
latest English poem is good or bad in virtue of its
possessing or lacking certain qualities that our experience of five centuries of English verse shows us to be
inseparable from good poetry; however personal a
new poet's outlook may be, his excellences, when we

isolate them by analysis, will be found to be, in essence, the excellences that are the essence of Chaucer and Shakespeare and Milton and Keats and Herrick. But is it possible to say of any new music that it is good or bad in virtue of its possessing or lacking certain things that make the excellence of the music of the past?

To appreciate the distinction more fully, let us imagine a lover of poetry and a lover of music each to have been suddenly transported into a century or two later than his own. A man of Chaucer's day—we might even say a man of Æschylus's day, had Europe known but one language for the last three thousand years—would find little difficulty in deciding whether *Hamlet* was a great work or not. The man of Herrick's time would find no difficulty in taking his bearings in the lyrical poetry of to-day. But what would a man of the twelfth century who knew (apart from folk-songs and dances) no music but plain song and the first experiments in organum have been able to make of a mass by Palestrina or a madrigal by Gesualdo? What would Peri or Caccini, or any other of the Florentine reformers, or even Monteverdi himself, have been able to make of *Tristan* had he been brought to life about 1870 and suddenly set down in a German opera house? Would the composer of *Sumer is icumen in,* had he been reanimated in Leipzig in the early eighteenth century, have been able to follow the complex figuration of a Bach chorale prelude? What would John Bull have been able to make of one of the late Beethoven quartets, or even of the *Eroica?* Would Corelli have been able to make head or tail of Bela Bartok's second violin sonata? Would the composer of any of the old German chorales be able to find his way about in a song like Hugo Wolf's *Auf dem grünen Balkon?* What would a great sixteenth-century contrapuntist like Byrd make of Schönberg's *Pierrot Lunaire?*

To ask these questions is to answer them. Any one of these re-visitors of the glimpses of the moon would, for a time at any rate, be completely at sea in the music of a few centuries or even a few generations later than his own. These cases, of course, are extreme ones; but it has been the experience of almost every generation to find the vocabulary, the grammar and the technique of music changing, as it were, before its eyes, to be called upon to pass judgment upon works of a type more or less new, and to wonder whether it was justified in doing so on the strength of the laws of beauty it had been able to deduce from the music of the past and the present.

*

* *

There are epochs in which this problem of judgment becomes particularly acute. The present is one of them,—and only the second, perhaps, in all musical history in which the past and the future of music have for the moment seemed to be irreconcilable. For some three hundred years no such problems have faced the critics as those that now confront us. During those three hundred years the development of music, despite the differences of genres, has been virtually along the one line, and from, say, 1610 to 1910, to judge fairly any new and "progressive" work of his day, a man had only to apply with just a little more elasticity the principles he had learned from the music of the immediate past. I do not mean that judgment was always easy; but this was only because of the difficulty this or that individual might find in making his own principles sufficiently elastic. But I do maintain that so gradual and so consistent was the evolution, so naturally did one style, one form, grow out of another, that the standards that had served for the judgment of previous music were equally applicable to the new music. Once the principle of canonic and other imitation had been discovered, it was a matter of quite gradual evolution to the complexities of the most advanced vocal and instrumental polyphonic forms. Once the harmonic sense had been started, it was only a matter of gradual evolution to the most complex harmonic thinking of yesterday. No ordinarily musical mind that had been brought up on Schütz could find much difficulty in Bach; nor need any man whose life stretched from 1700 to the day before yesterday have found the slightest difficulty in placing himself at the harmonic point of view of each successive innovator. I say "need not" advisedly. We know that almost every harmonic innovation has puzzled, and perhaps shocked, some contemporary listener or other. But the shocked ones have mostly been pedagogues and theorists, whose freedom of assimilation was hampered by their belief that the "laws" of their schools and their text-books were rooted in Nature itself. But whatever a few people of this kind may have said about the harmonic innovations, these presented no difficulty to the average man who, having escaped the petrifying intellectual influences of an academic musical education, listened with his ears and his imagination alone. Unfortunately the musical histories tell us nothing about these people—what, indeed, is there to tell about them?—while the historians go on making an absurd fuss over some pedant or some ignoramus whose inanities happen to have been recorded in print.

I am not contending, then, that harmonic and other innovations have not puzzled or outraged a few theorists or a few of the less musical people in each generation, but simply that there was no need for the average intelligent musical hearer to be puzzled or outraged by them. There is a logic in these things that is quite irresistible. Every new harmony that talks sense is merely an expansion or a subtilization of some previous familiar harmony, or a short cut between harmonies that once lay at a certain distance from each other; and the plain man who is unfettered by theory instinctively recognizes it as such. He knows that he is simply being taken a step or two farther along the well-known road, or by a shorter route than the old one; and though what he sees on the journey is new, it is not essentially different from the things he has been used to seeing all along the road he has so far traversed. If this were not so, indeed, how could any new harmony establish itself? We must always distinguish between harmony that, as I have put it, talks sense, and harmony that talks nonsense. Against the latter the horse sense, if I may so call it, of the average musical mind revolts at once. But in the case of harmony that is not nonsensical but merely unusual, it will generally be found that the opposition to it has come not from the plain man but from the hide-bound theoretician, who judged by the eye rather than by the ear. The plain man, knowing nothing of harmonic analysis or the "laws" of harmonic combination and progression, is as a rule hap-

pily ignorant whether a new texture *is* new or not, or
in what respect it is new; all he knows is whether it
pleases him or not, whether it does or does not carry
on the composer's thought logically.   There are tens
of thousands of unschooled hearers, for instance, who
have no notion that the harmony of Scriabine's
Prometheus and of other late works of his is largely
based on a chord-system of superimposed fourths.
But it is not necessary for them to know this, any more
than it is necessary for the lover of a simple song to
know that some of its harmonies are tonic, some
dominant, some sub-dominant, and all the rest of it.
All that is required is that he shall be able to follow
the composer's thought as expressed in the harmonies.
(Indeed, the composer himself would generally be
hard put to it to account theoretically for his new
chords; as Dr. Eaglefield Hull laments, "even down
to the present day musical composers have shown
themselves singularly ignorant of the laws of acous-
tics."   They have managed, however, to do their
work pretty well in spite of that.)   The theoretician,
on the other hand, is often debarred from the æsthetic
enjoyment of a passage by his purely intellectual revolt against something in it that flouts what he has
been taught to regard as the correct procedure.   Wagner long ago pointed this out in connexion with a
passage in *Lohengrin*.   These modulations, he says,

confused even a good musician like his friend Uhlig
when the latter first saw them in the score, but they
seemed quite natural to him when he heard them.
There have been many passages in music that have
puzzled the professors greatly, and the plain untheo-
retical and untheoritized listener not at all.

*

*   *

As with the vocabulary of the art, so with its forms.
Broadly speaking, each of these has grown so imper-
ceptibly out of its predecessor that no ordinarily intelligent musical mind that could think in terms of the
earlier form could find any difficulty in adapting itself
to the later.   Vocal music has gone stepwise from the
simplest folk-song to the subtly wrought songs of Hugo
Wolf, and from the most primitive piece of "imitation" to the intricate voice-weaving of the madrigal.
Instrumental music has gone stepwise from the primitive dance tune, with its simple balance of parts, to
the fugue of Bach and the symphony of Beethoven,
Brahms, Franck and Elgar.   Opera has progressed
stepwise from the *Euridice* of Peri, or those still
earlier quasi-dramatic tentatives of the sixteenth
century with which modern research has made us acquainted, to the opera of Verdi, of Wagner, of Strauss,

of Moussorgsky, of Debussy. In none of these instances has progress consisted of anything but putting old material to new uses, expanding it and adapting it as was necessary.

Moreover—and this is the point to which I have been working—in all this long evolution of three hundred years there was no point at which either composers or listeners felt any necessity to break with and contemn their predecessors. European musicians were as one family, engaged in a family business, in which each generation took up and carried further the work of the generation that preceded it. Nowhere and at no stage of the evolution did anyone hold that his forerunners had worked upon a fundamentally wrong conception of the nature of music, and feel that it was his duty to scrap some or all of them and make a new start along new lines. Naturally there have been periods when men thought comparatively lightly of this or that predecessor. But that was only because they felt that there was nothing more to be done along the predecessor's lines, and that salvation for themselves was to be found only along a road of their own. They sometimes thought their own work more vital than that of their fathers; and it is one of the laws of artistic and literary evolution, as of social and political evolution, that the generation with which men feel themselves to have least in common is the one immediately preceding their own. But the musicians who thought their own methods of art more advanced than those of their immediate forerunners did not regard these people's work as a mistake and a danger. Philipp Emmanuel Bach could refer to his father as "the old pig-tail." That is quite understandable. The Germany of the second half of the eighteenth century—the Germany of the *Aufklärung*—was so different from the old Germany of which Sebastian Bach was the final, indeed, the belated, summing-up that it could be excused for feeling that John Sebastian was a little old-fashioned and frowsy. But though Philipp Emmanuel, in his search for new forms and new expressions, may have missed a good deal of the greatness that the world to-day sees in his father, he never despised him: he might call him, with affectionate roughness, an old pig-tail, but he would never have called him an old fool. He was too well aware of his own indebtedness to him for that.

The history of those three hundred years is a history of the willing learning of the younger composers from the old. Even in that changed Germany of which I have just been speaking, we have the picture of the eager young Mozart, finding himself at Leipzig in possession of the separate parts of Bach's motets (there were no scores of them), distributing them around him and piecing the work together in his imagination. The forms in which his own genius impelled him to work were mostly different from those of Bach, but he could never have made the mistake of supposing that there was no bond of union between Bach and himself. Bach, again, was the humble pupil not only of his German predecessors and contemporaries but of the great Frenchmen and Italians. Mozart and Haydn did not disdain to learn from each other, nor Beethoven from both. Wagner's method of thematic working is in large part a conscious development from that of Beethoven, and no later symphonic writer has repudiated his own debt to these two forerunners. Every Italian opera composer of the last three centuries has followed unquestioningly in the footsteps of his predecessors. In France, even the revolutionary Berlioz based himself, in theory at any rate, on Beethoven and Gluck. The new methods of Liszt, so fruitful for modern music, merely tried to graft the poetic principles of one developed form of German art —the song—upon those of another—the instrumental form of Beethoven. Occasionally a highly original artist has made a sharp cut away from the main line— Moussorgsky, for instance, in his children's songs and Debussy in *Pelléas et Mélisande;* but these new organisms have proved, so far, practically unfruitful. The great things in music in the last three centuries were done by each successive artist reshaping to his own purposes the vocabulary, the idiom, and the forms of his predecessors in general and nourishing himself on some predecessor's spirit in particular; and though many of the new men flattered themselves that they had carried their forerunners' work a stage further, none of them flattered himself that in comparison with him his forerunners were idiots.

*

*   *

No critic who thinks at all about his work can feel anything but depression after twenty years or so at it. How little truth he seems to himself to have talked all this time, and how much error! It is, of course, some consolation to him to run over mentally the record of his colleagues and to recognize how much more of error they have talked than he, and how much less of truth. But if *they* reflect upon their business at all they are probably making a similar comparison and congratulating themselves that they are not as he is; so this leaves us all pretty well where we were. Is any criterion of judgment to be found? I myself, for instance, think Hugo Wolf a very great master of the song. But this morning some anonymous person sends me a cutting from which I see that A—— has the poorest possible opinion of Wolf. In my endeavour to account for this divergence of opinion I remember—and, I hope, give due weight to the fact —that A—— is himself a composer of songs, and very popular songs too, songs about "you" and "God" and "gardens" that are sung by the most admired of England's queens of song. This is more than can be said for Wolf; I cannot think, at the moment, of any of our queens of song who put his name on their programmes. I recognize, then, that, as a successful specialist himself, A—— has some right to treat a less successful colleague like Hugo Wolf *de haut en bas*. But even so my spirit is a little perturbed. For I have given some study to all the great song writers of the world (including, I need hardly add, A——), and I am bound to say that Wolf still strikes me as having the qualities of a master. And when I look round I find that a large number of people—singers, historians, critics and ordinary music-lovers—whose opinion on music I have learned to respect, think as I do on the matter. Wolf cannot be both a first-rate lyrist and a third-rate one. What then is the explanation of this difference of opinion?

Or look at a case of another kind. Stravinsky, whose genius I admired till, as it seemed to me, it began to decline for a time, brought out a few years ago a number of pieces in the smaller genres—songs, pieces for clarinet solo, music for strings, etc. I gave a good deal of careful study to these works, and the only conclusion I could come to was that they were mostly feeble in idea and experimental in expression. I felt that if these works had appeared under any signature but that of the composer of *Petrouchka,* most of them would have been laughed out of court in five minutes. But to my amazement one or two of my colleagues hailed them as revelations of a new spirit in music. One of these critics launched this staggering question at myself and other people of my way of thinking: Suppose we were presented with music in a completely unfamiliar idiom, such as Chinese, could we expect to grasp it in a moment? Would we not have to get used to its novel way of expression before we could be capable of judging it, or even comprehending it? Even so, we were given to understand, was it with these new works of Stravinsky. We poor dullards might, in time, have the felicity of comprehending them, even as B——— and C——— already did; but for the present we ought not to show our ignorance by condemning them out of hand.

In this particular case, however, one could perhaps fall back on some general principles. Moreover, we could apply what is known to logicians as the law of parsimony—the law that forbids us to hunt for a remote and complex explanation of a given phenomenon when a simple explanation lies close to our hand. For instance, if I find my cat dead and the remains of a poisoned mouse by her, it is more reasonable for me to suppose that the cat has died of eating the mouse than that the cook has slain both her and the mouse by witchcraft. Now in the case of these works of Stravinsky we can ask ourselves one or two eliminating questions in the vein of the law of parsimony. I talked about these works with a great many excellent musicians; I read a large number of critical notices of them in both the English and the foreign press. Nowhere did I find the works hailed as revelations by anyone of unquestioned standing in the world of music, with the solitary exception of one eminent conductor. Perhaps his liking for these works may not be incapable of explanation, for different men may like music for different reasons. But I just note the fact of his admiration, without feeling myself under the obligation to account for it. I am content with the basic fact that, so far as my researches went, he was the only musician of any standing to take these works seriously. Am I not entitled, then, to ask whether it is reasonable to suppose that he was right and everyone else—and I can vouch for it that "everyone else" in my own circle of acquaintance and in my own reading included many musicians of the first rank—was wrong?

By way of answer to this, of course, the argument from China may again be brought forward. But here too, surely, the law of parsimony should be invoked. In the whole history of music can anyone point to any works other than these of Stravinsky that their admirers have attempted to justify in such terms? Let us grant that now and then a work has given its first hearers the feeling that nothing of the kind had ever been heard upon the earth before. Any of us would no doubt have said this had we been present at the first performance of *Tristan*, or, to take perhaps a still more instructive instance, at the first performances of the first experiments of Peri and Caccini in the new *stilo rappresentativo*. But in neither of these cases would an ordinary cultivated musical hearer have felt that the music was so utterly unlike any other music that he had ever heard as to justify him in comparing it for strangeness with an art so remote from ours in mentality and methods as that of China. The man who heard *Tristan* for the first time might feel that here Wagner was often thinking far ahead of him and too rapidly for him, but he would know also that this rapidity was only an acceleration of the ordinary pulse of ordinary music, and that he would catch up with Wagner in a day or two. He would feel that the composer was here simply expanding and subtilizing the resources of his own earlier music and those of his predecessors. He would certainly not feel that here was a species of music to which the music of Beethoven, Schumann, Chopin, Liszt and others, as well as Wagner's own *Lohengrin* and *Rhinegold,* afforded no preparation and gave him no clue. And if—as there must have been—there were listeners to whom the new opera was hateful, we may be sure that the advocacy of none of its admirers took the form of comparing it, for novelty, to something so remote in time and space from the ordinary European musical mentality as Chinese music. Had they done so they would certainly have been laughed at. We may be sure that all they claimed for it was that it was in essence the same kind of operatic music as Europe had been listening to for generations, but very much better.

The *newest* thing in all music was assuredly the Florentine opera of the beginning of the seventeenth century: here, and only here, did the art deliberately turn its back on the past and consciously make a fresh start. Yet no such Chinese-art analogies and apologies were necessary to recommend the new music to its first hearers as have been thought necessary in the case of these particular minor works of Stravinsky. The new Florentine art became highly popular at once. No doubt a few of the old-fashioned contrapuntists turned up their noses at it; but that was because most of them thought it a thing too trifling for the consideration of serious musicians. They would have been astonished had they been told they were incapable of understanding it; nor would it have occurred to any of its partisans to claim that it was something to which only a few super-endowed initiates could hope to have the key.

There has never yet been a composer so greatly in advance of his time that only an initiate here and there —one or two out of a vast population of cultivated musicians and music lovers—could understand him. If Nature has never yet produced so extraordinary a phenomenon in all the past centuries in which men have been writing music, is it likely that she has done so to-day in the case of Stravinsky? We can, if we like, make this extravagant assumption; we can, if we like, assume that these small works of Stravinsky will be universally recognized as fine music as soon as the universe has risen to their height; we can, if we like, assume that something that has never before happened in the history of music has happened now—that thousands of men who, in other cases, know quite well good music from bad are in this case wrong, and one or two men alone are right. Or we can explain the divergence of opinion in another way: we can say that the one or two have blundered—perhaps from excessive partisanship of a particular style, perhaps from excessive loyalty to a composer who once deserved their loyalty and may deserve it again, perhaps from mere momentary failure of the critical faculty, or for any other of a score of good reasons; but anyhow that they are wrong and the thousands right. Can we not invoke the law of parsimony here?

This, however, is an extreme case and, for that reason, simple. But ninety-nine out of a hundred of the cases of conflicting opinion among the critics are not so easily accounted for. Is any certainty whatever possible in criticism? If so, by what means can any of us ensure this certainty for himself? If not, what is the value of our criticism?

*

*   *

Are there any objective criteria? The subjective school of criticism says "No"; criticism is nothing but "the adventures of the soul among masterpieces." But that famous phrase of Anatole France leaves a great deal to be desired. Why among masterpieces only? Is it not part of the business of the critic to distinguish between the works that are masterpieces and those that are not, and to make it clear that a given work is to be put in the one or the other class? And how can he do this if there are no criteria that are universally accepted as valid, or if not universally, at any rate among most people of culture and taste? Evidently a good deal depends on the quality of the soul that has the adventures.

I remember once refering satirically to some judgments upon Beethoven, that seemed to me absurd, of a writer who, as it also seemed to me, was inclined to over-rate what I regarded as second- or third-rate work by composers like Stravinsky and Casella.

Thereupon a third person rushed into the fray with the question: "If it is open to you to disparage Stravinsky, why is it not open to D—— to disparage Beethoven?"

The question appeared to me to testify to a certain innocence of mind. It is, of course, open to anyone to disparage anyone or anything. If I choose to say that the west front of Nôtre Dame is a truly despicable piece of architecture, no one can prevent me. But if I *should* choose to say this, it would presumably be because I wanted to convince my hearers that it is so; and they are not likely to be convinced by my mere assertion of something so flatly contradictory of the general opinion. I must give some reason for my own opinion; and the moment my opponents ask for reasons and I offer to give them, we both tacitly admit a criterion that is *not* purely subjective. Indeed, merely to speak of the "general opinion" implies some kind of objective criterion; for how have a multitude of people come to have the same opinion upon, say, the beauty of Nôtre Dame, except by their all feeling that it complies with certain conditions without which no building can be regarded as beautiful? They may not have considered in detail what these conditions are; indeed, it may be impossible to express them in terms that will satisfy everyone. But all the same there must exist between the many people who regard the west front as beautiful a definite if unconscious uniformity of standard; and it is in virtue of their tacit agreement upon this standard that they would agree to laugh at anyone who should say that the architect of the average Baptist chapel was a greater man in his line than the architect of Nôtre Dame.

I wonder if the correspondent who intervened in the

discussion to which I have just referred had ever considered all that his words implied. It may seem to him absurd that anyone should not think—I choose the example at random—the "Wind Symphonies" of Stravinsky a masterpiece, just as it seems absurd to me that anyone should think the best of Beethoven's broad and simple melodies merely commonplace, or should see, as some of the Russian "Nationalist" composers said they did, only a kind of "mathematics" in the working out of a great symphonic movement. But he, I imagine, would be as astonished as I to hear anyone say that Bishop's music was as great as Wagner's, or that Tosti's *Good-bye* was as fine an expression of sorrow as the aria "Have mercy, O Lord" in the *Matthew Passion*. But on the gentleman's own implied principles what right would he have to be astonished? If our judgments upon art are merely subjective, why should we smile at the person who prefers *Cavalleria Rusticana* to *Tristan?* Our smile is surely an implication that criticism is not, or should not be, merely subjective—that there *are* such things as objective criteria, valid for practically all people of knowledge and taste.

*

*   *

Every attempt to pooh-pooh objectivity in criticism ends, amusingly enough, with an unconscious assertion of it. I have just been reading a thoughtful and ably written article on criticism, the main thesis of which is that no "scientific" criteria are possible, that "all we are interested in [in criticism] is how a work of art has reacted on a temperament which we know is not

a common one, one that is a little abnormal, or super-
normal." Why, we may ask, *not* a common temperament? The writer forestalls the question: "through
such a temperament [i. e., an uncommon one] we may
not often see 'truth'—which, after all, is the collective
opinion of average humanity, and, in art at least, a
prosy matter—but we are sure to see the work of art
in a new light. And that is the real business of
criticism. Walter Pater found things in 'Monna
Lisa' that nobody before him, Leonardo da Vinci included, had ever seen."

That seems plausible enough—till we examine it in
detail. Here we have in its full glory the theory that
criticism is the play of the critic's mind upon the
masterpiece, and that this is all that criticism should
be. No one will deny that criticism that is worth
reading is so because of the play of a fine mind upon
the work of art. But why limit the field of play to
accepted masterpieces? Is not the critic often called
upon to decide whether a work is a masterpiece or
something inferior? And does not this imply his and
our having some common and generally accepted standard, something by which he and we can arrive at that
"truth" that the writer I have quoted seems to despise?
Nay, has not the great critic, whoever he may be, unconsciously acted upon this criterion when he writes
about the masterpiece? For how has he found the
masterpiece that is going to call out his fine writing?
How does he know it to be a masterpiece? By a
process, surely, of rejection, of deciding that certain
other works in the same genre are inferior, and inferior not merely for him but for the rest of us. How
did Pater come to be writing on the "Monna Lisa"
instead of on one of the many second-rate pictures in

which the Louvre abounds? Surely by a process of selection and rejection that implies a canon of objective judgment—for we all agree that he could have found nothing finer in the "Monna Lisa" room than the "Monna Lisa."

"We are sure to see the work in a new light," we are told, when it has reacted on "a temperament which we know is not a common one, one that is a little abnormal or super-normal." But suppose that the temperament is so far abnormal as to make its owner say, for example, not that the "Monna Lisa" is a fine picture but that it is a wretched one, or that one of Martin Tupper's didactic poems shows a better brain and a finer faculty of expression than are to be found in any of Goethe's "Xenien"? Suppose the temperament to be so abnormal that it sees a more wonderful significance in Blake's "Book of Los"—this sort of thing, for example:

> Coldness, darkness, obstruction, a Solid
> Without fluctuation, hard as adamant,
> Black as marble of Egypt, impenetrable,
> Bound in the fierce raging Immortal;
> And the separated fires, froze in
> A vast Solid, without fluctuation,
> Bound in his expanding clear senses;

than in his

> When the stars threw down their spears,
> And water'd heaven with their tears,
> Did he smile his work to see?
> Did he who made the Lamb make thee?

In that case the writer of the article to which I have referred would, I am sure, be among the first to break into a pitying smile. It is evident, then, that there must be limits to the abnormality or super-normality of the mind that is to criticize. There is, in fact, an abnormality that distorts the critic's sense of values and an abnormality that heightens it; but to say this is to recognize implicitly that there *are* objective criteria of value, independent of this individual or that. Indeed, the writer himself virtually makes this claim for himself in the very act of denying that it is permissible for others to make it. "Too much criticism," he says, "is merely pedagogic; the crude view of criticism largely prevails which would reduce it to a dull business of distributing good and bad conduct certificates." That is a charming example of how to make a thing look ridiculous by phrasing it in ridiculous terms—much as one can make a fine melody look nonsensical by jazzing it. But take the jazz out of the sentence I have quoted, and what we get is just this: that it is a crude view to take of criticism to say that it must distinguish between good and bad. But the chief object of the critic is surely to get other people to see the thing as he sees it; in other words, to get us to believe that he is *right* in calling this work good and the other bad. And how is this appeal of his judgment to ours to succeed unless he and we agree on certain standards of goodness, of rightness, that are independent of our own little subjectivities?

"The comparative method," the writer goes on, "of scientific criticism of Hennequin!—who believes in it all, who is attracted to it?" Well, many people still are, I fancy. They do not necessarily agree with all Hennequin's analyses; but at any rate they are interested in the attempts of that acute mind to find some positive criteria for sound critical judgment. And then our friend, I think, gives his case away.

"Professor Meiklejohn right, and Walter Pater wrong
—which is the more vital, the more fascinating?"
The answer to that may be that Pater had the more
fascinating mind—for some people and in some respects.   But we have to note that here the writer is
trying to ride two horses at once.   No one would
dispute that a lively mind may be more interesting on
the wrong side of a question than a plodding mind on
the right side of it.   The late John F. Runciman used
often to talk what many of us thought was nonsense
about certain modern composers; he would tell us,
for instance, that César Franck was "an industrious
schoolmaster and nothing more," and that Brahms
had no more intelligence than an antelope; and his
theory that *Parsifal* was an immoral and disgusting
work is well known.   But we always preferred Runciman when he was, as we thought, hopelessly wrong, to
certain other critics who, on the same subjects, we
thought hopelessly right.   It was the performance
that interested us, not the tune the man was playing.
Our preference of a clever writer to a dull one, however, has no bearing, so far as I can see, on whether
there are or are not objective criteria of values in art,
and whether it is not part of the business of the critic
to convince us that these criteria have entered into his
judgments.   But what follows *has* a decided bearing
on the question.   For the writer goes on to say:
"Mr. J. M. Robertson, himself a very able man, once
evolved a scientific method of criticism whereby one
might measure the arts just as a draper's assistant
measures cloth [another little excursion into jazz, by
the way], and how barren the result!   It did not
even give us certitude, for this same scientific method
found little poetry in the 'Ode to a Skylark' and heaps

of it in the most minor things of Edgar Allan Poe."
Evidently, for this writer, Mr. Robertson's sense of
poetic values—in this case at least—was at fault; and
it is clear from the tone of his remarks that he takes it
as a foregone conclusion that every reader who knows
what good poetry is will agree with him.   But surely
this is to take it for granted that there *are* objective
standards of value in art—that it is not sufficient for a
critic to say, "This, for me, is great art [Tosti's *Good-
bye,* for instance], and this, for me, is inferior art
[the "Liebestod," let us say]"; for by saying this he
runs counter to the general judgment of men of taste.
Mr. Robertson's method "did not even give us certitude," we are told.   Then there *is* such a thing as
certitude, it appears, and a critic is a good or a bad
critic according as he achieves certitude!   " '*A propos*
of Shakespeare,' Anatole France once said [our critic
continues] 'I will talk about myself.'   Does this reduce criticism, then, to a mere matter of taste?   Of
course it does, but it is the taste of the critic that
matters."   But if that be so, who is to decide between
tastes, and how?   It is not a matter now, be it observed, of dull or fascinating writing on the part of the
critic.   It is his taste, his discrimination between first-
rate things and second- or third-rate things, that is
now held to matter.   Our friend surely has no right
to object to Mr. Robertson thinking a minor poem of
Edgar Allan Poe's better than the "Ode to a Skylark,"
and to assume that everyone who knows anything
about poetry will support him in his objection, unless
there are some criteria or other in virtue of which
we can say not merely that *we* think poem A better
than poem B, but that poem A *is* better than poem B,
and that if a man does not think so his judgment is at

fault. The writer thinks that Mr. Robertson's method does not give "certitude" in this matter, but claims "certitude" for his own judgment. So there *are* certitudes, it seems, in criticism, after all! Apparently it is *not* all "a mere matter of taste"; something *does* matter besides "the taste of the critic."

*
*   *

Well, I shall have time to think this and other problems over in this heavenly solitude. My friend X has placed his house at my disposal for the summer. It contains one of the finest musical libraries in Europe. I shall find there all the material I may need. I shall not go outside the grounds for six weeks. I shall not have a single visitor. Except to a servant I shall not speak a word during the whole of the time —a priceless blessing to the busy journalist whose whole occupation is talking, either with the voice or through the pen, generally on subjects in which his interest is not very great, and to individuals, or to a public, in which his interest is less. I shall browse in the library, and try to get the same perspective of musical history as I do of the mountain slope beneath me and the wide bay beyond. How absurd the little daily things of one's London life seem when set against this serene spaciousness! Perhaps the little daily things of criticism will come to seem equally absurd when I can see them set against the spacious and serene background of history.

II

I SEE that one of the musical journals announces the coming of a series of articles intended as a "course" in musical criticism, for the benefit, presumably, of young enthusiasts who may be tempted to enter that dubious profession.

One smiles at the idea; but, after all, why? It is no doubt true that the higher art of criticism can no more be "taught" than the higher art of music or painting or sculpture or architecture can. A man is either a good critic or a good composer by the grace of God or he is not one at all, and never will be. Vision, imagination, sympathy, understanding, discrimination, these things cannot be "taught"; pedagogics are no more capable of turning a Smith or a Robinson into a Lessing, a Pater, or a Sainte-Beuve than they are of turning a Balfe into a Beethoven. All the same, pedagogics ought to have some right of entry into the field of criticism. Their place in creative art is admitted. A man might be born with the genius of Bach, Beethoven, Mozart and Wagner rolled into one; but he would not get very far without a technique. In a sense, it is true, every original composer makes his own technique; but he makes most of it out of the transmitted techniques of many earlier generations. A certain amount of teaching he must have, whether he gets it from a pedagogue, a textbook, or the works of the masters; there are certain fundamentals that are universally accepted in the making of music, as in the making of a cathedral or a ship.

There must surely be certain fundamentals in criticism, could we but discover them. Criticism being not merely the expression of an opinion but an attempt to induce others to see the thing as we see it—i. e., a virtual assumption that our view will in the long run, and by the mass of competent judges, be accepted as the right one—a "right" criticism must comply with the general conditions of all right judgments. It must see the whole of the case, and it must see all round it and right through it; and what it has finally to say about the case must be so grounded in reason that the average reasonable and receptive man, when he has had time to think it all over, will agree. A critic cannot, like the creative artist, say, "This is my view of things; take it or leave it, it is all one to me." For the artist does not pretend that his view expresses, or ought to express, anything but himself. The world is too vast, too complex, for any interpretation of it to be allowed to claim that it is the sole correct one. The artist's view of life matters nothing; what matters is simply his expression of his view. We do not go to him for a philosophy of the universe; we expect of him only that, for the hour or so we are concerned with him, he shall make his vision as real to us as it was to him; and whether he can do that or not depends solely on the intensity of his own belief in the vision and on his own power to give it such intensity of imaginative life that for the moment we too will believe in it. Artistic belief is not real belief: it is only belief—as the phrase ran in the late war— for the duration. As Coleridge put it *à propos* of the ghost in *Hamlet,* it is not that we believe in ghosts, but that we temporarily suspend our disbelief in them. And there are degrees of artistic as of every-day belief: the ghost in *Hamlet* is more real than the one in *The Canterville Ghost*. That is simply because Shakespeare is a more persuasive artist than Wilde. The imaginary world of art has its own laws and must be judged solely by those laws, not by the laws of life. Optimism may be a better philosophy than pessimism, but that does not prevent *The City of Dreadful Night* being a better poem than *A Psalm of Life*. Love may be a better boat than hate to sail life's seas in; but that does not prevent Swift from being a greater artist than Miss Ethel M. Dell.

All the creative artist asks us to do is to go with him for the moment. The critic, however, virtually asks us to go with him for all time. Brilliance or charm of treatment is in his case not sufficient: a critic every one of whose judgments was upset by time would be written down as a very bad critic, no matter how interesting his writing might be *qua* writing—until, of course, the time came when the things he had criticized were forgotten, and posterity could enjoy his writing purely as writing, without bringing it up to the bar of truth for trial. A man may be a very readable writer and a very bad critic. The critic's business, however, is to be not only an interesting writer but a sound judge. The creative artist, as I have said, asks us to go with him for the moment. He may himself go different ways on different days. To-day, in *Tristan*, Wagner may be the blackest of pessimists; to-morrow, in *The Meistersingers*, he may be the sunniest of optimists. We will gladly go both ways with him, so long as he is good company on each. But we will not allow the critic to go one way to-day and another to-morrow. As well ask us to trust the judge who on Monday acquits the prisoner and on Wednesday recalls him and sentences him to death as to ask us to have any faith in the critic for whom a certain work is a masterpiece on the third of January and a piece of commonplace by the middle of April. Insist as we will on the part that personality plays in making the difference between one critic and another, as it does between one composer and another, we still expect the ideal critical personality to function not at haphazard but according to universal law. The artist can be, to a large extent, a law unto himself. The critic cannot: he must not only deliver himself of a judgment, he must convince others that his judgment is a right one. He has to deal subjectively with objective things, and objectively with subjective things; a work is or is not a good work for reasons that are independent of his state of mind or body at the moment he comes into contact with it.

*

*   *

Surely, then, it is desirable that there should be a certain technical basis for criticism as there is for composition. By a technical basis I of course do not mean merely that a critic should be a trained musician. That goes without saying. I mean that just as a composer gets a certain grounding that helps him to think more quickly, more clearly, more securely, so a critic ought to be trained in certain fundamentals of judgment. If there were no science of composition, if each composer had to discover everything for himself —the nature of harmony, the devices of counterpoint, the principles of design, the making and handling of instrumental colour—none of them would get very far. Perhaps the art of criticism makes no sensible

progress because every critic has to discover its basic
principles for himself as he goes along, learning simply
by his own errors and those of other people.   Would
it not be better if there were some body of transmitted
technique that he could take as a fundamental,—even
if, at the worst, it were only a collection of negatives,
not a manual of things to be done but a compendium
of dreadful warnings of things to be avoided?

How would it do, as a beginning, to take a certain
critic or a certain period and study him or it as a
physician studies an organism, observing how it is con-
structed, how it functions, how it adapts or fails to
adapt itself to its environment, to what maladies it is
subject, how these originate, how they are to be cured,
and what other organisms of the same type should do
to avoid contracting the same maladies?   No critic
and no period could be taken as a model for criticism;
but what if we were to pick one out as a subject for a
post-mortem demonstration in morbid anatomy?

I was set thinking on these lines by a book I came
across in the library this morning,—the *Musikalische
Briefe, Wahrheit über Tonkunst und Tonkünstler, von
einem Wohlbekannten*, two volumes, Leipzig, 1852.
I already knew the work by name, but I had never
hitherto seen a copy.   The "Wellknown" who, in
these Musical Letters, undertook to tell "the Truth
about Music and Musicians," will perhaps be dimly
remembered by students of the Wagner-Liszt correspondence.   In one of his letters of August, 1859,
Liszt recommends Wagner not to worry about "Grenz-
botens, Wohlbekannten, Kreuzzeitungs and Gazette-
musicales," or any other critical scribbling, but rather
to "drink a bottle of good wine," and "work forward
to immortality."

The "Wellknown" was Johann Christian Lobe (1797–1881), "musician and writer on music of some eminence," as "Grove" truthfully if somewhat confusedly describes him. I learn also from "Grove" that although he composed five operas, two symphonies, and a quantity of other works, "it is as a littérateur that he is most interesting to us." He edited the *Allgemeine musikalische Zeitung* from 1846 to 1848, and after that the *Fliegende Blätter für Musik*. Later he became the musical critic of the Leipzig *Illustrirte Zeitung,* "and made endless contributions to other periodicals." He wrote several technical and other works besides the *Musikalische Briefe*.

*

*   *

I ran through his first letter as I stood in front of the shelf from which I had taken the book. This introductory letter intrigues me—I seem to recognize a kindred spirit in Lobe. Like so many of us to-day, he appears to have felt that music had come to rather a critical point in its development, and that it behoved those whose business it was to write about it to survey the whole situation calmly and find out where they stood. He calls his first letter "Lament." The young friend to whom the correspondence is addressed had told him that in his study of music he has arrived at a turning-point "where I must either cease to occupy myself with music or find some quite other way that will lead me to the desired goal. Before I give myself wholly up to despondency and despair, I would open my heart out to you and conjure you to show me the right way, give me light, give me truth, the unvarnished truth, the whole truth." The young man has come to the study of German music full of faith and enthusiasm; but both have evaporated. Doubts assail him; he has no star to guide him. He had heard that German music and German musicians were the best in the world. But what has he found? True, there is more music written and performed in Germany than in any other country; but is Germany now producing great composers as it used to do? (This is interesting, seeing that in 1852 Schumann was still alive and that Wagner had already produced *The Flying Dutchman, Tannhäuser* and *Lohengrin,* and was at work on *The Ring.*)

Which operas—to speak of this form alone—asks the young student, at present dominate the theatres of the civilized world? French and Italian, he replies; these are preferred to the German operas, even in Germany. "And what various judgments," he cries, "over a new German work! What contradictions!"

Evidently the young man is troubled, as we are, about the problem of judgment. "Are there no real laws of the beautiful and the true in music, that the judgments upon one and the same work differ so widely from each other? Or has the standard been lost by which good and bad in music are to be measured? Is music to become *a matter of faith,* and are the lovers of the art to split up into sects, each of which makes, not its God—for there can be only *one* God, as there can be only one *true* music—but its own idols, which it worships, while it reviles the idols of the other sects?"

One would think he was speaking of the situation at the present day!

He is troubled over the diversity of opinions upon

a new work. "Either the public is delighted with a new thing—Lortzing's *Czar und Zimmermann,* for instance—and the critics either ignore it or damn it utterly, or the critics fall into raptures over a work, praise the genius of the composer at the top of their voices, and assure us that he alone has discovered the truth, won clear of the beaten track and opened up new paths, while the public listens coldly to the be-lauded work, or else turns away from it with re-pugnance."

I rub my eyes and glance at the title page again. Yes, sure enough, the date is 1852.

The young man confesses that he is on the side of the public, for he likes a good deal of the music that critics say is no good, while much that they praise as the outpouring of genius leaves him cold, or repels him.   He is obviously referring to the "ultra-modern" music of that time.   "Do the public and myself, then, lack proper understanding, or do I lack the capacity for true feeling?   I have eagerly sought after enlight-enment, I have studied the critiques in the influential journals, but if before I was amazed at the difference between the opinions of the public and those of the critics, I am now astonished at the glaring contradic-toriness of the critics in their opinions upon one and the same work.   Contradictions between public and com-posers, between public and critics, between critics and composers, between critic and critic!   Honoured friend, whoever does not lose his reason in such a state of things has no reason to lose."

Poor young man, and poor us, who to-day are mak-ing the same complaints, are worried by the same doubts, and see no way out of our doubts!

*
*   *

I am getting interested in this book. Old Lobe
had evidently thought earnestly about the problems of
criticism. I shall be curious to see what light he can
shed on his young friend's difficulties. It strikes me
that this is the very book I have been looking for—one
in which a certain phase of criticism can be studied
complete, and by the light of which we can guide our
own footsteps. For a mere run of the eye over Lobe's
chapter-headings shows that he is going to discuss
every point in the problem of criticism as it still con-
fronts each of us to-day. What he was in 1852 I fancy
we are in 1924. We talk about other "new" composers than his, but ours present us with just the same
problems. He, like us, was called upon to judge a
new development of the art: he had to satisfy himself
that the tests he applied to the new music were as valid
as those he was accustomed to apply to the old. He
certainly went about his work with admirable thorough-
ness, judging from the headings of the letters.
"What is music, and what can it do?" he asks in the
first letter, beginning, like a good German, at the
foundation. He seems to answer his own question
in a series of letters on "German music," "The
newer German composers in general," "The present-
day German opera in general," "The German song,"
and "Church music." Then, apparently, he sets
himself to get to the roots of "Laws of art,"
"Form," and "Musical declamation." His scheme is
certainly beautifully lucid. He goes on to deal, in

the twelfth Letter, with the eternal question of "Too complicated!" In the thirteenth he discusses "Originality," in the fourteenth "Political Music" (I fancy this will be aimed, more or less, at Wagner), and in the fifteenth, "Classical and Romantic." Then, judging from the headings of the Letters, we get to still closer grips with the critical problem—"Progress in Music," "Youth and Age," "Musical Criticism," "Musical Coteries and Parties," and "Reflection and Unaffectedness." The remaining Letters, on such subjects as "Concerts and the Public," "The Singers," and "Virtuosi and Virtuosity," will not, I imagine, bear on the problem of criticism. But the others look decidedly promising. I will tackle the book in detail after lunch. It seems to me to be the very thing I have been looking for.

*

*   *

The more I read of old Lobe, the more I like him. I have a curious feeling of watching and listening to myself in some previous incarnation. So far I feel that if I had been in Leipzig in 1852 I would have thought, on the whole, very much like Lobe, and that if he were living in London in 1924 he would think very much as I do. He seems to have looked at the problem of criticism from much the same angle as myself, and to have come to much the same conclusions with regard to it.

Can it be that every generation is simply a repetition, in other forms, of the generation that went before,—that there is really nothing new under the sun? We quarrel to-day about German music and non-

German music, about emotional music and objective music, about impressionism and expressionism, about Strauss and Stravinsky.   Can it be that what the musicians, like the politicians and soldiers, have quarrelled about in every age has been merely the same thing under different names?   This war is nominally for the possession of Alsace, that for control of the Dardanelles, another to avenge a diplomatic insult or to secure the rights of traders.   Is it only the names that change, the moving forces being fundamentally the same throughout the ages, the things that made wars in modern Europe being essentially the same things that made wars in ancient Greece and Rome and Carthage?   And can it be that criticism is eternally faced with the same basic problems,—the fight, for instance, between expressionism and impressionism to-day being merely the old fight between classicism and romanticism fought in new uniforms and with new weapons?   "C'est un signe du temps!" says Anatole France.   "Or, j'ai retrouvé neuf fois sur dix les mêmes faits avec des circonstances analogues dans les vieux mémoires ou dans les vieilles histoires."

Well, let me work my way systematically through friend Lobe.

He has no doubt that there are many "significant talents" in the music of his day; but he thinks the poor results are attributable to the talents being wrongly employed.   The times are out of joint, and the talents suffer a sympathetic dislocation.   The brave Lobe will trace the trouble to its source and prescribe the right remedy.

It goes without saying that he puts part of the trouble down to the fact that composers now despise melody.   Many people diagnose the same trouble in the music of to-day. It is a curious thing, the cynic may reflect, that the music of every period lacks melody as compared with the music of the past. Yet there is any amount of melody in music. The explanation of this strange circumstance seems to be that melody is always in the music of the generation before, never in the present generation. People who reject Stravinsky or Schönberg because he "has no melody" hark back regretfully to the melodies of Strauss. But it was only a few years ago that we were being assured that Strauss had no melody,—that there had been no melody in music, in fact, since Wagner and Brahms and Schumann. Yet one seems to remember that Wagner and Schumann in their day were accused of melodic poverty or melodic ugliness; and no doubt the charge goes back long past St. Cecilia, to the very days of Tubal Cain. Some of the critics of fifteen or twenty years ago declared that Strauss's music was addressed to the intellect rather than to the heart. Here is Lobe making the same complaint with regard to the German composers of *his* day: their music is addressed, he says, only to the learned, and means nothing to the plain man. Music is not real music, he contends, unless it is true and beautiful. Quite so, friend Lobe; but what *is* true, what *is* beautiful? Is there a truth so true, a beauty so beautiful, that all lovers of truth and lovers of beauty must perforce recognize it when they see it? If so, what are its signs? "Apply this so simple criterion," he tells the young inquirer, "to any work that pretends to be an art-work, and you will never go wrong in your judgment of it, let art-fanatics, art-noodles, and art-liars chatter as they will." It seems simple enough. All we have to do is to apply the right criterion. But how can we be sure that *our* criterion *is* the right criterion? I hope friend Lobe will be able to tell me later.

Let me see what he has to say about "the new German composers in general."

*
*   *

I am bound to confess that this voice from the past makes me feel a little uncomfortable now and then. It seems to be always saying just what we are saying to-day; it is only the names that differ. But time has not exactly confirmed all Lobe's judgments. Will it be any kinder to ours? Lobe is certain, for instance, that there are no geniuses around him. "The present culminating point of music—I do not say it is a point beyond which music cannot go—is Beethoven. So far no composer has come who can be put beside him. If any people would give such a place to one of the moderns, just boldly call them shameless sycophants or blind idolators,"—which advice he will proceed to justify when he comes to deal with living composers. That is certainly "bold" enough; yet we cannot help remembering that Wagner and Schumann were alive when it was written.

Living composers, Lobe thinks, mostly fail in the matter of form. "Some do not know what form should be; they have, if I may so express it, no musical logic in their heads; others think the rule-less and the formless is new (and it certainly is, though it is not good), that this is the mark of genius, that this is making new paths." "Modern" composers, it seems, are given to restless modulation "through all possible

keys." Mozart, says Lobe, adapted his modulations
to the psychological problems of the moment: he would
not, for example, give the complex harmonies to
simple-minded Papageno that would be appropriate to
Don Giovanni. "But pick up any work of one of the
belauded moderns and you will not have long to search
before you find him using the most complicated harmonies and modulations to express the simplest feelings." And of course the wicked fellows who do
this also indulge in a gross excess of instrumental
colour.

We have heard something of this kind during the
last few years in connexion with Strauss. And as for
the complaint against the "moderns" of 1852 that they
"used the most complicated harmonies and modulations to express the simplest feelings," I remember
reading only yesterday, in Karl Storck's *Die Musik
der Gegenwart,* a protest against the same error on
the part of some of the "moderns" of to-day. "If,"
says Storck, "a composer wants to express in music
the agitated feelings that the work of Nietzsche has
aroused in him, and he does this in unprecedented
turns of musical speech, in tone-successions that go beyond anything yet heard, this may be accepted as the
perfectly natural and artistic expression of something
never imagined before. But when other composers
use this musical language for a harmless love-song,
that is pure falsity, a sin against genuine art." Lobe
puts the same thing in his own way and in terms of his
own epoch. "If a painter were to show a rose bush
in flower in a winter landscape, if he were to paint the
sky green and the water red, everybody would be hor-
rified at his craziness; but it is otherwise when a composer—as you can hear for yourself—sets the trump-

ets and trombones blaring during the gentle lament
of a maiden. Do not imagine that I am exaggerating.
The maiden's lament for her lost dove, in Kreutzer's
Nachtlager zu Granada, is accompanied by trumpets,
trombones, and kettledrums!"

In fact (to resume my reading of Lobe), "composers are bent on being free, and regard every rule
as a fetter. They not only throw aside the older
theory (to which I have no objection), but rebel
against the eternal laws of the true and beautiful . . .
and so find, not freedom, but unbridled licence."
Evidently to Lobe the beginning of the second half
of the nineteenth century was a period of something
like the same sort of Bolshevism in music that nervous
people see around them to-day. He puts a good deal
of it down to the bad influence of the Hegelian philosophy. "For just as many Hegelians think they have
said something very wise and clever when they have
clothed their little thoughts in unusual phrases that
scorn the plain human understanding, so that no one
knows what it was they really wanted to say, so some
composers think they have far surpassed the others
when they deviate from the ordinary language of
music and make a jargon of their own, out of which
no one can make sense."

And as a sound musician, old Lobe sees that a good
deal of the music of the time is so bad because it is the
work of dilettanti who think it unnecessary to go
through the grounding in the good old technique. It
is a superficial age, in fact, always trying to find the
shortest cut and the easiest path. Mozart, Haydn
and Beethoven thought long and hard about each new
work, always trying to improve it. Lobe's "moderns"
are incapable of a prolonged effort: "what it took the

ancients weeks and months to do, the new composers want to do in a moment, and the first idea that occurs to them they think the best." Rapid composition they regard as a mark of true genius. But the moderns, unlike the ancients, really do not know what it is they want to say in their music; and as they have nothing in particular to say, they say it as loudly and with as much variety of external effect as possible,—especially necessary is the brass to them. "They are always trying desperately to be original; lacking real originality of idea, they try to make up for it by unnatural, strained modes of expression, violently distorted ideas, unheard-of harmonic successions, and the flouting of all rules." And as all these misguided people insist on being heard, a vast quantity of inferior, unripe music is published and performed, and receives excessive praise from the coteries and the log-rolling journalists.

Really, it might be the present day that the man was writing about!

Then, as now, the mortality-rate of the new music was distressingly high; few of the bantlings that were hailed with such enthusiasm at their birth survived even the first trials of childhood. One of the reasons for this, thinks Lobe, is that many of the young composers have so poor an opinion of their own time that they prefer to write for the future (I suspect a dig at Wagner here). Then, as now, composers were writing badly for the voice and relying too much on the expressive powers of the orchestra. Then, as now, everyone was writing songs, because songs—of a kind—are at once the easiest form of music to write and the quickest way into the affections of the big public; but then, as now, composers were writing songs with their heads instead of with their hearts. Then, as now, the main interest of the song was not where it should be, in the voice part, but in the accompaniment. "Hence those innumerable songs in which hardly any melody is given to the singer, who has only detached declamatory phrases to sing—or rather to ejaculate— to a wandering and confused pictorial accompaniment." Composers do not set a poem as a whole, but merely illustrate it point by point; an honourable exception is Robert Franz, who tries first of all to get at the central idea of the poem, and then makes every bar take a part in the expression of this idea. I seem to remember that the complaint most frequently heard about the songs of to-day is that the composers set the poems line by line, point by point, instead of making an organic musical whole of them, and that what masquerades as a song is often merely a piano solo with a badly fitted-in voice part. Lobe is evidently an earnest and lucid thinker on these matters. He points out, for example, that Heine is a peculiarly difficult poet for the composer to tackle, inasmuch as in many of his poems the real point—often an unexpected one—comes at the end, and the composer who takes the earlier lines at their face value, and so misses the irony or the bitterness of the final line, has falsified the whole poem in his music. Franz, he says, does not fall into this error.

*

* *

In a letter about "Art Rules" Lobe advises the young man to seek out the eternal "art-maxims" that are unconsciously embedded in the works of the masters.

But the study of these masters must not be a blind one; it must be clear-eyed and searching, otherwise the student may mistake the false for the true. For even the masters, being but men, are fallible; in particular each has his mannerisms that must not be imitated,—Spohr's passion for enharmonic modulations, for instance. Effects in art should come out of causes; Spohr indulges in effect for its own sake. And there comes a time in every art when artists, trying at all costs to be new, mistake false maxims for true ones; and this is the beginning of the downfall of the art. At times like these the only salvation is in looking back to the art of the genuine masters. Time, of course, brings many changes. Music must always *sound well;* but we have to recognize that each generation has its own idea of what constitutes sounding well. Still, no music that does not sound well can be good music; therefore rough and dissonant orchestration is a sign either that a composer has never known the eternal truth or that he has not known how to imprint it on his work.

I am getting a little uneasy, however. How can Lobe be sure that what does not "sound well" to him may not sound perfectly well to someone else? Suppose the young man had asked him squarely, "But, master, there are people who say that a certain work that you declare to be ill-sounding is to them well-sounding. By what infallible criterion do you decide that you are right and they are wrong?" What would Lobe have answered? He seems to have anticipated some such question, for in his next paragraph he says that "never will a time come when monotony, overcrowding, unclearness, over-refinement, confused part-writing, incongruity, want of definite character, excessive length, dryness, careless structure of periods, unrecognizable connexion, too much variety without perceptible reference to a unity, rambling modulation, etc. etc., will have the validity of genuine art-maxims."

True; but, the young man might timidly have gone on to inquire, may not different people feel differently about some of these things? May not, for example, a work that seems "dry" to one hearer be full of sap for another? And in that case what right has either of them to say the other is wrong? But the excellent Lobe is so sure of himself, so confident that, whatever mistakes other people may make, *he* can always be trusted to know the geniune article from the imitation, that I have no doubt he will let us into the secret later. For evidently musical controversy in his day ran on much the same lines as in ours; Lobe speaks of "ignorant critics and shameless coteries" who err pitifully about values, and of contemporary composers who are hailed by these people as great geniuses without being anything of the kind. Yes, that is how we are all inclined to regard those who differ from us; and I should not be surprised to hear that these people in their turn think in the same kind way about us. What then is the infallible criterion in virtue of which the Lobes declare that they are right and their opponents wrong? There must be such a criterion, and Lobe must have been in possession of it, or he would not have been so positive.

It was only the other day that one of the brightest of our young English composers described how he and his fellows were always searching anxiously for new methods of expression,—which remark, I regret to say, drew from more than one of those cynical fellows the critics the suggestion that before these young

gentlemen began worrying about a new medium for
the expression of their great thoughts they had better
find the great thoughts to express, there being, indeed,
a strong probability that if one of these composers
did happen to be favoured with a striking new idea
it would find of itself its own new manner of expression without his worrying very much about it. Apparently there was the same confusion of cause and
effect in Lobe's time among certain young composers
and the critics who made a practice of aiding and
abetting them (Lobe evidently looks with no favourable eye on this sort of "critic," for he ironically
italicizes the word); these people, he says, "seek progress in music in new forms instead of in new ideas."
Lobe goes on to show that, at bottom, all musical
forms are very much the same, and that only *ideas*
can be really new; he cites, in support of his conten-
tion, the Strauss and Lanner waltzes and the first
eight symphonies of Beethoven, in which the "form"
is virtually always the same. This is what we are
still saying to-day,—that a work may be patently new
in build and in texture and yet be worthless, while
another may be in a transmitted form and yet speak
with a voice of its own. And the complaint of so
many of the modern composers that their wonderful
revolutionary ideas do not get their proper chance
because of the opposition of the "conservatives" is
met by anticipation by Lobe in a quite charming sentence *à propos* of the "modernists" of his day: they
are, he says, like the authors we used to have among
us, who, when the political censorship was active, used
to assure us that were it not for this they would write
the most marvellous works, and then, when the censor-

ship was abolished, had nothing to say that was particularly worth saying.

He seems rather a bright old fellow, this Lobe.

*

*   *

I skip the chapter on musical declamation, and settle on the next, entitled "Too Complicated."

In those days, as in these, conscientious critics declared themselves unable to judge a big work at a mere first hearing. The robust Lobe, as I might have expected, goes straight to the real point. It does not necessarily follow that because a work is not clear at a first hearing the fault is with the hearer. It is not a matter of mere depth of thought, for a deep pool that is pure can be clearer than a shallow one that is muddy. The truth is that the modern composers are mostly "too complicated," resorting to ingenuities and piquancies and audacities because they know that if they were to talk simply about simple things their poverty of idea would be found out. Still, there *are* works that are recognized as excellent, even at a first hearing, by both critics and public: for example, Gade's first symphony, "which pleased at its performance in Leipzig, and goes on pleasing everywhere."

I am pulled up with a jerk; my blood runs cold.

Gade's first symphony! Where is that symphony now? as Hans Breitmann might ask. I begin to ask myself whether our good Lobe's judgment is quite so infallible as he thought, especially when I find him, in this same chapter, hinting that the bigger works of

Schumann were among those that indiscreet admirers regarded as too "deep" to be understood all at once. Well, Schumann's symphonies may not be in the very front rank of their genre, but at any rate they are still alive, which is more than can be said, I am afraid, for the Number One of the estimable Gade.

The thirteenth letter, on "Originality," promises to be interesting.

Lobe begins by pointing out how easy it is to be "original" in the sense of merely saying what no one else has said.   Quite so; but how are we to know the true originality from the false?   Lobe thinks it a sign of mere striving-to-be-original when a composer "sins against the laws of musical form, as when he writes six little four-bar phrases and follows them up with phrases of thirty or forty bars, or when he gives a whole work the same instrumentation throughout, or prescribes the same unvarying dynamics—a constant *forte* or a constant *piano*—or makes every phrase begin *piano* and end *forte*"—and so on.

Yes, there is something in all this that is not wholly inapplicable to the present day, when one composer imagines he is original because he dispenses with the strings, another because he uses the voice purely as a musical instrument without words, another because he has introduced a typewriter into the orchestra.   But after all, few people would be taken in merely by devices of this sort.   The serious question is, how are we to distinguish between the sterile novelties of the charlatan and the fruitful new ideas of the genius? Can Lobe help us here?   It is all very well to say that the difference between good music and bad music is that the former is sincerely felt and the latter is not;

but what *is* "sincere" in this connexion? Is it not probable that Ethelbert Nevin was as sincerely moved when he wrote *The Rosary* as Wagner was when he wrote *Tristan?* "True originality," says our Lobe, "consists then not in the form but in the ideas that speak through the form"; and he follows up this truism with an analogy that I myself have often used. The poet or prose writer does not think it necessary to make a fresh form of his own, a fresh syntax of his own, a fresh vocabulary of his own, a fresh system of punctuation of his own, for each of his works; he takes the ordinary words and the ordinary grammar, and somehow or other manages to express himself fully in them, to make it clear to us that his mentality is different from that of other men, that he has felt for himself, that he has seen the world from his own angle. Swinburne may not use a single word that Tennyson has not used, his nouns and verbs and adjectives and adverbs may stand in precisely the same grammatical relation to each other; but there is no danger of our mistaking a page of Swinburne for a page of Tennyson. Why then should it be necessary for the composer, in order to be original, to invent a vocabulary, a syntax and a form that can come under no suspicion of being anyone's but his?

But to recognize that it is the ideas, not the dressing of them, that really matter, does not of itself help us, surely, to discriminate between the ideas. We may say that a certain simple little piece of diatonic music is, in the final sense of the word, more truly original than a particular page of bad Schönberg, inasmuch as any of us might have been able to put the Schönberg page together by a little reflection, whereas if the other thing—the main theme of the finale of the Ninth Symphony, for example—had not occurred to its own composer it would never have occurred to anyone else. But by what infallible criterion do we presume to separate the music of our own day into the good and the bad, the true original and the false original? Lobe is quite certain that *he* has such a criterion, and that he can pass it on to his young friend. But I am bound to confess that I do not discover it among the generalities in which he indulges, unimpeachable as these are.

Indeed, the more I read of Lobe the more I have my doubts whether sound principles of judgment necessarily ensure sound judgments. He quotes from Griepenkerl, who in the mid-nineteenth century was doing what some critics enjoy doing to-day—exhorting composers to write "contemporary" music, to express the spirit of their own time. Griepenkerl particularly demanded this of the opera composer. But my confidence in Griepenkerl's judgment is sorely shaken when I find that he can discover only one contemporary opera that really expresses the life of the time— the *Huguenots!* Here, of course, we have the half-literary, half-musical dilettante, blundering bumptiously into an art of which he knows comparatively little. Griepenkerl's enthusiasm for the *Huguenots* (and, I gather, for *Masaniello*) came from the fact that the libretti of those operas deal with such political problems of faith and freedom as were agitating men's minds in his day. Lobe has no difficulty in making mincemeat of Griepenkerl's theories. He easily shows that there is no such thing as "the spirit of the times"—that in no country do the whole of the inhabitants think alike on any subject, and that what is a vital question for some of them is a matter of trifling importance for others—a point we may well bear in mind to-day.   For some of our young bloods are woefully intolerant.   Because they themselves have not as much emotion as would set the heart of a tortoise throbbing, they would deny the right of richer-natured people to feel strongly about life and death; because they are over-intellectual they fancy romanticism is dead; because they are expressionistically virtuous, there shall be no more impressionist cakes and ale.   It is interesting to find that in the Germany of Lobe's time also there were coteries each of which claimed to be doing the only musical thinking that could really matter, and that the calm sense of Lobe sees them all just as they are, as fragments of the immensity that we call the contemporary soul.   We know from Wagner's prose works (and I suspect that it is at Wagner that Lobe is now aiming his shafts) that, as in these queer latter days, there was a strong feeling in some quarters that music should be "democratic."   But granting, says the liberal Lobe, that there *can* be such a thing as "democratic" music, has not aristocratic music an equal right to exist?   Or in the end must each party, each church, each caste have its own music?   And will the principle be applied to the other arts?   Will Raphael's *Madonna,* for instance, be put aside as representing a standpoint that is out-of-date, and not worthy of comparison with Hübner's *Silesian Weavers?*

I shall pass over the chapter on "Classic and Romantic," because I fancy it will be better to take this later, when I come to read what Lobe has to say about the leading composers of his time.

*
*   *

His next chapter is on "Progress in Music."

It begins very well with the maxim, "Nicht jeder Vorschritt ist ein Fortschritt," which is no doubt what the future historian of music will say as he turns over some typical scores of the nineteen-twenties, and reads what was said about them by the contemporary critics who made a point of hailing every work as a masterpiece if only it sounded different from everything else that had ever been written.

According to Lobe, there were three parties in his day—those who said that music had attained its highest possible perfection, and that it must return to the great masters of the past; those who said that music was still a long way from perfection and must hurry forward; and those who said that music was on the wrong path, and that the right one must be found forthwith. For Lobe, apparently, there is only one formula for good music—something clearly conceived and clearly expressed. This, he says, will be found to be the case in all the acknowledged masterpieces of every period. But I am afraid the formula is insufficient; it seems to me that in many of the works that are failures the composer has expressed himself so clearly that there can be no mistaking what was in his mind. Time has rejected these works, surely, not because they are unclear, but because they are so clear that we can see how empty they are. So that we get back once more to the vital questions, What are good ideas? What are poor ideas? How can we be sure of knowing which is which? Lobe does not seem to be troubled by any doubts in the matter; but perhaps the musicians of his time who disagreed with him were equally confident of their own infallibility. All that Lobe has to say on the necessity for truth and clarity in musical expression is admirable; but I am afraid it does not help us to discover a criterion by which we shall all know truth from error, or explain why a work that to one hearer sounds confused is to another perfectly clear.

In his seventeenth letter, Lobe deals with the problem of the eternal conflict between the old and the young. He sees the necessity for both, the former defending the masterpieces of the past against those who, as a rule, have not yet had the experience of life and of art that would fit them to understand them, the latter, by their restlessness, their love of adventure, preventing the art from stagnating. He feels that it is useless for either party to hope to have a complete understanding of the other. What endears the old music to the older men is, in part, a certain association of ideas. "With the well-known tones there comes back to the older man the beautiful days of his youth. . . . The remembrance of one's youth is always a glimpse of heaven, a return to happiness, of blessedness; in recollection all one's youth seems lovely, as are all Springs remembered in Winter." To these men, most new music, lacking such associations, seems cold; they feel themselves to be among men who speak another language than theirs. To old men who feel like this he gives the counsel to lock themselves up with their memories and not attempt to judge the new.

But, he continues, there is a progressive type of age that does not lose its zest for the new, but only tries to separate the true from the false in it. It does not ask that the new music shall be like the old, but only that in its own way it shall be as good as the old.

Youth, on the other hand, lacks experience. If the older man, filled as he is with music, perhaps sated with it, may sometimes see less in a new work than there really is, the youth may see more in it than there really is, because he mistakes his own emotional fullness for a fullness in the work itself. And never, says Lobe, has there been a period in which youth was so sure of itself as now, so certain that it knows everything and is alone fit to govern the world. (Yet the date of the book is 1852!) Lobe can only recommend youth to steady itself by studying the older works and finding out for itself what it is in them that makes them endure—"the essential, eternal laws"—and then judging the new works by these "laws." There need be no conflict between youth and age. "To shake oneself free of the disposition and the bias natural to each age is indeed difficult, but still possible, since there are old people who know how to enjoy and estimate rightly *everything* good, whether old or new, and there are young people who are also capable of this."

*

*　*

Next comes a chapter on "Musical Criticism." Once more Lobe describes by anticipation the situation of to-day. There is too much writing *about* music, he says: "Whoever does not withdraw from it and isolate himself absolutely is lost." The criticism is mostly negative; it gives the masses a sort of half-culture, but for the man of distinguished talent it is poisonous, an obstacle to his free and healthy growth. This is how Goethe described the literary world of *his* day, in a conversation with Eckermann; but that time was one of innocence compared with ours [Lobe's]. "Each coterie, each critical tribunal has its masked emissaries, whom it sends out to summon the artist to appear before the court, and be condemned for offending against its arbitrary and unauthorized laws." Then comes a sentence that makes us think once more about our own situation. We complain to-day that criticism has outstripped creation—that our critical faculties have become so sharpened and subtilized by exercise upon the great art of four centuries that very little of the music produced to-day can satisfy us. But evidently people were saying much the same thing in 1852; and Lobe's answer to them is that it is not the lack of creative talent that gives rise to the criticism, but the noxiousness of criticism that prevents many a talent from developing to its full possibilities. "Until the pernicious power of the Press is broken, until the earlier innocent and ingenuous times of art-creation and art-enjoyment come again, we cannot hope to get the old productive power in its old freshness, youthful strength, and purity"; at present not only the public but the composers are confused by the contradictoriness, the incompetence, and often the dishonesty of criticism.

If this were true in Lobe's day, how much truer is it in ours! How many good composers have been momentarily discouraged, how many bad ones permanently encouraged, by unintelligent criticism?

For the majority of critics, says Lobe, are mere dilettanti, mere bunglers; no one can find to-day such critics as Lessing, Goethe, the two Schlegels, Schiller, and, in music, Rochlitz, Hoffmann, etc. He divides the generality of critics into four species: the art-enthusiasts, who merely, so to speak, enthuse; the art-chatterers, without knowledge and without judgment, who just repeat parrot-like the phrases of the day; the art-hypocrites, who think one thing and say another, for fear of being thought ignorant; and the art-liars, "the most dangerous, the most mischievous of all, who form coteries and deserve a Letter to themselves." The number of people writing about music who are competent to do so is very small. Lobe proceeds to give some specimens of the critical inanities of his time, which are astonishingly like the things we meet with in the articles of to-day. And evidently the critics not only had their catchwords then as they have now, but they were the same catchwords: "genius must be free"; this composer's standpoint is "antiquated"; this other has "opened new paths"; and so on. Judgments of this sort, says the pithy old Lobe, are like certain hard nuts; you crack them with difficulty, and find in them only a poor little withered kernal, or a maggot, or—nothing at all. The outcome of it all is confusion for both the public and the artist. Especially bad is it for the young composer, who is told that the old masterpieces are played out, and that he must, for good or evil, find a "new standpoint of his own," "break new paths."

It is all as true now as it was then; but is there anything more now than there was then in the good Lobe's recommendation to the young composer to seek out the eternal laws in the works of the old masters and follow these? What *are* the eternal laws, and how can we be sure that an apparent flouting of them in a particular case is not really an extension of them?

Once more Lobe seems to be describing our own day by anticipation when he speaks of "Musical Coteries and Parties." Everyone, he says, who wants to assert himself chooses from among the journalists a band of retainers to precede and surround him on his artistic path, to announce his coming with trumpets, to extol at the top of their voices the wonders he is going to perform, to exalt his past achievement above everything that has been, is, or ever shall be, and to disparage his rivals; "even when he sneezes, the whole band cries out: 'Listen to the great man! Only a genius can sneeze like that!'" It was this type of uncritical enthusiast that once provoked a savage outburst from Hugo Wolf, in one of his articles in the Vienna *Salonblatt*. When Brahms's fourth symphony was first produced, the official Brahms incense-bearers drew the attention of the world to the portentous fact that neither Mozart nor Beethoven nor Schubert nor Mendelssohn nor Schumann ever wrote a symphony in the key of E minor. "A colossal revelation!" cried Wolf sarcastically. "What an original, profound composer Brahms must be, to be able not merely to write, like Beethoven, in C, D, or F, but, for the first time, in E minor! Heavens! I am beginning to tremble before the uncanny genius of Herr Brahms!" And only a year or two ago were we not assured, by a distinguished English critic, that Ravel's sneeze had a potency in it that the uninitiated would never have suspected? "Ravel," we were told, "is not only a prince of classicists, he is the saviour of classicism. He has rescued the distressed maiden

from the attentions of the dragon of portentous drab-
ness. After listening to Ravel we can still believe that
the classics were human beings." To think that we
might never have felt we could really be sure of the
humanity of Bach and Mozart had Ravel not conde-
scended to be born!

There are, continues Lobe, journalistic factories for
the manufacture and marketing of a composer's fame.
Lobe's advice to the public is not to be taken in by
these publicity campaigns, but to use its own judgment upon the music it hears.

Rather better than the cliques and the claques are
the parties—the assemblies of people who cannot exist
without a god, or at least a demigod, and who are
prepared to fight all other sects in the name of their
own deity. Lobe cites the Gluckists and Piccinists
as typical of these sects: "Neither is in possession of
the whole truth, yet neither is wholly wrong. Each
is driven into extremes by the opposition of the
other. . . . In our days we have the Mendelssohn
and the Schumann parties. . . . They judge not according to the works but according to the names, for
the Mendelssohnians regard every work of their idol
as excellent merely because it is by Mendelssohn."
Ergo, concludes Lobe, *censeo claquas, cliquas et cot-
terias esse delendas*—a sentiment that everyone who
has followed the musical wrangles of to-day will echo
from the bottom of his heart.

*
* *

The further I dip into Lobe the more similarities I
find between his point of view and that of many of us

to-day. In his next chapter, on "Reflection and Ingen-uousness," he remarks: "Everyone knows, feels and laments that no really great works are being written in our day, or at all events that they are very scarce. There is any amount of capable writing—so much, indeed, that it is harder now for a composer to attract attention to himself than in the old days when the general level was not so high; as Goethe said: 'I am thankful that I am not eighteen now. When I was eighteen, Germany also was eighteen; something could still be done then; but now an incredible amount is expected of one, and every path is barred.'"

Lobe will not have it that the composer of the present [his] day fails through "reflection" as op-posed to the (fictitious) "ingenuousness" of the older masters, for a certain amount of "taking thought" there must be in the freest and most spontaneous out-pouring of artistic emotion. The trouble rather is that the young artists of to-day "reflect" in the wrong way. "They do not reflect how they can say some-thing true and beautiful, but how they can say some-thing out of the common, something never said before, and thereby draw attention to themselves and make a noise in the world; . . . they imagine that the music that gives pleasure is too ordinary, too easy, too *démodé* in its standpoint." In Lobe's day this "new spirit" took the form of a noisy and confused expression of the *Weltschmerz;* in our later day it takes other forms; but in each case, as Lobe says, a system is first of all consciously evolved, and then works are written to illustrate the system; "they re-gard all the music written before to-day as imperfect, exert themselves to lead the art into quite new paths, try to create a 'music of the future,' and make their music as little like the preceding 'false' music as possible.   They fail in part because their thinking is wrong, in part because their technique is not equal to their task."

Really, this old Leipzig musician of 1852 seems to have thought of everything some three generations before us!   He anticipates the modern critic even in his remarks on the minor grievances of the musical life; he tells us, for instance, that "most concerts are too long"; that the orchestra should spare us the usual horrible preliminary noises by tuning up before it comes on to the platform; that programme notes are helpful to some extent, but would be more helpful still if the public could read them before instead of during the performance; in this matter the Press could do good service by writing about the work before the performance rather than after it; and so on.   Lobe even anticipated those bright spirits of to-day who hold that the only way to ensure that people shall listen to a work without prejudice and without pre-possessions is to keep the composer's name out of the programme: "Leipzig hissed an Overture by Bach when it did not know the work was by that revered old composer. . . . In Paris several things of the kind have happened, and we can boldly assert that every public would be painfully embarrassed if for some time works were performed before it without the composers' names."   It would be a good way to test the alleged good taste of the public: "If the Directors of the Leipzig concerts, for instance, believe firmly in the often-praised judgment of their public, let them refrain from giving a single composer's name through one whole winter, and we shall then see whether it knows good work from bad."

But I need not follow Lobe in all his anticipations of modern musical criticism. What I want to see now is how he applies in his own practice the excellent maxims he has been unloading so generously upon the young man who had sought his advice.

*

* *

The second volume of his work consists of discussions of sixteen composers of his own and an earlier time. In all his judgments he shows himself a sound musician, and of uncompromising honesty. Now and then it is a little difficult to weigh him accurately because we cannot quite place ourselves at his point of view and that of his time. He has a vigorous chapter on "Bach Mania." The deification of Bach was just beginning, and Lobe felt that it was his duty to utter a warning against it. We now get our first hint of how too complete an absorption in a particular technique of composition can affect a critic's point of view. Lobe reveals himself everywhere as a man of what we may call the sonata-form period. Instrumental music, he virtually implies, began with Haydn, was developed by Mozart, and came to a climax in Beethoven. He has a subconscious prejudice against polyphony for polyphony's sake, of which he finds too many examples in Bach. "We have only to look with expert and unprejudiced eyes at Bach's Suites for orchestra, his concerto for two claviers, etc., to see already the tasteless, stiff, old-fashioned quality of the ideas. Listen to them and dare to tell the truth as to what you have heard. Certainly there can be no question of 'pleasure' here for people who have heard

the works of Mozart, Beethoven, etc.; if they profess
to have received pleasure they are either hypocrites, or
are deceiving themselves, or really do not know what
music is, will be, and can be. Bach, from this point
of view, loses none of his *historical* greatness; only
the language of the Bachianers, Forkel, the elder
Griepenkerl, Marx, Hilgenfeldt and their echoes appears in the harshest conflict with the impression that
the Bach works make on the cultivated and unprejudiced hearer."   Bach was "a great talent; he was the
best of his time; but it is a ludicrous exaggeration to
regard him as *the best of all times,* as an 'eternal
model' for music."

We have to remember that comparatively little of
Bach was known even then (the Bach-Gesellschaft
was only just commencing its labours on the complete
edition of his works).   But it seems clear that what
Lobe most objected to in Bach was his excessive de-
votion to counterpoint, resulting sometimes in music
that is not clear to the ear, however impressive it may
be to the eye.   He has been, says Lobe, a bad influence
on many modern composers—among them Schumann,
"in whose later large works there is hardly a trace of
expressive melody, but more and more of over-
subtilized part-writing."   Too much Bach study, in
fact, "kills the feeling for pure melody, and awakes
the delight in ingenious contrapuntal combinations for
which any idea, even the most trivial, will serve, although it expresses nothing and has not the least
melodic charm."   The point of view, as I have said,
is that of the man brought up on the classical symphony and its allied forms.   Lobe sees a happy and
fruitful future for instrumental music only in the de-

velopment of these forms, that for him mean beauty, expressiveness, and clarity.

On Haydn, Mozart and Beethoven he writes soundly and well. But about the latter he has some curious things to say. Beethoven has indeed completed the stately building begun by Haydn and developed by Mozart; "but it was he also who, in the later days, began the destruction of the building." He goes unreservedly with Beethoven only as far as his second period; the third period he regards as one of doubt, confusion, and partial failure; he refers to the later quartets, the Mass in D, and the Ninth Symphony. He particularly objects to the new passion for the polyphonic in Beethoven's later works, which results, he holds, in a good deal of confused writing. "His last works are more for the eye than the ear; they read better than they sound." Lobe has no doubt whatever as to the rightness of his judgment; he relies on those "eternal laws" of beauty that he has already expounded at such length; and anyone who disagrees with him as regards these later works of Beethoven is either incompetent or a hypocrite. It follows, for him, that the influence of Beethoven on contemporary composers is in large measure a bad one; they attempt to carry still further the wrong principles of the third period, instead of developing the principles of the second. The side-blow, I fancy, is at Wagner.

Lobe's studies of Schubert, Weber, Spohr, Marschner, and others, excellent as they are, do not closely concern my present purpose, which is to see how his admirable theoretic principles of criticism served or failed him when he tried to put them in practice. (He is particularly sound, let me remark, on Spohr, whom, although the composer was still living, he sees steadily and whole.) About Mendelssohn he writes sensibly. Meyerbeer he over-praises, to our modern thinking; "he possesses more true talent and genuine inner force than all the young composers who now contend with him; his works have therefore a much higher value than all those of the so-called new reformers. . . . Meyerbeer is unquestionably the most significant figure in the present transition period of music"; he may go wrong now and then, but in the main he follows the true paths of the art.

In the article on Lortzing and Flotow he makes a comparison that seems odd to us of to-day. "Lortzing incontestably had neither so great a talent nor so good a schooling as, for example, Schumann or Wagner; but he had a purer simplicity, a better knowledge of himself, more discretion, and a more cheerful spirit. He knew his limitations, and did not expect from himself more than there was in him—which cannot be said of some others. . . . Only in one thing is Lortzing like Wagner—like the latter he wrote his own texts, which are better than the music."

Of Gade he thinks a great deal. "He is one of the most gifted and certainly the soundest of the new men. . . . If he is no Beethoven, yet in the main he surpasses the much-praised new composers, especially in his adherence to rational maxims." Gade considers the public, which is praiseworthy of him, but the young people think little of him—much less than they do of Schumann; "and this I regard as a dubious sign of the times, for it shows that the unintelligible now counts for more with youth, and has more attraction for it, than the intelligible and clear."

Lobe's last two Letters are devoted to the two musicians whom he evidently regards as the most important of the day, if not necessarily in the sense that they are the greatest, at any rate in the sense that they have attracted the most attention. He is more critical of each of them than of any of the other composers whom he has been discussing.

Schumann's fame he puts down in large part to the coterie spirit—the anti-Mendelssohn party wanted a leader to fight under, and it chose Schumann—and in part also to the vigorous journalism conducted on his behalf by the young Romantic school. Lobe thinks well of the early sonata (op. 11)—"this work has not received the consideration it deserves, for everything that is characteristic of Schumann is already visible in it, his good qualities as well as his faults and weaknesses"—and of the first symphony. But "in his second symphony he had already departed from the right way, and so, in spite of all the journalistic clamour, it did not make the effect of the first. The third symphony and his latest work, the *Requiem for Mignon,* I do not know." His opera *Genoveva* failed because of his lack of feeling for the stage. He has written a number of very good songs and smaller piano pieces; "but he writes too much, too quickly, too incessantly. He relies too much on his name; he is not particular enough in his choice, and has not patience enough to use the file. In a word, like the majority of the new composers, he is too indulgent a father to the children of his own imagination." His themes are not always significant, and instead of developing them as Beethoven does his he trusts to mere repetition of them; he resembles Beethoven only in the weakness of his fugal writing. "His harmony and

modulation are sometimes interesting, piquant and surprising, sometimes harsh and painful to the ear."
He has a genuine gift for simple, moving melody, but
it does not appear very often in his larger works,
especially his symphonies; Gade is superior to him in
this respect, not to mention Schubert. His sense of
form is naturally good, as the first symphony and the
D minor trio show; but in his later works, through
attempting to be deep and original, his form goes to
pieces. Lobe finishes up with a warning. The only
way to bring music home to the people is not, as many
of the new spirits seem to think, to make it more complex, but to keep it simple. "If Schumann continues
upon the path he has lately entered upon, in which he
is less and less particular about clear form and the
melodic element, he will become, I am afraid, like
Sisyphus, who vainly tried to roll the stone uphill, or
Icarus, who would fly to the sky on waxen wings.
But if he will give himself a little rest, work as the
true geniuses, the great masters, have done, does not
accept each and every idea that comes to him no matter how and when, but chooses and tests and files it
as Beethoven did his, if he returns to melody, clarity
and intelligibility, then, I doubt not, he will produce
works that will really deserve the acclamations and
the laurels that are now undeservedly showered on him
by his clique."

The fact that Lobe reserves Wagner for the last
study of all in his volume shows that he was sensible
of his importance. He admires him, however, with
reservations. "Richard Wagner is undoubtedly the
most significant talent of our time; but he overtops all
his colleagues not merely by the greatness of his gifts
but by the greatness of the error to which he is a

victim.   That a talent like Wagner should press forward in his art is very natural and quite intelligible;
his mistake and his misfortune are that he goes too
far, he does not preserve moderation, but goes to excess . . . How easy it would be for him to surpass
all the new men and become the darling of the whole
German public.   But he *will* not, because he has a
false conception of art."   Lobe proceeds to analyse
Wagner's theories as set forth in *Opera and Drama,*
and concludes his study and his book thus:

"I have insisted on the element of error in Wagner,
and given less attention to the many beauties of his
works, because all these beauties do *not* derive from
his system but from the maxims of other good masters
that I have already set before you in this volume; and
my final judgment of him is this: Wagner is a
genius, or at any rate certainly an extraordinary double-
talent, both composer and poet.   But the passion for
novelty, the desire to do something unusual, the pre-
dominance of fantasy, the want of a clear, untroubled,
tranquil sense of reality, have unfortunately led him
into wrong paths."

III

So much for Lobe. He has interested me enormously. What can we learn from him? Little that he fain would teach us, perhaps, but a good deal of which he himself was quite unconscious. He is a complete "case"; he is like some dead animal that has been preserved whole into a later century than its own, for the benefit of the scientist. Can we use him, profit by him, as the scientist would by the animal survival?

Of his competence, as of his honesty, there can be no doubt. He is a thoroughly trained musician; I have just been skimming another book of his, the fourth volume of his *Lehrbuch der musikalischen Komposition.* This is a searching study of the technique of the opera, and is full of sound judgments upon every constituent of that genre. It was published in 1867, and was evidently still so highly esteemed twenty years later that no less an authority than Hermann Kretzschmar brought out a new and enlarged edition of it. (It is this second edition that is in my friend's library, and apparently it needs to be used with a little caution, for there is nothing to indicate that the chapters dealing with the later Wagner are not by Lobe but by Kretzschmar.) Of the soundness of Lobe's musicianship there can be no question; this, indeed, is apparent enough from the *Briefe* of 1852. In that year Lobe was about fifty-five years of age, a man of real standing in the German musical world, not a journalist dealing casually with the affairs of the moment, but an author working carefully and shrewdly over the whole field of the German music

75

of his time. His probity is as undoubted as his competence. Plainly he belongs to no party, and some of the composers whom he discusses so frankly were, or had been, his personal friends or acquaintances.

There is very little in his theory of criticism that is not as valid to-day, or in any day, as it was then. He is, as I have said, a shade too evidently a man of the classical symphonic period; but his bias towards the tradition of Haydn, Mozart, and Beethoven scarcely affects his judgments of music in general. He was quite certain that he had discovered the immutable laws of good music, and that his own criticism of his contemporaries was firmly based on these. If, then, such a man fails to appraise his contemporaries rightly, what hope can there be that the soundness of the theoretical principles of any of us to-day will ensure correct judgment? How, then, when all is said, does Lobe stand as a critic of the new men of his time, and when he goes wrong can we discover why? If we can, we shall be at any rate the richer by a negative principle or two for our own work. If the post-mortem shows us what the critic and his criticism died of, we shall at all events get a hint of what to avoid in our own way of critical living.

In the main, Lobe's judgments are sound. The one thing it is really difficult for us to understand to-day is his high opinion of Meyerbeer. His over-estimate of Gade is perhaps more easily explicable. He is not blind to Gade's weaknesses, but there was something in the general spirit of the Dane's music that appealed to him. May we conjecture that this first tang of northern "national" feeling had a charm for German musicians of that day that it no longer has for us? Did people, meeting with this new accent for the first time, fall victims to its piquancy very much in the way that English people have been known to fall victims to Russian national music at their first encounter with it? Schumann also, it will be remembered, had hopes of Gade that were not realized; the Dane impressed Schumann in 1843, as he did Lobe in 1852, as one of the most original and promising of the younger composers of the day; "we can only express," he said, "our hopes for the worthiest and finest things to come from such remarkable talent." This is one of the instances in which it is hard for a later generation to place itself at the point of view of an earlier one; how are we to account, for example, for the enormous reputation of Telemann in his own day? It would be worth the while of some student to make a special study of cases of this kind, with a view to discovering just what it was in the music of such men that gave them the hold they had on the imagination of their contemporaries.

It is when Lobe comes to deal with Wagner and Schumann that we feel his judgment to have been most at fault. Yet certain considerations must not be overlooked. Contemporary criticism is always more apt to fasten on the weaknesses of a composer than on the virtues that will assure his immortality. The contemporary critic is not far enough away from his subject to see him quite in the round; for one thing, the composer's work is not yet finished. The excellences in it are savoured quietly; the faults in it stir deeper reactions. It is too often forgotten that a good deal of contemporary critical fault-finding was perfectly justified; if we do not insist on the faults now it is because the perception of them is so universal that there is no necessity to talk about them. To-day one would almost as little think of censuring Wagner for his mannerisms of style, such as his sequences, as one would of rushing into print to say that Queen Anne was dead; but a contemporary critic would have had every justification for pointing to these sequences as weakness on the composer's part and advising him not to indulge so copiously in them.   Much that Lobe says in dispraise of Schumann is perfectly true, and was well worth saying at that time.   As for Wagner, we must remember in the first place that in 1852 the only works by which Lobe could judge him were *Rienzi, The Flying Dutchman, Tannhäuser, and Lohengrin.* The later Wagner had not yet so much as given a hint of himself; for some years after the production of *Lohengrin* in 1850 he appeared before the public only as a prose writer.   Lobe's criticism of him is based mostly on *Opera and Drama,* which had just been published; and it is easy to imagine the effect that this and others of Wagner's prose works must have had on the average musician of the day, with their involved style, their rambling and hysterical political and social disquisitions, their dubious literary views, their disparagement of so many dead and living composers, and their exceedingly confused presentment of a new theory of opera the validity of which could only be tested when the work written to illustrate it—the *Ring*—was given to the world many years later.   If we examine Lobe's criticism in detail, we see that it is practically all justified.   Neither he nor anyone else at that time could know that however muddled a thinker Wagner might be in politics or sociology, however inclined he might be to regard his own peculiarities of æsthetic psychology as laws for the rest of the world, the *musician* in him was developing steadily and sanely in secret.   All in all, for his time Lobe judged him pretty fairly. At any rate he was conscious of his unusual quality.

But these pages of Lobe's contain, I think, a valuable lesson for us, if only a negative one. It is clear that his judgment tended to be deflected at times by the stupidity of many of the critics of the day, and by the folly of the partisans of this or that composer. His irritation at these people is always showing itself unknown to him. He tells us that some of the Schumann partisans not only ranked their idol with Beethoven, but placed him above him. Lobe's sense of workmanship alone would make him jib at this. He saw Schumann being used by one clique as a weapon with which to beat the Mendelssohn clique; and his sense of the injustice that must often have been done to Mendelssohn must have made him subconsciously inclined to stress to the utmost any point he could legitimately raise against Schumann. The blindly partisan journalists must have been the half-comic, half-serious irritation then that their successors are now. It must have been an irritation to see Schumann lauded as the "reformer of opera" when all he had done was to produce one conspicuous failure in that genre and to demonstrate to every impartial observer that though he could write good music here and there to an operatic text he really had no genius for the stage. And the *Weltschmerz* that the Schumannians so admired in him, and on the strength of which they declared him to be a deeper thinker than Beethoven, must have affected many of the better balanced spirits of that period as disagreeably as it sometimes does the anti-Romantic mind of to-day.

IV

THE test to which we put a critic of the past is this—
did he see his own age *sub specie aeternitatis?*   Did
he pierce through all the little things of the day that
did not matter and get to the heart of the things that
really did?   This is the test, we may depend upon it,
to which each critic of to-day will be put in the next
generation or the one after that by anyone who may
have the curiosity to make research into contemporary
critical opinion.   And the critic of to-day may perhaps
be helped to strip the little problems of his own time
of their inessentials and get to the *Ding an sich* by
discovering what it was that prevented otherwise
sound critics from doing so in the past.   One of the
causes, I am sure, was excess of reaction due to pure
irritation at the follies of the more extreme partisans
on each side.   And what may be called the classical
party is always specially prone to this irritation.
"Classic" and "romantic" are better terms than "conservative" and "radical," or "reactionary" and "progressive," or "age" and "youth."   All these other
terms beg the question; they correspond to no real
antithesis.   There never was a time in which all the
younger people were on one side and all the older
people on the other, and there never will be such a
time.   It is pure fancy to paint the present period,
for instance, in these crudely contrasted colours.   A
considerable number of young people are pro-
Schönberg and anti-Beethoven; but there are just as
many people of the same age of the opposite way of
thinking.   There are young conservatives and elderly

radicals. "Reactionary" and "progressive," again, are terms devoid of real meaning in music, for the simple reason that since none of us knows what line the music of even the next ten years will take, none of us can say which among the many lines that music is taking to-day is the line of progress. All we can be sure of is that music is changing; and "progress" is only the term given by excitable and self-complacent people to the form of change with which they happen to be most in sympathy; the man who calls himself a "progressive" is merely indulging in a not very subtle form of self-flattery; he implies that he has a prophetic insight into the future that is denied to less gifted mortals. "Reactionary" is a meaningless epithet in art. Reaction does not always and necessarily mean stagnation; it may mean simply the healthy perception that one is on the wrong path and a healthy determination to shift to the right one. If in the middle of a run that I am enjoying immensely I suddenly find myself at the edge of a precipice, and I pull myself up sharply, I am indeed reacting; but to become a "reactionary" is, under these circumstances, the most sensible thing I could do. A "reactionary," in fact, is simply and literally one who reacts; and whether his reaction is good or bad for him and other people depends entirely on what it is that he reacts against. He very wisely "reacts" against a cold in the head, and takes quinine to help him in the reaction, instead of letting the fever "progress." If we apply the term "reactionary" in an opprobrious sense to someone else, we mean no more, in our simplicity, than that he shows his lack of intelligence by not thinking as we think; we get back to the innocent self-flattery involved in calling ourselves "progressive."

It is for the future, not for us, to decide whether the way we are taking is the way of progress, or whether we should not have done better in the long run to have refrained from taking it. *Nicht jeder Vorschritt ist ein Fortschritt.*

"Classic" and "romantic" are not open to any of these objections. They carry with them no moral implications; they merely define two frames of mind that have been more or less in opposition ever since art began. There is no need to attempt definitions of them; everybody is familiar with the type of mind that, at the end of a great period of art, compares what has been done in the past with what is being done in the present and finds the former superior, and the type of mind that is at once much less sensitive to the great art of the past and much more ready to be thrilled by the art of the moment merely because it *is* of the moment. There is really no reason why the two types should be regarded as hopelessly irreconcilable; and, indeed, if the mind of the ordinary cultivated man in any period were critically examined it would probably be found that he was neither wholly classically minded nor wholly romantically minded, but that he combined a keen enjoyment of the past with a lively interest in the present.

But the history of art shows that the extremes of the two types always come into sharp conflict with each other, and the extravagances of the one type set up reactions of irritation in the other. History does not tell us the full story, because it fastens only on the broad features of the conflict; it does not show us quite how the conflict appeared to the men who were in the thick of it. Least of all does it do justice to the classicists; it is much too prone to assume that they were mere "reactionaries." It fails to take account of the enormous amount of sheer foolishness that is indulged in by the young romantics of every age, and of the pardonable contempt that the classicist must feel for all this foolishness. Every new movement, not only in art but in politics and in social affairs, throws up a large number of not very intelligent people who are infected by the excitement around them and stimulated by it to a self-expression that may be excellent as a safety-valve for themselves, but does not add very much to the world's store of wisdom. They are like the bits of paper on the platform of the suburban station that are caught up and set whirling in the track of an express train; they are not, as they fancy, the cause of the motion, but one of the minor consequences of it. It is this swarm of voluble and futile people that makes every new movement a trifle ridiculous in the eyes of the classicist.

It is on this point that posterity does not quite do justice to the classicist critics of a bygone epoch. Posterity sees only the two or three bigger figures that have emerged from a period of storm and stress; it knows nothing of the crowd of foolish, or abortive, or pathetic little figures that surrounded them, and were, to the eyes of the time, sometimes indistinguishable from them. No study of this type of secondary artist has yet been made in music. Perhaps it would hardly be worth anyone's while to undertake it; it would mean laboriously working through a huge mass of music that has perished through sheer inanition; and why should anyone waste his time on old dead music when there is so much old music that is still alive and to the secret of which he never has time to penetrate? But a literary epoch here and there supplies us with the data we require—the romantic movement in France, for instance, in the early years of the nineteenth century.

*

*   *

All epochs of ferment and expansion are essentially alike; the names change, the formulæ change, but the points at issue are eternally the same; Victor Hugo's famous preface to *Cromwell* is, in essence, the manifesto of the new spirit in every age.   But while history records in full the victory of the main forces in these eternal conflicts, it is almost silent as to the ineffective little revolters who tried to assert themselves here and there, and who, we may be sure, did much more than the great and really vital figures to arouse the antipathy of the classicists.   Nowhere does history repeat itself with such monotonous uniformity as in this eternal resurgence of the romantic in art.   A set of formulæ could be worked out that would embrace every period of the kind; the same types come forward, the same battle cries are uttered, the same banners are unfurled, there are the same casualties on both sides, and the final peace leaves things very much as they were before the war broke out.   We recognize the present period of revolt in music in another form in M. Léo Claretie's description of the romantic revolt in French literature in the early nineteenth century: "Literature felt this necessity for liberalism.   Vocabulary, syntax, prosody, all were set free.   No more 'grand seigneur' words, no more 'roturier' words.   The rigid alexandrine was broken up, smashed; rhythms and cadences took on a free and disengaged gait (as in *Les Orientales*, the *Ballade à la Lune, A la Rime*), to

the point of virtuosity and jugglery." And behind
the leaders was a great host of men-at-arms, sharp-
shooters, camp followers, and what not, who aped the
manner of their betters, and claimed for themselves
the same liberty of expression. As M. Claretie says,
if you are going to ask the public to take a passionate
interest in yourself, your self must be worth taking an
interest in. A Lamartine, a Hugo, a de Musset, yes;
"but the others, the poets of the second rank, what
had *they* wherewith to attract the indifferent crowd?
They created themselves; they forged a factitious
originality for themselves *à toutes pièces;* and in this
way they thought to prove themselves original, whereas as a matter of fact they were only 'originals.' " . . .
"They drew the attention of the public to themselves
by their manner, their aspect, their *façons d'être*
and *façons de dire.* They were the *enfants terribles*
of romanticism." One recalls the description of
the early Prokoviev as an *enfant terrible* tweak-
ing the noses of the academics. Unfortunately
it is so easy to tweak noses, especially if the owners
of the noses refuse to take you seriously and
only smile indulgently at you while you are doing
it. Much of this nose-tweaking in art, this display of
terrible infantilism, is merely the natural ebullience of
youth before it has come to the age of discretion. In
the early nineteenth century it took the form of
wrenching off door-knockers and upsetting watchmen's
huts. In the eighteenth century, as we learn from
Steele, it took the form of jostling people off the pavement, "roasting porters, smoking cobblers, knocking
down watchmen, overturning constables, breaking
windows, blackening sign-posts, and the like immortal
enterprises, that dispersed their reputation through-

out the whole kingdom," and in smashing windows by projecting halfpennies through them; as Gay sings in his *Trivia, or The Art of Walking the Streets of London:*

> His scatter'd Pence the flying *Nicker* flings,
> And with the Copper Show'r the Casement rings.
> Who has not heard the *Scowrer's* Midnight Fame?
> Who has not trembled at the *Mohock's* name?

In the days of Alcibiades it took the form of roystering and bullying one's way through the streets of Athens, to the danger and terror of respectable citizens. In the London of to-day it takes the form, each Boat Race night, of rowdyism in the theatres and an arm-in-arm sweeping of the pavements in Shaftesbury Avenue. In circles that are devoted to less physical and more intellectual delights it takes the form of writing consecutive fifths, or, more lately, of doing fearsome things in the way of atonality and polytonality. But always the spirit is the same—the eternal, admirable, joyous spirit that prompts youth to bash established things for the pure joy of bashing.

But the system has its drawbacks. Just as now and then a sober citizen, on Boat Race night, objects to being pushed off the pavement or to the spoiling of the theatrical entertainment to which he has taken his wife and daughters at considerable expense to himself, so it sometimes happens that the sober classicist feels a slight annoyance at the hullabaloo kicked up by the young romanticist—a hullabaloo that, as an entertainment, hardly seems to the classicist to be worth watching, still less worth paying for. He finds that the less there is in the young romanticist the more seriously does he take himself. There is a certain modesty

about a Hugo or a Gautier in spite of his exuberance;
for exuberance without modesty, for a conceit, indeed,
that passes all limits of the permissible, we have to
go to a Petrus Borel.

> "Je veux, au siècle paraître,
>   Etaler ma nudité,"

he cries in one of his *Rapsodies* (1831). The
"blood" in art is always displaying his nudity. He
always innocently assumes that the world is, or ought
to be, passionately interested in the spectacle. It
never occurs to him that his figure may not have that
perfection of proportion that alone could justify so
confident a claim on the attention of mankind. There
are Borels in every new movement. The music of
to-day is full of them. There is, for instance, the
Red Russian composer, Leopold Herwen, who tells
us that we must destroy everything and begin all over
again, and that he is the person to do the destroying.
He has "abolished" tonality: "if it pleases me to sup-
press tonality, I do so," he loftily told an interviewer.
He has composed, he proudly confesses, a sonata in
C sharp minor in which C sharp is never once used.
He is frankly contemptuous of so effete a gang as
"The Six." For centuries the musical ear has been
perverted by "monstrous falsehoods" of melody,
harmony, and rhythm; it is his mission in life to re-
store the ear to its primal soundness.

The Borels and the Herwens are perhaps extreme
specimens, but the type is familiar to the student of
every period of ferment in the arts. The crowd of
little hangers-on, of pretentious half-talents, of abortive no-talents, that we see taking part in the artistic

movements of to-day are merely the descendants of
the people who brought into ridicule, for their contemporaries, such movements as that of French
romanticism in the eighteen-thirties, or of the German
musical romanticism of the mid-nineteenth century.
Each party to the conflict is inclined, in the heat of
the moment, to a confusion of the standards of value.
For the young French Romanticist, all the writers of
the preceding age were, without distinction, *vieux jeu;*
while the classicists, sinking minor differences in
face of the common enemy, as a nation does when it
is attacked, welcomed all under their banner who were
not romantic. "Neither the classics nor the romantics," says M. Claretie, "distinguished between Boileau
and Voltaire, or Voltaire and Viennet . . ."; and
"the romantics thought it necessary to demolish Racine
to crush M. de Jon," just as some of the revolters of
to-day think it necessary to reject Beethoven and
Brahms in order to make it clear that they have a
soul above Tchaikovski and Puccini. It is these extravagances on either side that confuse what is always,
in reality, quite a simple situation. The romantics
being themselves unable to distinguish between the
seminal forces and the impotencies within their own
ranks, it is hardly to be wondered at that the classicists often confuse the two. What is generally not
taken into consideration, in writing the history of
artistic "movements," is that the so-called reactionaries were perfectly right in their disparagement of
nineteen-twentieths of the so-called progressives.
Time has amply justified them; but since the mediocrities have been forgotten, it is also forgotten that
much of the opposition of the new movement was di-

rected against them rather than against the three or
four truly big figures of the time.

Théophile Gautier's *Histoire du Romanticisme* has
this value among others, that it shows us how a movement of revolt appeared in later years to one who had
taken a prominent part in it. Gautier himself has to
admit that in the trail of the half-dozen artists of
the time who really mattered came an army of little
people of whom their contemporaries and they themselves took much too flattering a view. Even Petrus
Borel—a fourth-rate mind if ever there was one—inspired the young Gautier with "exceeding awe"; he
treated Borel, he says, "with an amount of respect
quite unusual between young fellows of nearly an
age. . . . I thought him remarkably clever, and had
concluded that he would be the particular great man
of our company. He was slowly elaborating the
Rapsodies in mysterious secrecy, intending that they
should suddenly blaze forth like lightning, or at least
dazzle the astounded bourgeoisie." The Borels we
have always with us; who does not recognize a hundred
specimens of the type in the music of to-day? They
are always about to blaze; always, like Mr. Snodgrass,
taking off their coats and announcing that they are
going to begin. And an admiring world waits ex-
pectantly; but the coat never gets any lower than the
shoulders, the blaze never becomes more than the
spluttering of a squib.

Where are Philothée O'Neddy and the other bright
young spirits of those ardent years of the romantic
movement? Where are even the second- and the
third-rate artists who for a moment promised so well?
Devéria is typical of them all. "Nascent romantic-

ism," said Gautier in the later days, "built the highest
hopes upon Eugène Devéria. Darkness and forget-
fulness have long since fallen upon his fame, which
arose in a blaze of splendour, admiration and enthusiasm. No man ever started so brilliantly, or held out
fairer promise." He was, in fact, one of the kind
we have seen in such profusion in music during the
last decade or two—geniuses at eighteen, mediocrities
at thirty, and nonentities at forty. Louis Boulanger
was another of the romantics who "died almost un-
noticed after having blazed at their beginnings in the
splendour of lightnings. . . . Everyone believed that
he was destined to have a brilliant future, and his
splendid success at the outset justified the highest
hopes."

It is easy enough to "place" your young contemporaries twenty or thirty years afterwards. But is
it not probable that many a despised classicist "placed"
these young romantics accurately at the time? Look
at so eternal a type as Philothée O' Neddy; he appears
in the music of to-day under many names. "No one
more than Philothée O'Neddy," says Gautier, "ex-
hibited these characteristics of extravagance and ten-
sion. The expression 'paroxyst,' first employed by
Nestor Roqueplan, seems to have been invented
specially for Philothée. In all he did the tone was
excessive, the colouring exaggerated and violent, the
utmost bounds of expression reached, the very originality aggressive, and the whole almost dripping with
incredibility, as Xavier Aubryet used to say. Never-
theless, the feeling for the poetic period and the harmony of rhythm made itself felt through the absurd
paradoxes, the sophisticated maxims, the incoherent

metaphors, the turgid hyperboles and the six-foot words."

*

*   *

In short, every movement is bound to throw up a large number of essentially mediocre people who attract attention for an hour or two by their energy and vehemence, but have no staying power. It is the business of the contemporary critic to distinguish between these people and the innovators who really matter. It would be well for him, indeed, if he could ignore the mediocrities, for they are apt to provoke reactions in him that may extend to the two or three greater artists of whom these lesser artists are only the ineffective echoes. I am certain that Lobe, for instance, would have seen Schumann and Wagner more steadily had his gaze not been deflected by the antics of the merely noisy mediocrities. As one reads Lobe, one is struck by the frequent recurrence of the expression "the new men." This does not refer to the leaders, but to the swarm of minor composers and to the journalists who were booming these. There must have been dozens of these composers in Germany; we have only to turn up the musical magazines of the time to realize that. How little they really counted for is shown by the fact that not one out of a score among them is now known to the average man even by name. They are of no significance whatever now; they were of no significance whatever then. The truly wise critic of the day would have been the one who saw that they were of no significance, and refused to waste his time on them. By bothering about them as he did, Lobe only allowed them to work him into a state of irritation in which it was difficult for him to see clearly and calmly the really seminal forces of the period.

Every age has an enormous deadweight of insignificant art to carry. I run through the index of the new Jahn-Abert life of Mozart, and note a few of the composers of the age most of whose very names are now forgotten—Abel, Abos, Anfossi, Agrell, Accorimboni, Bonno, Badia, Bambini, Beck, Beecke, Binder, Calegari, Cambini, Cannabich, Champein, Cirri, Coignet, Conti, Caffaro, Dezède, Fabrizi, Ferrandini, Friberth, Gardi, Gassmann, Gauss, Gazzaniga, Graf, Guglielmi, Hertel, Hoffmeister, Holzbauer, Honauer, Hurlebusch, Kirchoff, Knecht, the two Kozeluchs, Lampugnani, Latilla, Le Tellier, van Maldere, Maschek, Meissner, Manna, the two di Majos, Pallavicini, Paradisi, Perez, Pescetti, Pleyel, Raupach, Ricci, Rinaldo da Capua, Rutini, Schlöger, Schulz, Schwindel, Starzer, Steffan, Tarantino, Terradellas, Tuma, Umlauf, Vogler, Wranitzky, Zach, Zelenka. The majority of these were not even the distinguished talents of the time, such as Paisiello, Schobert, Sacchini, Salieri, Dittersdorf, Schenk, and so on. Yet they were persons who made a certain noise in the world in their own generation; and to-day the very names of most of them are unknown except to one student in ten thousand. It has been so in every age. We may take it as certain that it is so in ours. The critic who wants to get a sure sense of values and preserve it will turn away from the vast majority of contemporary composers after a glance or two at them, and refuse to concern himself with them again. They amount to nothing whatever on a broad view

of things; and to spend much time studying them is
to get a false perspective.   I look from the window
of this house, down the noble hill, and take in the vast
curve of the sea coast.   If I am going to make a
properly proportionate map of the district I must be
careful not to put in every insect on every leaf, every
swimmer in the bay.

This, of course, is where it becomes so difficult to be
both critic and journalist.   The latter cannot help a
good deal of his time and energy being wasted on the
mediocrities of the hour; but it is all to the detriment
of the fineness of his perceptions and his sense of proportion as a critic.   The shopkeeper, taking in and
dealing out small change all day, gets no sort of train-
ing for thinking in thousands.   But it is only in thousands that the critic must think, for it is only the
thousands that ultimately matter, not the small change
of art.   I know it is said that the critic should do all
he can to encourage the small composer, with a view
to preparing the field for the big composer.   All this,
however, comes from a confusion of ideas.   One need
neither encourage nor discourage the small composer;
he will go on whether we trouble about him or not.
The point is not whether we shall permit him to compose—to that there can be no objection—but whether
the critic, as distinguished from the musical reporter,
should concern himself with his compositions.   I have
never been able to see how a multitude of insignificant
composers can do anything towards making a significant one.   Precisely how, for instance, did the activity
of a Gassmann, a Kozeluch, a Schulz, or a Schwindel
assist the making of a Mozart?   It is as if we were
to imagine that by breeding a sufficiently large flock
of geese we should some day get from them a swan.

The swans do not come in that way; they are another species altogether. The thousand or so German composers, now forgotten, who were writing between, say, 1820 and 1880—how did they help Wagner, or help the world to get a Wagner? How could "encouraging" them help to make a Wagner what he was? The theory of "encouragement" of mediocrities leaves out of account the most important consideration, the one vital consideration—the higher circles of art are an aristocracy into which no one can be promoted by the crowd; one has to be born into it or one never gets into it. Over the production of a Bach, a Mozart, a Wagner, a Chopin, we have not the slightest control; he is the one-in-a-million chance of a one-in-a-million father and mother.

Does any rational person suppose that if any one of the big men had not been born, or had died in his childhood, somehow or other his work would have got itself done by the others? By no means. His work was not an inevitable necessity from what had gone before; it was the product of his own unique personality. It is quite true that had the work of his predecessors not been there his own work would not have been what it was; no one imagines that had Beethoven, for instance, been born in the sixteenth century, while instrumental music was in its earliest infancy, he would have developed the close musical logic of his symphonies. That the greatest artist is conditioned by his environment is universally recognized; and it would be still truer to say that he is conditioned by his legacy from the past. It is not at all improbable that certain composers of folk-song—the unknown author of the best of the Hebridean songs, for instance—had a natural lyrical endowment equal to that of Schubert;

but the folk-singer had not the vocabulary to work upon, the technique to work with, that Schubert had. But the fact of the great artist's dependence upon the legacy bequeathed to him by the past does not imply that this legacy would have multiplied itself in the same way without him.

We derive Wagner, in a rough-and-ready way, from Beethoven; we say, and truly, that the texture of his later works is the symphonic tissue of Beethoven applied to a dramatic action. But to trace one thing to another *a posteriori* is not the same thing as to deduce it *a priori*. Now that the thing has been done we can see that B has come out of A; but no one, before it was done, could say that out of A would necessarily come B—and for this reason, that though B may have been implicit in A, it would never have come out of it but for the chance that Nature threw out, among her millions, one particular being who acted as a spark that liberated the dormant and till then unsuspected energy in the mass called A. To suppose otherwise is to suppose, for instance, that had Wagner not been born the Wagnerian music drama would still have come into existence. There is no reason whatever to suppose this. If theorizing could have solved the problem of the opera it would have been solved long before Wagner. There is very little, indeed, in his theory of the opera that had not been already set forth by other people. In the very year of his birth (1813) there was published a *Versuch einer Aesthetik des dramatischen Tonsatzes* by one Ignaz Franz Mosel, in which the whole theory of music drama was expounded with the utmost clearness; a good deal of the book might have been written by Wagner himself. Who can doubt that if Wagner had never been born, or if he had died young, we should still have been theorizing as Hoffmann and Mosel and a hundred others had done, and still been as far as they were from realizing the true music drama, or perceiving how alone it could be realized? It was a lucky throw of Nature's that sent into the world just then one musician—and only one—who saw the dramatic uses to which Beethoven's system of thematic development could be put, and had, moreover, the ability to put it to these uses. Wagner himself could not have created the Wagnerian music drama had he been born a hundred years earlier; and had he not been born when he was, the whole development of music since Beethoven would have been different. All the minor composers of the period from 1830 to 1870 might have called a public meeting and debated the problem, without their getting any further on with it than Gluck and Mozart and Weber had done. The journalists might have "encouraged" these small fry for fifty years without thereby endowing them collectively with the power to produce from among them or from the community as a whole the seminal force that was Richard Wagner.

V

BUT is any age capable of distinguishing between its own first-rate composers and its second- and third-rate? Have not past generations blundered badly in this respect? And is our own luck likely to be any better in the eyes of our successors?

At breakfast I turned over the pages of a musical magazine, and was not only interested in but somewhat amused by an article in which were quoted a number of contemporary criticisms of Beethoven—the object, of course, being in the first place to show how little perception of Beethoven's genius his contemporaries had, and in the second place to cast ridicule on, or at any rate inspire doubt as to, the present-day criticism of contemporaries.

We critics are always being warned that we must not attempt to forecast the verdict of posterity. We are always being told that no great composer's greatness has been recognized by his contemporaries, that every great artist has had a hard struggle against the innate conservatism of his time. If that be so we may well be cautious, both with our enthusiasms and with our disparagements. For according to this reading of history, the mere fact that a composer has a great vogue in his own day is a pretty sure proof that he is a mediocrity, while somewhere in his shadow will be found an as yet barely visible form that will be the shining light for the generations to come.

What are we to make, for instance, of the case of Telemann, that has been set forth so fully for us in M. Romain Rolland's essay on *A Forgotten Master,*

in his book, *Voyage Musical au Pays du Passé?*   Telemann's vogue was infinitely greater than that of his
contemporary Bach.   Yet Bach to-day is—Bach; and
Telemann is forgotten except by a historian here and
there.   Has it been thus in every age, the glib talent
being acclaimed and the seminal genius being ignored
or opposed?

One would gather from the writings of a certain
order of critic that it is so.   But are not these people
just a little hasty in drawing their conclusions?   A
scientist asks for a large body of facts before he begins
deducing general principles.   In the case of music,
such a body of facts would be afforded by a comprehensive history of musical opinion.   But we possess
no such history; what passes for it is only a collection
of anecdotes; and it seems to me rather unscientific
to make sweeping generalizations about the past and
the present on the basis of nothing more substantial
than fragments of gossip—I suspect them to be hardly
more than that—that have been started by Heaven
knows whom, and repeated, as it seems to me, by one
docile writer after another without the slightest attempt to investigate for himself the real value of them.

I believe that this theory of the inevitable failure of
any generation to recognize its great composers is a
fallacy, and a modern fallacy at that.   I imagine it
to be a product of the late nineteenth century, and to
have had its origin among the Wagnerians.   I fancy
that if you had gone to a music-lover of any period
between, say, 1500 and 1850, and told him, with tears
in your eyes, that it was a sure sign of a composer's
genius that the world ridiculed and reviled him, and
that the great composer can only look to posterity for
recognition, he would have laughed in your face.

Every age, I think, has had a pretty accurate idea as to which composers were the greatest credit to it. The men who were most highly praised by their contemporaries were, in the vast majority of cases, the men whom the world recognizes to-day as the biggest figures of their epoch.

I run my mind's eye over the history of music from about 1550 to 1800, and I can discover no cases of genius alleged to have been neglected or misunderstood by their contemporaries, except Monteverdi, Bach and Mozart. I do not say that these men *were* neglected or misunderstood, but only that the historians allege them to have been. For the rest, after spending a whole morning diligently turning over the historians, I have failed to find a single great name that was not idolized in its own day. "Whatever private disputes and troubles Byrd may have endured," says Dr. Fellowes, "there can be no doubt at all that he was held in the highest esteem and veneration by all the musicians of his own time; and not by musicians only, for the list of patrons to whom his eight published volumes were dedicated is in itself evidence that he commanded great respect in aristocratic circles." Morley declared that Byrd was "never without reverence to be named of the musicians." Thomas Tomkins described him as his "ancient and much revered Master." An anonymous contemporary writer called him "the parent of British music." To John Baldwin, the Windsor lay-clerk and copyist, he was "homo mirabilis"; in Baldwin's poem he is ranked above all the composers of his time, English or foreign. Even "the clerk who recorded Byrd's death in the Chapel Royal cheque-book" was moved to add "to the bare entry of Byrd's name the significant tribute, 'A Father of Musicke.'" The testimony is abundant enough that, as Dr. Fellowes says, Byrd "stood supreme among English musicians in the minds of the ordinary people."

Every one of the sixteenth century composers whom the world now sees to have been the greatest of his time and place was recognized as such by his contemporaries; and each great new figure, so far from having his way made difficult for him, was hailed as marking an advance on his predecessors. Among his numerous fellows Clemens non Papa stood out like a mountain among hills; but the vogue of Clemens himself diminished as the work of Orlando Lasso became known. As Ambros puts it, "The sixteenth century was not in the habit of disparaging each new master in comparison with the older ones until he had won the right to exist by hard fighting; rather did it rejoice in each great new apparition, and think that *now* the golden age of music had come; and so the age was even a little unjust towards the earlier masters. See, for instance, the introduction to Hermann Finck's *Practica musica* (1556). When Orlando Lasso appeared he dimmed the glory of all his predecessors in the eyes of his contemporaries." He was the "plus que divin Orland."

Cyprian de Rore, Willaert, Palestrina, the two Gabrieli and Schütz were, to their own generations, what Byrd was to musicians in England. A fair indication of the regard in which these and other of the old masters were held by their contemporaries is the fact that they were given the best official appointments of the time, Courts and churches competing for the glory of employing them. Their works were performed all over Europe. And the more sharply a man's music marked him off from his contemporaries, the more personal his spirit and the more novel his style, the more rapturously was he acclaimed.

*

*   *

I suspect the sentimental legend of the hard struggle of genius against the stupidity of its contemporaries to be in the main, the creation of the Wagnerians, and, once fairly established, to have been extended to other composers of the more distant past.   No one seems to have taken the slightest trouble to investigate this legend, or rather these various legends; one biographical parrot merely goes on repeating them after another.   I suppose that what is at the back of most people's minds who talk in this way is the feeling that if the theory can be established with regard to the geniuses of the past, it will put courage into them in their fight for the composers whom they regard as the towering but unappreciated geniuses of the present. A little while ago a minor poet printed some contemporary denigration of Keats and Shelley side by side with the unfavorable reviews of his own work, the public being expected, I take it, to draw the inference that as the critics had been proved to have been wrong in the one case, time would prove them to have been wrong in the other.   The good man forgot that a horse-chestnut is not the same thing as a chestnut horse.   If a genius now and then has been despised and rejected, it does not follow that every poet or composer who is despised and rejected is a genius. Yet some such innocent assumption as this is apparently made by those critics who, irritated at the failure of their fellows and the public to see a swan in each of their geese, shake a warning finger and bid us ponder the case of Wagner—a true swan if ever there was one, yet, according to them, branded "goose" for practically the whole of his life.

It may be worth while to make a first-hand examination of some of these legends. It would help us very much if we could find a single instance in history of a great musical innovator having had a hard time of it *by reason of his innovations.* I stress "by reason of his innovations" because, it goes without saying, the innovation in itself is only half the story. A new man can talk new sense or new nonsense. My own feeling is that if he talks sense he will get a respectful hearing at once, no matter how novel his method of expression may be; while if he talks nonsense it is more reasonable to put the rejection of his message down to this fact than to the fact that his grammar and his vocabulary are new. I doubt whether any innovator in music who has had something vital to say has ever been denied, from the mass of plain music-lovers, a sympathetic and appreciative hearing. Since Nature never does anything once only, it might help us a little to decide the question whether this or that composer of the present day is a genius whose innovations are above the comprehension of his contemporaries if we could find a solitary case of the kind in the past.

Is there one case that can be proved beyond dispute? I propose to examine a few of them in detail.

VI

I BEGIN with Wagner. I take down from my friend's shelves Wilhelm Tappert's so-called *Schimpflexikon,* and read once more that choice collection of the abusive epithets that were hurled at poor Wagner's head for something like thirty or forty years. Read only the nasty things the critics said about him, and you will wonder how he ever managed to keep going. But surely we would feel the same wonder in the case of every big man if we read only the evidence of the hostile witnesses and the speeches of the counsel for the prosecution? If some biographer with a passion for the darker colours of portraiture were to publish, fifty years hence, a *Schimpflexikon* of the nasty things that were said about Mr. Gladstone in his time, the sympathetic reader would probably wonder how it was that a man so universally hated managed to become Prime Minister as often as he did, and to finish with a public funeral. And the mystery, both in Mr. Gladstone's case and in Wagner's, would indeed be insoluble if the *Schimpflexikon* told the whole story. But obviously it does not. It does not even tell a quarter of the story. Opinions differed about Wagner as they differ about everything else under the sun; but all the same, whatever the makers of myth and legend may say, he was the most popular composer of the day with the plain man.

The picture we get of him from a too trustful reading of the sentimental biographers is that of a composer so far in advance of the taste of his day that each of his works, as it appeared, was almost hooted off the boards, and that in consequence the German theatres were mostly closed to him.   The simple truth, I find, is that he could have had as many performances of his works as he liked, had he not been so exacting as to the quality of the performances, and so insistent on the operas, long as they were, being given without cuts.   I have just been turning over the pages of the Wagner-Liszt correspondence from 1849 onwards. Wagner at the time, and for some ten years afterwards, had everything against him.   He was a political exile, with a price on his head.   He could do nothing himself to get his works performed in Germany; he could operate only through Liszt.   The great Court theatres, especially those that set the fashion for the rest of Germany—Berlin, Dresden, Vienna—were virtually closed to him because of his republican writings and his supposed complicity in the revolution of 1849.   Yet opera house after opera house was anxious to give his works, and wherever they were given they were successful.   If they were not given oftener, it was because Wagner himself refused his permission, on the ground that he could not trust the conductor and the singers to do his work justice if he or Liszt were not there to explain his intentions.   It is not he who is imploring the Intendants to give his operas; it is they who apply to him, and are, as often as not, refused.

I turn over the pages of the Correspondence hurriedly, and note a few of the salient facts.

26 Feb., 1849. Liszt to Wagner. *Tannhäuser* has made a great impression at Weimar. (Two performances.)

28 Oct., 1849. L. to W. Difficult to find a purchaser for *Lohengrin* and *Siegfrieds Tod* (not yet

written, by the way), because "these operas being essentially, I may say exclusively, Germanic, they could be given only in four or five German towns at the most. Now you cannot be unaware that, after the Dresden events, *official* Germany is hardly favourable to your name. Dresden, Berlin and Vienna will be, for some time at any rate, virtually impossible for your works."

5 Dec., 1849. W. to L. Sees himself that Paris is impossible for him, as his work is so purely German. His subjects would not attract there.

14 Jan., 1850. L. to W. Difficulties as regards London, where Italian opera is all the vogue. The Weimar public, "by some miracle of taste," is clamouring for more *Tannhäuser*.

2 July, 1850. W. to L. If *Lohengrin* is to be given, it must be without cuts.

2 Sept., 1850. L. to W. *Lohengrin* has been given in Weimar (first production on any stage, 28 Aug.). "Relatively satisfactory." The Court and the "intelligent people" full of sympathy and admiration. The general public will applaud what it does not understand.

8 Sept., 1850. W. to L. Letters from Weimar have made it clear to him that the work has fatigued people by its length. He puts this down to the tempi being too slow, and is doubtful whether the singers have made their parts fully intelligible. Still refuses to permit cuts; if *Lohengrin* can be made a success only by this means, he will not have it given at all, and "I have written my last opera."

3 Jan., 1851. L. to W. Tells Wagner not to allow Brussels to give *Lohengrin* unless he himself can

revise the translation and supervise the final rehearsals.

29 June, 1851.   W. to L.   Breitkopf and Härtel have offered to publish the *full* score of *Lohengrin,* as well as the vocal score.   Wagner is almost dumb with astonishment.   "It seems to me almost like a fairy tale—to publish the full score of an opera that has been performed only in Weimar!"

15 Jan., 1852.   L. to W.   Pretty well satisfied with the *sixth* performance of *Lohengrin.*   Admits that the first was very feeble and faulty, but things now go better; not only the public but the singers are beginning to understand the work.   The seventh performance (on the 24th) will certainly be an improvement.

29 May, 1852.   W. to L.   The *Flying Dutchman* has been given four times in Zürich in one week, and made "an indescribable effect; Philistines who could never be induced to go to the theatre or to concerts attended all four performances."   Vocal scores have been ordered in half-dozen lots.

23 Aug., 1852.   L. to W.   Berlin wants *Tannhäuser.*   Liszt wholly approves of Wagner's "exceptional" demand of 1,000 thalers, and his stipulation that Liszt shall conduct.   (An audacious condition to lay down to a Court theatre with which Liszt had no connexion!)

8 Sept., 1852.   W. to L.   Would not allow *Rienzi* to be revived if he were asked.   Disgusted with the generally bad performances of the *Flying Dutchman, Tannhäuser* and *Lohengrin,* that

made it impossible for the public to understand them.

12 Sept., 1852. W. to L. Insists on a guarantee from Berlin that *ten* performances of *Tannhäuser* shall be given that winter, otherwise he will withdraw the score.

7 Oct., 1852. L. to W. *Lohengrin* given again at Weimar. The theatre "again crowded."

13 Oct., 1852. W. to L. "Great success" of *Tannhäuser* at Breslau.

22/24 Dec., 1852. W. to L. Breslau wants *Lohengrin,* and Dresden and Schwerin the *Flying Dutchman.*

27 Dec., 1852. L. to W. *Tannhäuser* given at Weimar again. "Overcrowded house, with *abonnement suspendu.*" "Extraordinary effect." "Decisive success." Public interest in *Lohengrin* increasing. Hotels full on *Lohengrin* nights.

13 Jan., 1853. W. to L. Leipzig and Frankfort going to give *Lohengrin.*

11 Feb., 1853. W. to L. Dissatisfied with the German theatres. Sometimes sorry he has allowed any performances outside Weimar. Cassel asking for *Tannhäuser.* Has no longer any hope of spreading the true knowledge of his works. He would refuse them to theatres like Munich, etc., as the conductors would only ruin them.

18 Feb., 1853. L. to W. First Weimar performance of the *Flying Dutchman.* Reception "warm and sympathetic." The overture made such an effect that in spite of the etiquette of the occasion (it was the *Festtag* of the Grand

Duchess) the audience broke out into enthusias-
tic applause.

19 Feb., 1853. W. to L. *Tannhäuser* withdrawn at
Prague, through the intervention of some highly-
placed personage. But it has been given in Riga.

8 April, 1853. L. to W. The *Tannhäuser* overture encored at Prague.

—May, 1853. L. to W. *Lohengrin* to be produced
in Wiesbaden, and the *Flying Dutchman* in
Schwerin.

30 May, 1853. W. to L. The *Tannhäuser* overture
and the *Lohengrin* prelude and other fragments
given in Zürich. "A tremendous popular success." Three concerts given: "I might have
repeated them six times, and they would have
been full each time."

14 June, 1853. W. to L. *Tannhäuser* a "striking
success" again in Posen. Four performances in
six days with maximum receipts.

15 July, 1853.   W. to L. Wagner publicly fêted:
"I almost wish you could have heard the speeches;
they were extraordinarily sincere and true-
hearted; I was hailed as a complete saviour."

19 Sept., 1853.   L. to W. *Lohengrin* to be given in
Leipzig in November; Liszt anticipates a warm
public welcome for it. "The Leipzig fortress
has been conquered." "Even the *Wohlbekannte*"
(our friend Lobe), told Liszt that he had been
moved to tears by the finale.

31 Oct., 1853.   L. to W.   A "Wagner week" in Weimar; the *Flying Dutchman, Tannhäuser* and
Lohengrin "have taken firm ground here and cast
deep roots." The *Flying Dutchman* given yesterday; "increased public satisfaction."

16 Nov., 1853. W. to L. ". . . it is now pretty certain that my two last operas will be given at all the German theatres, as *Tannhäuser* has already been in most of them. . . ." He has already sold *Tannhäuser* to twenty-two theatres; he is dealing with fifteen others. He had told Breitkopf and Härtel that there was no chance for his operas. Now the circumstances are so altered that he wants good terms.

Finds an unexpected source of income in the sale of the text-books of the operas; 6,000 copies of *Tannhäuser* ordered for Breslau in one winter alone.

29 Dec., 1853. L. to W. *Tannhäuser* at Weimar. *Abonnement suspendu*—"an unprecedented event in Weimar for an opera that has already had fifteen performances." For the first time, many people unable to get admission. Enormous effect on the public.

8 Jan., 1854. L. to W. First performance of *Lohengrin* in Leipzig. Big audience at *double prices*. Performance only passable. "The great success of the work can no longer be denied."

15 Jan., 1854. W. to L. The success of *Tannhäuser* had emboldened him to live more luxuriously; "my income seemed to me an infallible thing." But the expected orders for *Lohengrin* had not come in. Regards *Lohengrin* as having failed at Leipzig. (It is to be observed that he makes no complaints against the public, but blames the theatre management and the performers.)

[Letter No. 143.] W. to L. "While here I chew a beggar's crust, I hear from Boston of 'Wagner nights.'"

9 April, 1854. W. to L. Vetoes performance of *Tannhäuser* by the Königsberg Company in Berlin. *Tannhäuser* at Augsburg. Way paved for Munich. "As *Tannhäuser* has everywhere proved a draw," he wants bigger fees.

[Letter No. 150.] L. to W. *Tannhäuser,* as usual, drew a full house; many unable to get tickets for *Lohengrin.*

[Letter No. 167.] W. to L. Has been asked to conduct London Philharmonic concerts.

16 Feb., 1855. L. to W. Success of *Lohengrin* at Cologne. Hamburg being educated up to it.

[Letter No. 178.] W. to L. Allowing performances of *Tannhäuser* and *Lohengrin* at last to get money. (Not a word as to any difficulty in getting performances; the theatres are all anxious to give the operas.)

[Letter 183.] W. to L. In London the journalists abuse his music, but the public "does not let itself be misled."

8 May, 1857. W. to L. Invitation from the Emperor of Brazil to go to Rio de Janeiro, where he shall have everything he wants.

[Letter 251.] W. to L. Breitkopf and Härtel going to have the full score of *Tristan* engraved *before* performance. (In Jan 1858 *only the first act* was as yet written.)

9 Oct., 1858. L. to W. Vocal score of *Tristan* being engraved by B. and H. (The composition of the opera was not finished until the summer of 1859.)

21 Nov., 1858. W. to L. *Tannhäuser* and *Lohengrin* his "old capital."

*
* *

It is the same with the later works. I open the sixth volume of Glasenapp at random. The *Ring*— first produced at Bayreuth in 1876—is being given, either as a whole or in parts, in town after town, rarely in a way that satisfies the exacting composer, but always with popular success. In the spring of 1878, the *Rhinegold* and *Valkyrie* are given in Leipzig. "The extraordinary excitement and expectation had seized not only upon the Leipzig public, but upon large numbers of people elsewhere; numberless were the bookings from every part of Germany, especially Berlin, Breslau, Frankfort, Weimar, Halle, Schwerin, etc." Wagner sent a congratulatory telegram to his native town. Small theatres, like that of Königsberg, wanted to give the whole *Ring*. Weimar took up the *Rhinegold*, Schwerin and Hamburg the *Valkyrie*, Munich and Vienna *Siegfried*. Brunswick and other towns followed suit. In Munich, says Glasenapp, the *Gätterdämmerung* aroused a frenetic and endless enthusiasm. Malvida von Meysenburg, who is staying with Wagner at Bayreuth, writes to a friend that "the Master is in good humour; he has been greatly pleased by the unheard-of success of *Siegfried* and the *Götterdämmerung* in Munich and Leipzig." In November *Siegfried* is given for the first time in Vienna to "tempestuous applause."

"The separate parts of the *Ring*," says Glasenapp, "took possession that autumn of the theatres like some irresistible force of nature." Vienna gave many per-

formances of *Siegfried* to full houses.   In Munich, in
November, the *Ring* was given in its entirety for the
first time outside Bayreuth; the theatre was sold out
in advance.   For the next year the story is the same.
Cologne alone gives eighteen performances of the
Rhinegold between February and May.   In March it
produces the *Valkyrie,* and the two operas alternate
on successive evenings for some time.   Mannheim
gives the whole *Ring,* and congratulatory telegrams
rain upon the conductor.   So it is with the other
operas of his prime; the *Meistersinger,* for instance,
is given without cuts in Mannheim, "with unheard-of
success."

In the face of records like this, what *is* the use of the
sentimental historians quoting disparaging remarks
from this or that forgotten critic, this or that negli-
gible pedant, as if that were the whole story?   Many
of these disparagements came from people of no importance in the musical world.   Dr. Paul Stefan, in
his book *Die Feindschaft gegen Wagner,* quotes with
bated breath a contemptuous estimate of the composer
in J. L. Klein's *Geschichte des Dramas,* and others by
Ludwig Speidel, Gutzkow, Wilhelm Lübke (the historian of painting) and people of that sort.   Precisely
what authority is supposed to attach to the utterances
of these non-musical or half-musical men on the subject
of music is not clear.   Sometimes it is the musical
pedant who speaks, as in the case of Moritz Haupt-
mann, who, after the *Tannhäuser* overture, we are
told, had serious doubts as to Wagner's future (I have
not checked the reference).   Occasionally a voice to
which we are compelled to pay respect makes itself
heard; it is a shock, for example, to find the great historian of music, Ambros, saying that "the charivari

of sound in the *Meistersinger* overture is a real distress to us." But we must allow for these differences of taste among men; there are anti-Wagnerians even to-day. Nothing can alter the fact that Wagner's music was immensely popular all over Germany.

The comforting view is sometimes taken that it was only the professional musicians and the critics who were opposed to Wagner; and the opportunity is seized to harp once more on the old theme of the futility of "criticism." As for the composers, these gentry are notoriously inappreciative of each other; the very individuality that makes their own music what it is makes it generally impossible for them to see either life or art from anyone else's point of view. As for the critics, is it necessary to point out once more that the historians and biographers mostly quote only the passages that suit them? There was any amount of kind and flattering things said about Wagner by the critics; but these do not suit the sentimental biographer's purpose, which is to depict his hero as the good man struggling with adversity, with no hope except of posthumous justification. That Wagner received an immense amount of disparagement cannot be denied. But there were reasons for this. In the first place, he was for something like thirty-five years the most frequently discussed of German musicians. In the second place, a great deal of the enmity he roused was his own fault, and, though apparently directed against the musician, was primarily inspired by detestation of the man. He could live in no town for long without making enemies of the journalists; and, human nature being what it is, we cannot be surprised that some of them seized the first opportunity that came their way of paying back his rudeness in his own coin.   A good deal of the Press was in the hands of the Jews; and Wagner's violent anti-Semitism was not exactly calculated to endear these people to him. He did not know the meaning of compromise, of tact, of common prudence.   It is perhaps as well for us that he did not, for had he been made of gentler stuff he would never have won through; though, to be sure, he would not have had so hard a fight of it had his character been different.   It is useless to blind ourselves to the fact that most of his difficulties were of his own making.   No composer with a grain of sense would have invited Hanslick to a private reading of the *Meistersinger* libretto, in which, it was evident to everyone in the room, the critic was satirized in the part of Beckmesser.   (It may not be generally known that in the first manuscript sketch of the text the Marker is actually called "Hanslich.")   If a composer hits out like this at his critics he cannot complain if some of them hit back.   Had Hanslick been a bigger man and a better critic, of course, he would not have let Wagner's malicious hostility affect his view of his music; but in a world like this it is hardly to be wondered at that, even if only subconsciously, he afterwards looked at the music rather to discover in it things he could snap at than to discover things he could praise.

Apart from all this, Wagner's private life earned for him more active enemies than fell to the lot, perhaps, of all other composers of the nineteenth century put together.   We have to remember that the people in a great man's entourage do not see him through the veil of historic idealism in which he is wrapped for future generations.   A later day sees only the great-

ness of the artist, not the smallness of the man.   We
smile now at the story of Beethoven picking his teeth
with the candle-snuffers in a great lady's drawing-
room; but it must have been difficult for the spectators
of the incident to smile, however many fine symphonies
and sonatas the delinquent may have had to his credit.
Most of Wagner's contemporaries who came into contact with him were astonished at the discrepancy between the man and the artist.   Some of them turned
away from the former and concentrated their gaze on
the latter.   Others could not do this; their dislike of,
and contempt for, the man made it impossible for them
to do justice to the composer.   Wherever he went he
left a trail of debts; wherever he went, until, in his
middle age, Cosima laid her firm hand upon him, there
was, to put it crudely, trouble with some woman or
other.   His name stank in a good many nostrils.
The difficulties he made for himself by his defects of
manners and of morals account for much of the opposition he met with in the Press, in private, and in
the theatres.   One of the stories that used to move
the good Wagnerian to tears was that of the vain attempt to get *Tristan* produced in Vienna in 1862–3—
how after fifty-four rehearsals the work was given up
as "impossible."   That the singers and the orchestra
found the music difficult can easily be believed—it is
difficult to-day; but Julius Kapp suggests that the true
explanation of the abandonment of the production
must be sought elsewhere.   Wagner had created a
great deal of comment in Viennese musical circles by
his liaison with the actress, Friederike Meyer.
Friederike's sister was Frau Dustmann, the Isolde of
the opera; and Frau Dustmann strongly objected to

the affair and the scandal it aroused. It was probably her increasing repugnance to Wagner that made it in the end impossible to produce *Tristan* in Vienna.

He made other enemies by his political opinions and activities, and others again by his constant carping at the theatre Intendants, the Kapellmeisters, and the singers. No doubt many of his criticisms were justified; no doubt, from his own point of view, he was right in protesting against performances that did not present his work as he had conceived it. But neither can there be any doubt that his tactlessness, his congenital inability to behave even with reasonable courtesy towards people who did not share his view that the rest of mankind had been sent into the world simply to further his aims, deprived him of a good deal of service that would willingly have been placed at the disposal of any other composer of the same genius. His later works presented everyone—singers, players, conductors, producers, machinists, scene painters, theatrical treasurers—with difficulties hitherto unheard of. And yet, in spite of everything, in spite of his personal *intrasigeance,* his unsavoury reputation, his political and social indiscretions, his unprecedented demands upon the resources of the theatres, the venom of his personal enemies, he had nothing whatever to complain of as regards general public recognition of his work. There might be difficulties in the way of producing a given opera in a given town; but once it was produced it became immensely popular. Of all musical careers, that of Wagner lends least support to the theory that the man of genius is so far in advance of his time that posterity alone can appreciate him.

*
*   *

The very records of the biographers themselves
prove that some other explanation must be sought for
the neglect of this or that work in this or that town
than the immovable conservatism of the musical public
and its hostility towards the innovating man of genius.
Mr. Finck imparts to us what he calls an "extraordinary fact"—so extraordinary that he has to put it in
italics: *"Vienna did not hear a single one of Wagner's operas till he was forty-four years old and had
composed Rienzi, Dutchman, Tannhäuser, Lohengrin,
Rheingold, Valkyrie, half of Siegfried, and all of
Tristan—all but three of his works! It seems incredible—yet two other German capitals, Munich and
Stuttgart, were in the same predicament."* But on
analysis the indictment becomes rather less devastating.   Vienna could not be blamed any more than any
other town for not having produced in 1857 the as
yet unfinished *Ring*.   In that year, when Wagner was
forty-four years old, *Tristan* also was still unfinished;
it was not completed until August, 1859.   There remain only the four earlier works—*Rienzi* (produced
in 1842), the *Flying Dutchman* (1843), *Tannhäuser*
(1845) and *Lohengrin* (1850).   From 1849 to 1860
he was a political exile from Germany, with a warrant
out for his arrest.   As the correspondence with Liszt
shows, during the greater part of this time he was
persona non grata with the big Court theatres; Mr.
Finck himself goes on to point out that "when Vienna
did at last hear *Tannhäuser* (1857), it was not at the

Imperial Opera, but at a suburban theatre"; and he gives another reason, besides the political one, for his neglect—" 'religious' objections (the references to the Pope and Rome!) had kept him quarantined from the Imperial Theatre!"

The Vienna public, in fact, was prevented from hearing these earlier works by the people in authority, whose reasons for the ban were other than musical. The ban at the Imperial Opera was raised in 1858, when *Lohengrin* was given, to be followed by *Tannhäuser* in 1859. Both of them, says Mr. Finck, were "received with enthusiasm"—a rather mild description of what happened, as the contemporary records show. Anyhow, we see once again that Wagner's music had only to be put before the public for it to be taken to the public's heart.

The most diligent search on my part has failed to discover in the whole of Wagner's letters and prose works a single complaint from him that the public was against him, or even inappreciative of him. His grievance is always against the theatre directors, who will not give his operas as he thinks they ought to be given. His *Epilogue to the Ring of the Nibelung* (published in 1872), throws a light on his attitude towards the theatres. He is speaking of the "surprise visit" to Vienna in 1861, when, to celebrate the occasion, he was given the opportunity of hearing for the first time (owing to his long exile from Germany) the thirteen-year-old *Lohengrin*. He describes the reception of the work by the public as "truly moving." Encouraged by this, he ventured to ask the management for a few more stage rehearsals in order to correct certain errors in the presentation of the opera. He met with a refusal; and when he offered to write a new opera expressly for Vienna he was told, in writing, that after due consideration they thought they had given sufficient attention for the present to the name "Wagner," and that it would be as well to give another composer a chance of speaking. This other, he says, was Offenbach! Yet this treatment, he adds, was humane in comparison with that accorded to him in Berlin, where the Intendant simply refused to see him should he call upon him.

Is it not clear enough that, for this reason and that, he had become the kind of composer whom, no matter how popular he may be, the theatre Intendants have come to regard as rather a nuisance personally? He himself speaks of the "assiduously circulated charge" that he was "insatiable in his demands." He seeks to refute the charge; but the justice of it is proved to the hilt by his own letters. And his incurable ill-breeding comes out in the story he tells of his answer to the invitation of the Hamburg management to attend the fiftieth performance of *Tannhäuser* "in order to receive the same ovation as had just been given to Herr Gounod for his *Faust*." He evidently objected to being associated with a composer of whom he had so poor an opinion; and he "declined with thanks, saying that I would regard the honour paid to my Parisian friend as received by him for me also." This episode is simply another illustration of the prejudice he raised against himself everywhere in official circles by his tactlessness.

VII

WHEN we look into the Wagner case, then, we find it to be mostly legend, and I suspect that the other pseudo-historical cases will prove to be legends also. These legends flourish because no one takes the trouble to examine them in detail. I find Mr. H. A. Scott, for example, in an otherwise sound study of our normal attitude towards music, writing thus: "That difficulty is to be expected in understanding and enjoying all new music of serious aim goes without saying, and the whole history of the art affords evidence to this effect. Hardly a composer of any eminence has failed to puzzle his contemporaries at first." The citations I have just run through show that, as regards at any rate the works of his early and middle period, Wagner did *not* "puzzle his contemporaries," who found no difficulty in "understanding and enjoying" this "new music of serious aim."

Quite lately Mr. Bernard Shaw has joined the ranks of the myth-makers. He is reported, in a speech to the British Music Society's Congress, to have claimed that "he could remember all the Wagnerian musical criticism that occurred in his lifetime, and, generally speaking, it urged upon Wagner in the most abusive terms that he was no composer and had better go and sweep a crossing; that he could not produce a single bar of melody; that his harmony was a mass of abominable discord, and that he himself was a most offensive charlatan; that instead of bringing up a respectable family he bought silk dressing-gowns. He did not know why he should not have bought them, but the whole criticism had since been proved a mass of errors. They found the same thing applied to every man who was a poineer in art. The mass of critics attacked him."

Mr. Shaw, I am afraid, would be hard put to it to give evidence for these last confident assertions. But even about Wagner he is demonstrably wrong. Had Mr. Shaw accomplished the stupendous feat of reading "all the Wagnerian criticism that appeared in his lifetime" he might have found little time for anything else, but he would at all events have discovered that not all this criticism was stupid or anti-Wagnerian. A good deal of it was undoubtedly hostile; but on what subject, pray, do we ever expect all humanity to be of the same opinion? There are thousands of music-lovers even to-day who do not care for Wagner; is it surprising that many of his own contemporaries did not care for him? Is not the simple truth of the matter just this, that people differed about Wagner as they do about every subject under the sun—though the controversy over him was more acrimonious than the average, because of his unhappy gift of making enemies and wounding susceptibilities—but that, in spite of all this, he was the most popular German composer of his time? We are invited by Mr. Calvocoressi, in his thoughtful book, *Musical Criticism,* to read this, from d'Ortigue (1861), and to stand astonied: "No form, no design, no rhythm, no symmetry" [in Wagner]. But really, I see no more reason to regard this as typical of the general opinion of the time than I do to regard the first sentence that may meet my eye in this morning's leading article in *Le Matin* as typical of the general European political opinion of to-day.

Mr. Bernard Shaw has had some devastating things said about him in his time. Suppose some historian, fifty or a hundred years hence, were to dig out a few of these and attempt to prove from them that Mr. Shaw met with nothing but misunderstanding and vilification during his lifetime; would not that be a sad perversion of the real fact, which is that Mr. Shaw is recognized all the world over as one of the half-dozen most vital minds of our time? Why should we take too seriously what a d'Ortigue said about a Wagner? D'Ortigue was a busy French journalist of the mid-nineteenth century, with no particular claim to be regarded as an authority on music; and his anti-Wagnerism is perhaps not unconnected with his blind Berlioz partisanship. And if ten thousand d'Ortigues had said that they could see "no form, no design, no rhythm, no symmetry" in Wagner, that would not alter the fact, against which we are brought up again and again, that more than half of the intelligent music-lovers of the period were solid for Wagner. Mr. Calvocoressi thinks that this and other remarks of the same type that he quotes about other composers "reduce themselves to three statements: the [new] music heard tried the ear, ran contrary to the hearers' customs and tenets, and did not make sense for them." One gets from this a troubled vision of a puzzled Europe straining its ears to follow Wagner's new harmonies and understand his new forms, of a Europe striving desperately, and, one gathers, unsuccessfully, to adjust its "customs and tenets" to a new music that did not "make sense" for it.

Such a Europe, however, exists only in the imagination of the biographers and historians who prefer repeating old *clichés* to looking into the facts for themselves.   Such a Europe was unknown to at any rate one person of the period—Richard Wagner.   I can find no complaint anywhere on *his* part that his music was beyond the comprehension of the public.   On the contrary, he always contended that it was merely those malignant fellows the critics and rival composers who, actuated by personal enmity, persistently ran him down, while the public was always for him.   At the final dress rehearsal of *Tristan,* at which a select audience was present, he made a speech from the stage in which he said: "And now, for the first actual performance, there remains to be seen only the effect on the real public—for to-day the audience is an invited one.   I feel no anxiety as to this contact with the public proper.   It was the German public that everywhere upheld me against the most extraordinary enmities of the cliques."

Tristan probably presented more new problems and difficulties to its first audience than any work had done since musical history began.   We need not be surprised, therefore, if its reception by the Press was mixed, and that many of the critics were completely confused by it; people listening to it for the first time even at the present day have been known to emerge in the same frame of mind; the music is complex, the text often anything but clear.   Some of the articles were favourable; but if anyone wishes to insist that the majority were unfavourable I shall not say him nay, because the more stress is laid on this fact the more remarkable does another fact become—that the general public was profoundly impressed.   After the first performance there was a little hissing and a great deal of applause.   This performance took place on June 10, 1865.   The unfavourable reports appeared the next day. Had they been representative of public opinion, had they had any power to influence public opinion, the second performance would have been a failure. But this second performance, which took place on June 13, was, says Röckl, who has gone straight to the newspaper records of the time, "a triumph for Wagner." The third performance, on the 19th, drew a full house and created immense enthusiasm. Wagner was deeply moved. These three were all the performances that had been arranged for; the Tristan and the Isolde—Schnorr von Carolsfeld and his wife—belonged to the Dresden Opera, and the King of Bavaria had been able to obtain leave of absence for them for no longer period. Ludwig, however, wanted to hear yet another performance, and obtained from the King of Saxony an extension of the Schnorrs' leave. This fourth performance was given on July 1, with "extraordinary success"; the *abonnement* was suspended, yet the house was practically full. On the 12th, Schnorr sang a number of extracts from Wagner's works at a private audition for the king. The great tenor returned to Dresden, and on the 21st was dead of fever. With his death, *Tristan* of necessity disappeared from the stage for a long time. Its difficulties made every theatre fight shy of it—to say nothing of the awe it inspired in the tenors and sopranos of the day. It was revived in Munich in 1869, again with success.

*
* *

There is nothing in this veracious record of the facts to support the sentimental legend that *Tristan,* difficult as it admittedly was and still is, was completely beyond the comprehension of its generation. Nor does the record of the *Ring* lend any countenance to what we may now call the great Wagner myth. We may pass over the first reception of the work at Bayreuth in 1876, for it may be urged that those performances were given before the faithful Wagnerian band. But what happened to the *Ring* when it left Bayreuth?

The story may be read in the reminiscences of the impresario who first took it up—Angelo Neumann, who was at that time stationed at Leipzig. He begins by telling us that there were two parties in the town, one as violently anti-Wagner as the other was pro-Wagner. Fears were entertained that the production of the work would lead to "scenes" in the theatre. The *Rhinegold* and the *Valkyrie* were given in the spring of 1878, with such success, says Neumann, that even the Wagner partisans were amazed. The success was so "astonishing" that Neumann conceived the idea of taking the two productions to Berlin, a capital that, for political and other reasons, had never been particularly favourable to Wagner. Meanwhile *Siegfried* and the *Götterdämmerung* were in rehearsal in Leipzig; they were given there in September with the usual "enormous success." Then came the well-known tour during which Neumann gave the *Ring* all over Europe. The Berlin production was the first, and was typical of the others. The quaint modern belief that Wagner was a solitary Titan struggling against a world of evil gods will hardly survive a perusal of Neumann's first-hand narrative of what he saw with his own eyes:

"And now I must describe the great Berlin *Ring*

days—days of which one can hardly form an accurate idea now. Even the approach to the theatre was in itself a kind of strange drama. Unter den Linden, from the imperial palace onwards, was a dense lane of people; from the windows thousands of eyes looked out on the crowd. . . . There were spectators in the tops of the trees. . . . The jubilation reached its climax when Wagner became visible in his carriage, with his wife and Countess Schleinitz. Brilliant in the extreme was the sight of the theatre, that was full to the roof. The Court and all Berlin seemed to have made a point of being present." [There follows a long list of the notabilities and celebrities.] "Scarcely had Wagner entered his box . . . when the public greeted him tumultuously. . . . The reception of the work was brilliant. Wagner himself applauded the artists with an air of great satisfaction. The public, however, would not be satisfied until the composer himself at last gave way to the general demand and appeared on the stage." He made a speech, thanking the artists and the public. "As he left the theatre the crowd gave him a great ovation. Thus ended the first *Ring* day in a glorious victory, that moved even the stubborn sceptic von Hülsen [the Intendant] to say to me next day: 'Since you made such a success of the *Rhinegold* yesterday, which I never should have thought possible, I no longer have any doubt as to the success of the whole *Ring*.' As a matter of fact, the *Valkyrie* evening was even more festive. This time Wagner did not appear among the singers, but thanked the public for its enthusiasm from his box with a gesture towards the stage." *Siegfried* did not go so well; Jäger (the Siegfried) was hoarse, and sang consistently out of tune; Neumann had implored Wag-

ner to let him transfer Jäger to the second cycle, but
the composer had obstinately refused.   When he saw
in what bad condition the singer was, he insisted on
Vogl replacing him the next day in the *Götterdämmerung;* but this time it was Neumann who refused.
As it happened, Jäger was now rather better.   At the
conclusion of the performance there was the usual wild
enthusiasm, and Wagner had to make another speech
from the stage.   "Of the tremendous tumult," said
the *Berliner Zeitung,* "that broke out at the finish of
the mighty work, the reader can hardly form a conception.   Rarely have we seen anything like it."

Look where we will, we find the same record.   In
face of all this, what in the name of reason is the use
of quoting a fatuous sentence from this or that insignificant journalist of the time and trying to prove from
it that Wagner's music, like that of every other innovator, "tried the ear, ran contrary to the hearers'
customs and tenets, and did not make sense for them"?

An objector may say, "Yes, no doubt the general
public was mostly for Wagner, but that does not alter
the fact that the critics were almost to a man against
him."   But this really will not do.   No one is entitled
to say that most of the critics were against Wagner
until the whole Press of Europe from, say, 1840 to
1883, has been ransacked.   The sentimental historians
have so far done nothing but quote the uncompliment-
ary criticisms; but we know that several critics were
quite complimentary, and we may be pretty sure that
we should find many others if we were to look for
them.   When all allowances had been made for the
special enmities that Wagner called forth for political,
social, religious, personal and other reasons—enmities
that no other composer has had to face—we should

probably find that just about as much sense was talked about him in the Press as nonsense. That is, I fancy, the rough truth in connexion with every composer of genius. We cannot, as some good people think, make a distinction between "the critics" and "the public," the former being generally wrong and the latter generally right. Apart from the fact that the critics do not, any more than the public, all say the same thing at the same moment, there is really no dividing line between the two classes. The critic is merely one of the public who expresses his opinion in print instead of in conversation. His judgment has merely the same chances of being right or wrong as the judgment of any ordinarily cultivated musician in the audience; it is absurd to suppose that Jones or Brown, so long as he is a member of the public, is a reliable judge of values, but that his sense of values goes to the devil the moment he begins to express his opinions in print.

VIII

IF the legend of the hard struggle of the man of genius against the conservatism and the incomprehension of the public of his own day does not hold good in the case of Wagner, in whose case does it hold good? Mozart's? Dr. Paul Stefan, in the full flood of his weeping over the sad lot of Wagner, yet manages to distil a tear for the latter's great predecessor. "To-day," says Dr. Stefan, "we are told that only a generation led astray by Wagner can show us how much in the right were the good musicians of the past. They would hold up, as models, Mozart and Beethoven, to whom we of to-day must once more 'go back.' But the eternal Men of Yesterday played the same game with that very Mozart who is now played off against Wagner as an idol. Kapellmeister Sarti said of Mozart that 'music is bound to go to the dogs when such barbarians take it into their heads to compose . . . Mozart, who does not know D sharp from E flat, must have ears cased with iron'—just as the J. L. Klein whom I have already mentioned spoke of the iron-fronted Wagner, cased in wood and brass! And of a string quartet of Mozart's a contemporary musical journal asked: 'Is this the best way to write music? And can anyone really be found to print such music?' "

Well, I look up the old familiar story in Jahn again. The case is really quite simple. As we might

have anticipated, Mozart was in his own day regarded
not as the model of simplicity and clarity that he has become for us, but as a rather advanced thinker. His
own father, the Emperor Joseph, and Dittersdorf
compared him with Klopstock, and Haydn with Gellert; both these, as the Emperor said, "were great
poets, but one had to read Klopstock again and again to
understand all his beauties, while those of Gellert
were evident at a first glance." A writer in Cramer's
Magazin der Musik thought it a pity that Mozart was
too intent on novelty, at the cost of feeling; "his new
quartets, that are dedicated to Haydn, are too
strongly spiced, and what palate can stand that for
long?" Count Krazalkovicz, a well-known amateur,
had the quartets performed, and repeatedly called out
to the players that they were making mistakes; and
when he was convinced that they were only playing
what was printed he was furious and tore up the parts.
From Italy the parts were returned to the publishers,
as being full of errors. The great stone of stumbling
was the introduction to the C major quartet of 1785—
one of the six dedicated to Haydn.

We know the controversy that once raged over this
passage. Fétis attacked it in the next century, and
was in turn attacked by several writers. Gottfried
Weber subjected it to a close analysis, and finally declared that *his* ear was not comfortable under such
harmonies. The point, long before this, had been
referred to Haydn, who only said that if Mozart
wrote the passage like that he must have had his
reasons for doing so—which is a little ambiguous.
Oulibicheff, like Fétis, "corrected" the passage. Let
us look at it:

Its theoretical justification needs no labouring for the modern student of harmony; our ears do not demand, as those of some of the early protesters did, that the A natural in the first violin in the second bar shall be altered to A flat, or, with others, that the entry of the A should be postponed until the third beat of the bar. But may we not ask whether the objection to the passage was *primarily* on theoretical grounds? Our way with unaccustomed harmonies is very much our way with people we are meeting for the first time. We do not analyse these psychologically and then say whether we like them or not; we instinctively take to them or are repelled by them, and then try to find psychological reasons for our liking or disliking. If these harmonies of Mozart had talked sense and given pleasure to the contemporaries who heard them for the first time there would have been no hunting about for a theoretical justification of them. They were tried in the name of theory because they did *not* talk sense to these good people. And why?

For two main reasons, we may conjecture. One is that what Mozart is driving at in this introduction becomes clear only in the light of the later stages of the quartet. (It is, by the way, the only one of the set that has an introduction.) The work appears to be concerned, as the programme annotator would put it

in these days, with the contest between a principle of
gloom and depression and one of light and cheerful-
ness; and the object of the introduction is to establish
the atmosphere of gloom, of struggle. Therefore
only when what we may call the spiritual design of the
whole quartet is understood can the purpose of the
introduction be seen and its justification found. This
is easier for us than it was for the average listener of
the eighteenth century, because of the large number
of Romantic and post-Romantic works that follow
this principle of design. It is not to be wondered at
that people who heard this introduction for the first
time were puzzled and perhaps revolted by it; but it is
at least probable that, if not less puzzled by it, they
became relatively reconciled to it as their acquaintance
with the whole quartet grew.

The second reason, I think, carries us rather further.
Theoretical analysis, in a case of this kind, is
æsthetically quite futile. If the passage—this or any
other—says something to us that both sounds like sense
and is something absorbingly interesting, it does not
matter in the least whether the theory of the period
can explain it or not; we know, as a matter of fact,
that different theorists will often give quite different
explanations of the same harmonies, and that the
theory of one century is often seen to be erroneous by
the next. On the other hand, if the passage in question does not appeal to us purely as a piece of expression, justification of it on theoretical grounds amounts
to nothing; a page of music is not necessarily a page
of good music because we can name every chord in it
and demonstrate that one harmony succeeds another
correctly. It is therefore quite beside the *æsthetic*
point—no matter how interesting it may be as a piece

of cold theory—to show, as Jahn does, that both the turbid, troubled

and the clearer, aspiring

strive towards the same resolution in

or to say, with Hermann Abert, "the introduction strives, like most movements of its kind, towards the dominant key, which it finally reaches after a deep plunge into the region of the sub-dominant. As so often in the older music, the bass descends chromatically a fourth, and—again after the old fashion—there is a regular sequence-structure in the first nine bars. Only Mozart is not satisfied with the step of a fourth in the bass, but inserts a further part, which reaches the dominant indirectly by way of E flat major and C minor, i. e., by way of the sub-dominant. Upon this harmonic foundation there takes place a spiritual episode of quite incomparable pregnancy. First of all the tonality remains quite ambiguous; the two middle parts come in tired and resigned, to revolve about the fifth of the tonic and the dominant, then the first violin cuts athwart them with its A natural like a flashing sword. . . ."

All perfectly true, from an analytical point of view. But does this kind of truth really matter in such a case as this? What if, in spite of the theoretical correctness of the harmony, the passage has something wrong about it *from the æsthetic point of view?* For my part, I have always felt that it has. It seems to me to be trying to say something and not quite succeeding; and it has ugly moments in it. I am convinced that if it were put before us without any hint that it was by Mozart we should be pretty severe on it. No doubt the people who heard it for the first time in 1785 or thereabouts felt very much like that about it; and we must remember that Mozart was not for them the ideal figure, almost immune from criticism, that he now is for us. For posterity, a great artist is always privileged; he can safely do things that it would not be permitted to a living artist to do. For the men of 1785 Mozart was one of themselves, a young man of about twenty-nine who was indeed unmistakably gifted beyond the generality of his colleagues, but who was not yet a figure in a stained-glass window, not yet a master who had produced so many immortal things that one could afford to look with a tolerant eye on his lapses—nay, even regard as a virtue in him what would be looked upon as a lapse in another. That generation was franker towards its great contemporaries than ours can possibly be. I imagine that it did not particularly like this introducton to the C major quartet, and said so; and then the theorists began finding legal reasons either for or against the popular verdict. But the reasons do not matter, while the instinctive dislike does. I venture to say that this introduction is *not* good Mozart, that it has an uncertainty about it—not so much harmonic as æsthetic

—that we do not often find in him; that the men of his own day were conscious that it was not good Mozart; and that they were quite justified in saying so.

And Hermann Abert, in his new redaction of Jahn, says a good deal that supports me in this opinion. "The first impression," he writes, "that contemporaries had of these quartets was one of confusion, obscurity, artificiality. Instead of smiling at this, we shall do better to try to understand it. As a matter of fact, there is a certain amount of justification for it. Every school-relationship implies a certain lack of freedom, at any rate in respect of technique; and it is evident from Mozart's own words that he found it difficult to adapt the new Haydn technique to his own kind of artistic experience. As we shall see later, he never quite solved this problem. . . . His own kind of artistic experience was quite different from that of Haydn; it was much more inclined to the irrational, to the divagations of fancy and to sudden spiritual catastrophes that were alien to Haydn, who had been brought up in the North German school. What had gradually developed in Haydn as the natural fruit of his whole artistic growth, Mozart had to make his inward own; and this task was all the more difficult for him the greater was the purpose in these quartets, the deeper his own inner experience. We can take his word for it that the six quartets were the result of long and painful labour. The Haydn technique in itself, thanks to his extraordinary adaptability, he could pretty soon make his own; the great difficulty was to make it the servant of his own world of feeling. It is always one of the most difficult things for a great master to take over the style of another and at the same time preserve his spiritual independence—so to transmute this style into himself that it appears to be the natural expression of his own being, and therefore, at bottom, something new. Whenever Mozart succeeds in this, whenever his personality appears clearly and definitely behind the Haydnesque manner of writing, we get works that are not merely the peers of Haydn's, but that even gave Haydn powerful incitements for his own later works." But it almost goes without saying that here and there in these quartets a conflict is evident between the new manner and the old matter, that here and there the wine and the bottle do not agree. Such a passage, I think, is this famous introduction to the C major quartet. Even in the ears of to-day it does not ring quite true; it has not the felicity, the inevitable rightness, we expect of Mozart. The ears of 1785 must have been conscious of this also; and it was *this* that the men of that day were driving at when they tried to account on purely theoretical grounds for what was really an æsthetic discomfort.

It is easy, then, to attach too much importance to Sarti's famous attack on the quartets. In the first place it may be, as Abert points out, that Sarti's article was merely an illustration of how far the average Italian musician had lost contact with German music in general and with instrumental music in particular. In the second place, Sarti, we are told, was an envious spirit who was always venting his spleen on his superiors. At a later date he fell foul of Beethoven.

*
*   *

But I am not quite satisfied on this Sarti matter.   I
have seen so many of these old disparagements, that
have become the historians' and critics' *clichés,* turn
out, once they are studied at first hand, to have nothing
like the significance that in the course of generations
has become attached to them, that I should like to examine the original document for myself.   I must try
to get on the track of it.

No modern history or biography tells us any more
about the Sarti affair than Jahn did some sixty years
ago, and Oulibicheff thirty years before that.   The
story was current before then, but it was Jahn who
first put it into general circulation; and everyone who
has written on Mozart since then has simply copied
from him.   All that Jahn does is to summarize Sarti's
criticism thus:

"The good man later wrote a bitter and malicious
critique of some passages in Mozart's quartets, con-
cerning which——revolted that 'barbarians without any
ear permit themselves to compose music'——he asks,
'Si può far di più per far stonar i professori?'   He
points out fault after fault 'that could be made only
by a clavier player who could not distinguish between
D sharp and E flat'; and he clinches the matter with,
'Dirò anch'io come l'immortale Rousseau: De la
musique pour faire boucher les oreilles.' "

The source of all these stories is Nissen, Mozart's
first biographer (1828), who married the composer's
widow.   He was not very musical, and probably had
only a very dim idea of what the fuss about the quartets had been some forty years before; he merely repeated what he had been told, and apparently there
was already in existence, in the second decade of the

nineteenth century, a legend about these quartets corresponding to the Wagner legend of our own time.

Every modern writer upon Mozart dutifully re-tells the old story; but apparently not one of them has thought it incumbent upon him to look into the matter for himself, to find out what it was that Sarti really did say, and why he said it. Apparently Sarti's Italian manuscript, which he wrote for a Milanese lady, has never been printed. But in the early eighteenthirties there was a recrudescence of the old controversy—caused, I think, by Fétis's suggested emendations of the offending passage—and one writer, who had very sensibly thought it time some one consulted the manuscript, gave a German summary of it in the *Allgemeine Musikalische Zeitung* of June 6, 1832. Suppose, then, we brush aside Jahn and Oulibicheff and Nissen and Paul Stefan and the rest of them, and, for our information about Sarti, go straight to Sarti?

He begins by positing two fundamental laws of the older masters: (1) Perfect consonances must not follow each other in direct motion, because this makes a deficiency of harmony; (2) False relations that make a bad effect are strictly forbidden. The first rule is discretional, since a penury of harmony does not outrage the ear. A false relation, on the other hand, is directly contrary to the aim of music, which is to please. Certain new composers pride themselves on not observing these rules, so as to annoy us with barbarisms; they believe that all that is necessary is to avoid consecutive fifths. This rule, however, as a consequence from the first of the maxims given above, is discretional. It has been proved physicomathematically that, certain cases apart, the violation of this rule is not contrary to the above-mentioned aim of music. But in conformity with this aim false relations must absolutely be avoided; whoever indulges in them must have ears cased with iron.

After an analysis of false relations, Sarti goes on to say that the old masters occasionally allowed themselves these licences, but always made the ear the judge, since they proceeded from the unshakable principle that there can never be a composer without a good ear. But they were wrong. Now that barbarians have begun to write music, we get passages that make us shudder.

Apart from the ear, we learn from physico-mathematics which false relations are tolerable and which are to be avoided. Here let us consider those that apply to the present case, i. e. the progressions of Apotome and Minimo and their inversions.

Apotome—also called the small semitone and the false unison—is that which has the same name—e. g. F, F sharp, or E, E flat. Minimo is an interval with two step-names, the under note having a sharp and the upper a flat—e. g. D sharp and E flat, or F sharp and G flat. It is clear that false relations of this kind are among the most horrible, though there are cases where they are hidden, and so do not make such a bad effect.

Then he proceeds to analyse the introduction to the C major quartet.

Bar 2. The first violin at its entry makes an Apotome false relation with the viola and is dissonant, because the beginning suggests the soft key and the violin the hard; moreover, the violin begins with an interval of a second to the viola; this is one of the most horrible of entries.

Bar 3. The C sharp in the second violin makes an Apotome false relation with the previous C in the bass.

Bar 4. The B flat in the first violin makes an Apotome false relation with the preceding B natural in the bass; for although F sharp comes between them, a quaver does not suffice to make us forget the B natural.

Bars 6, 7, 8 are *rosalie* of the preceding bars, and contain the same faults.

Bar 9. The A in the viola makes a false octave with the A flat in the bass, which, in an adagio, lasts a fair while and so becomes noticeable. The false octave is the inversion of the Apotome.

Bar 11. The F sharp in the first violin, with the F in the bass, produces the same fault.

Bar 14. The viola enters badly with the flat, since it makes an Apotome with the previous B in the bass.

Bar 20. The A sharp of the second violin, as the augmented third of the F in the viola, is very bad in an adagio.

Bar 21. The A sharp in the viola, as diminished sixth to the F in the violin, gives the inverse fault to the one just mentioned.

Then Sarti quotes the following bars from another of the quartets dedicated to Haydn—the D minor—and comments upon them:

Bar 4. The E natural not going into F after the E flat is an arrant Apotome monodico, and one of the worst faults. To permit of such a transition, E flat must become D sharp, which could have happened here if the E flat were not absolutely defined by the D in the first crotchet of the bar and the two preceding bars (2 and 3); it is thus impossible for the listener

to believe that he hears D sharp, and be spared the
horrible sensation at the entry of the E. Do not imagine (as many clavier players do) that E flat and
D sharp are a unison; there is a real interval between
them, but one which, as harmonic doctrine proves, is
the most disagreeable that can occur. The effect of
the hackneyed cadence

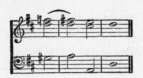

is good when the F can appear before the F sharp as
E sharp; if it does not create this illusion, the effect is
bad. The Apotome is not laid bare when it immediately precedes the Limma, or diatonic semitone, e. g.,

or

also when it falls on the heptachord (the harmonically
divided small seventh), e. g.,

or, inverted,

Bar 13.   The dissonance of the small second between the second violin and the viola hurts the ear by its long duration.   The teachers of counterpoint allow a dissonance to last at the most half a bar, and that in *tempo di cappella;* harmonic science teaches that the dissonance should not last longer than one second. This dissonant bar, though *allegro,* lasts at least two seconds, which is all the less permissible as it is a semitone, and therefore the most unpleasant of all dissonances.   The G sharp in the viola, though it lasts only a moment, is very harsh.

Bar 14.   The trill on the flat in the second violin is in bad taste, since it has the C sharp of the first violin above it; the C of the trill makes with the C sharp a false octave, the inversion of which is the Apotome.

Sarti sums up thus: From these two fragments we can decide that the composer ("whom I do not know and do not   want to know") is only a clavier player with a depraved [unsound, *goaste* in the Italian] ear; he is a sectary (*settatore*) of the false system that divides the octave into twelve equal semitones, a system sufficiently well known to intelligent artists, and one proved false by harmonic science.

"Could a sound taste allow the first violin to enter so dissonantly as in the second and sixth bars of the first quotation [i. e., the introduction to the C major quartet]?   Has the composer done it to cover the player with shame, or that the hearers may cry out: 'He is out of tune'?   Is this the best way to write music?   And will anyone be found to print such music?   In short, if this composer packs his works with such capital errors (19 in 36 bars) as he has been shown to have done in these two fragments, we may be sure that they will be rejected by everyone who has a good and unspoilt ear. I would say with the immortal Rousseau, 'De la musique à faire boucher les oreilles.' "

*

* *

It was worth while disinterring this fragment. When we meet it face to face we see that it is not so terrible as we might infer from the dark hints of the dutiful biographers of Mozart. Its tone is unpleasant; but we have to remember first of all that musical controversy has always been a little acrimonious, and in the second place that, as I have already said, Mozart could not possibly be for his contemporaries the idealized, almost sacred figure he is for us. We may freely admit that Sarti was an envious and somewhat malicious man, who found it difficult to admire his superiors unreservedly. But putting the personal element on one side, is there very much wrong with his criticism *qua* criticism? It is all very well for the 1832 translator of the manuscript for the *Allgemeine Musikalische Zeitung* to exclaim indignantly: "Nineteen faults in thirty-six bars! And the remaining thousands of heavenly bars in these six quartets—how did *these* strike Kapellmeister Sarti?" That is beside the question; if we are trying a man for embezzlement it is not relevant to the issue to ask us to take into consideration his kindness to the office staff. Sarti is not attempting an æsthetic appreciation of the quartets as a whole; he is simply subjecting certain bars of them to a technical examination. And is not a good deal of his criticism justified from the technical

point of view, especially that of his period? Our ears
are less sensitive to-day than those of the older
musicians were; we have come to feel that little things
of this sort are mostly not worth worrying about.
But they evidently worried about them in the
eighteenth century. The deeper we go into this
Mozart case, does it not become clearer that the whole
trouble was this—not that they picked a quarrel with
the quartets in the name of theory, but that certain
things in the quartets offended the ears of the time,
and that *then* the listeners looked to theory for a
justification of their feeling of offence? Have we not
all felt, in many an admired piece of music, that this
passage or that does not fall as graciously upon the
ear as we should like? But our feeling this does not
imply that we are utterly opposed to the composer
and all his works. Why then should we assume that
Mozart's contemporaries were unable to appreciate
his genius as a whole because they objected to a bar
or two here and there as harsh or ill-written? In
spite of the fact that Mozart was Mozart, and they
were only they, may not they have been in large part
right, and he, for once, wrong? The introduction to
the C major quartet has always been, and still is, a
rather dubious piece of writing; we see what Mozart
was driving at, but it does not quite "come off." It
was forty or fifty years after the quartet was written
that Fétis began to theorize about it and to suggest
altering it; he tells us that when it was played in Paris
by the Baillot Quartet—who may be presumed to have
known their business—a tumult broke out in the
audience over the introduction. Fétis's conjectural
emendations drew on him the wrath of several of the
German musicians. In the very same volume of the

Allgemeine Musikalische Zeitung in which I found the translation of Sarti there are two replies to Fétis, one by Balthasar, the other by Leduc. Each gives his reasons for declining to accept Fétis's theories, and justifies Mozart's harmonies from the schoolroom point of view. But each is silent as to the quality of the passage *as music*. Leduc, indeed, as good as admits that the passage needs defence—it was now, be it remembered, close on fifty years after the first publication of the quartet, when the work had become the common property of quartet players and audiences, and when, therefore, there could be no question of a novelty to which men's ears could not, for the moment, adjust themselves. "Without doubt," says Leduc, "it occurs to no one to deny this effect [i. e., of strangeness]; it was intended by the composer, and he could easily have avoided it had he wanted to do so. We may like it or dislike it—every hearer must be allowed his freedom in this respect; but we can never subscribe to the theory that the effect came about through sinning [as Fétis had alleged] against the laws of counterpoint." We can easily read between the lines. Leduc himself found the passage a little *rébarbatif;* but he was unwilling to admit this, partly because the music came from so great a master as Mozart, partly because he would not have it made the pretext for academic dogmatism on Fétis's part.

And that the passage had always been a stumbling-block is evident from Fétis's taking up the question as he did and at the time he did. He had seen Sarti's manuscript, or a copy of it. His complaint against Sarti was not that the latter had objected to the passage, but that he had objected to it on the wrong grounds; Sarti's purpose, he said, was not so much to explain these faults of Mozart by the rules of art as to express his ill-humour at what had "put his own ausonian ear on the rack" Even to-day no one comes forward and says: "The passage sounds excellent, and there is an end to the matter." Everybody feels that there is something wrong with it, but is content to accept it either because Mozart wrote it or because it can be shown to make theoretic sense. But with the passage still æsthetically as much in doubt in 1924 as it was in 1830, it is surely going a little too far to say that the hearers who jibbed at it in 1785 merely wrote themselves down as "reactionaries" who were unable to keep pace with the new spirit that Mozart was bringing into music. The Mozart legend, in fact, like the Wagner legend, collapses the moment it is critically examined.

*

*   *

I have run once more through the latest Mozart literature to see if any writer on the subject addresses himself frankly to the æsthetic question involved in the introduction to the C major quartet. I can find none; but the paragraph on the matter in Sir Henry Hadow's volume on *The Viennese Period* in the *Oxford History of Music* is very interesting. After speaking of the "colour" in Mozart's and Haydn's chamber music, he says: "Yet it is on a point of colour that Mozart has most directly challenged critical opinion. The famous introduction to the C major quartet was an enigma in his own day, it remains an enigma in ours. Technically, no doubt, it is easy of explanation; it aims, for once, at obscuring tonality, in order that the key when established may stand more salient by contrast; it effects this by playing upon two notes which are, for many purposes, harmonically interchangeable. But the direct result is a false relation[1] which, even after a century of experience, it is easier to understand than to enjoy, and of which our safest judgment is the verdict of Haydn, that 'if Mozart wrote thus he must have done so with good reason.' Far too much coil has been raised over a few bars which, whether we like them or not, are evidently intentional, and of which the momentary harshness only enhances our pleasure in the radiant melody that follows them."

I respectfully dissent. A composer either says clearly and convincingly what it was in his mind to say or he does not. If he does not, the proper term for the result is not enigma but failure. That is what we should call it in the case of Smith or Jones; I see no reason to call it by any other word because the perpetrator of the failure happens to be named Mozart. Are there, indeed, any "enigmas" in music—at all events any that withhold their elucidation from the whole race of musicians for a century and a half?

On examination, then, Sarti turns out to have been mostly right and Mozart wrong. Our first thought, when we read in the biographies that Sarti accused Mozart of not knowing D sharp from E flat, is that the smaller man had been guilty of a mere impertinence towards the greater. But we see now that all that Sarti was doing was to state again the eternal problem of pure string intonation as against the tempered scale of keyed instruments; we have only to

---

[1] "The opening triad gives us the erroneous impression that the key is A flat major, an impression somewhat rudely dispelled by the A natural of the first violin."

turn to Sarti's treatise to see, indeed, that the account usually given of the episode is quite misleading. Sarti did *not* say that Mozart was incapable of distinguishing in general between D sharp and E flat; he said, what is perfectly true, that these two notes are not really the same, but that *clavier players,* using the tempered intonation, are inclined to persuade themselves that they are. In the eighteenth century, as the instruction books of the period show, the musical ear was much more sensitive in these matters than the modern ear is; and Sarti must have been speaking for thousands of musicians who felt that, however one might justify it by theory, the introduction to the C major quartet was a piece of clumsy and ugly writing for strings.

As for the passage from Cramer's *Magazin der Musik* that Jahn cites—and all the other biographers after him—really one can only wonder at the solemn childishness of these good people. I have hunted out the old volumes in the library. The *Magazin der Musik, herausgegeben von Carl Friedrich Cramer, Professor in Kiel,* was a small and short-lived sheet published in Hamburg. The reference to Mozart occurs in the Vienna letter of June 29, 1787, of a Vienna correspondent who signs himself "A." It runs thus: "He [Mozart] is the best and cleverest clavier player I have ever heard; but it is a pity that in his ingenious and really beautiful compositions he goes too far in his attempt to be new, so that feeling and heart come off rather badly [*wenig gewinnen*]. His new quartets, dedicated to Haydn, are too strongly spiced—and what palate can stand that for long?" That is all! Let us put aside the old question as to whether this correspondent and others who thought

like him were right about the quartets (the point in
debate seems always to have been the introduction to
the C major).   The really interesting thing to observe
is that this is just a passage from an anonymous correspondent's letter.   What would posterity think of
some biographer of the year 2000 who, desirous of
giving his readers an idea of what the musical world
in general thought about Stravinsky in 1924, quoted
a solitary sentence from the anonymous London correspondent of a Birmingham paper?   It is high time
someone undertook a genuine history of musical
opinion.   What has hitherto passed for this seems
mostly to have been written by children for children.

IX

STILL in search of even one case of a great composer being so far in advance of his contemporaries that only misunderstanding was his lot in his own day, I turn to Monteverdi. The Wagner legend and the Mozart legend have both failed to substantiate themselves. Will the Monteverdi legend be able to bear up against a similar scrutiny of its bases?

One biographer after another goes on dutifully quoting Artusi's censure of certain "crudities" in Monteverdi as typical of the opposition, the misunderstanding, that the innovating genius is fated to meet with in every age; and the innocent student is taught to see Monteverdi as a solitary figure fighting desperately for the new truth against an army of fools and knaves. An hour's research would have shown the second-hand historians that they were mistaken. Monteverdi's popularity exceeded that of any of his Italian contemporaries in the same field; and it was precisely after he had become recognized as the most daring innovator of the day that his popularity was greatest. His *Lament of Ariadne* was the Italian "best-seller" during a whole generation. When the Kapellmeistership of St. Mark's, Venice (the most coveted post in Italy), became vacant through the death of Martinengo in 1613, the Senate discovered, after inquiries in Rome, Milan, Mantua and elsewhere, that the unanimous opinion was that Monteverdi was the musician who would bring most glory to the town. The salary of all his great predecessors—Willaert, Cyprian, Zarlino, etc.—had been 200 ducats. Monte-

verdi, as an inducement to accept the post, was offered
300 ducats from the first, and in 1614 his stipend was
raised to 400 ducats. His music was everywhere in
demand. In 1619 the Court of Mantua tried to win
him back again from Venice, but in vain. The learned
academies heaped honours on him. Few composers
have enjoyed such dominion over their contemporaries
as the one who is so often and so ignorantly cited,
along with Wagner, as the supreme type of genius
misunderstood and hounded down.

His case is really an astonishing one. Never has
so large a mountain been made out of so small a mole-
hill. M. Louis Schneider, in his recent book on
Monteverdi, may be taken as typical of the senti-
mentalizing historian. "Critics, critics, my brothers,"
he cries dramatically, after an account of the Artusi
episode, "meditate on the Artusi-Monteverdi case; it
recurs under the form of La Harpe-Gluck, Hanslick-
Wagner, and many others; and let us, like wise men,
dip our pen seven times in the ink-pot before we enun-
ciate these definite judgments that it will be the business of posterity to correct." True to type, M.
Schneider, before this, has given unwary readers the
impression of a general revolt among the "conserva-
toires" of the day against the novelties and audacities
of Monteverdi. "The mediocre people," he says,
"the partisans of facile effect, those who insist on art
being submitted to a rigorous discipline, the false
masters who are really only scholars kept in leading-
strings during their whole career, were indignant at
the sight of a young and newly-appointed head of the
ducal Chapel permitting himself an æsthetic different
from theirs, or exhibiting a personality superior to their

talent, which had got used to following too-beaten paths."

Could the chivalrous reader help feeling, after reading this, very much as the mediæval knight-errant must have felt when he learned that a virtuous damsel had been carried off by a regiment of dragons? He burns to take up arms and fly to the persecuted one's rescue. Knowing nothing of the circumstances of the times, the young student's heated imagination pictures poor Monteverdi assailed, like Wagner, by a horde of stupid enemies. But on investigation the regiment of dragons thins down to one, and that rather an insignificant specimen of the fauna. It was Artusi, and Artusi alone, so far as history records, who took upon himself to censure Monteverdi in the name of tradition. It is true that in his dialogue he makes one of the interlocutors say that at a recent performance of some madrigals [Monteverdi's] in the house of a young gentleman of Ferrara there were a number of connoisseurs who were revolted at the badness of some of the writing; but this multiplication of his own personality is one of the privileges of the controver-sialist. Whether the whole room did or did not share the indignation of Artusi we cannot say; certain it is that we have no written record of any criticism of this order from anyone but him. It is possible that in Monteverdi's punning dedication of one of his church compositions to Pope Clemens VIII there is a hint at other critics besides Artusi; but if such there were, their criticism must have been delivered in private; history knows nothing of it. And what has the solitary Artusi to say against Monteverdi's novelties? Simply that they are contrary to the ancient rules.

He criticizes the madrigal *O Mirtillo,* to quote M. Schneider again, "as a professor of harmony would criticize a pupil's exercise; and he finishes by saying that he cannot understand how a musician can permit himself to perpetrate faults that would leap to the eyes of quite little children."

Well, who *was* Artusi? He was a pedagogue of the type that abounds in every art and every age. He had written a treatise on counterpoint, and he had turned out some madrigals of his own that we shall probably be safe in assuming to have been as correct and as dull as the music of the professor generally is. He censures Monteverdi for having infringed the school rules. Suppose now that some three hundred years hence some historian were to dig out a pamphlet in which a Macfarren, let us say, found fault, in the name of school theory, with the harmonization of half a dozen bars of *Tristan.* That historian would be giving his readers a very wrong idea of the true state of things about 1870 if, on the strength of this one passage, he argued that all Wagner's contemporaries were against him. We know that if there is one person whose æsthetic judgment is completely unrepresentative of the opinion of the average man it is the schoolman pure and simple, the theorist who ignores expression and tests everything by theory. We know that the good Jadassohn, to whom Breitkopf and Härtel sent the manuscript of some of Hugo Wolf's early songs, advised the firm not to publish them; "they are among the most nonsensical things," he said in his report, "that the extreme Left of the New German School has yet perpetrated, and in my opinion they have nothing in common with the art of music except that they contain tones and rhythms." But we know also that this was not how the songs struck other people who were less fettered by theory; it is highly probable, indeed, that Jadassohn was the only man of any standing in the musical world who saw or heard the songs who got that impression of them. It would be foolish to assume that the pedantry of a Jadassohn or a Macfarren was typical of the attitude of the world in general towards a Wolf or a Wagner. It is equally foolish to assume that "criticism" made an ass of itself over Monteverdi, merely because a single irritated pedant objected, in the name of theory, to one or two things he did not understand. The simple truth is that Monteverdi was recognized from the first as one of the greatest of Italian composers, and for perhaps the last forty years of his long life as the greatest of those then living. Edition after edition of his madrigals was called for during his lifetime and in the years immediately following his death; and even M. Schneider, after picturing him as moving about in a world always ready to try him for "crimes de lèse-grammaire," after moralizing that "not to be understood is not invariably the sign of the beautiful, but it is often the price that genius has to pay," ends his book thus: "And yet this innovator, this precursor, presents us with an example unique in the history of art; he was understood by his time, he was admired during his lifetime! It seems as if posterity had been more unjust to him than his contemporaries were, for it has ignored him for some two centuries and a half." To which it only needs to be added, for the sake of completeness, that in the matter of recognition by his contemporaries Monteverdi was *not* "an example unique in the history of art." The really unique phenomenon—if we could find it—would be a great composer who was not "admired during his lifetime" —to the extent, of course, that his work was known; for obviously a generation cannot be blamed for not admiring a composer *en masse* if, as happened in the case of Hugo Wolf, his music is not generally accessible.

*

*   *

It is a pity that the literature of all these old controversies is not within the ordinary student's reach; it would be so much better if he could look into them for himself instead of having to be content with a mere citation here and there, and even that shown him through the distorting lens of a biographer or historian who, even if he has happened to go to the original documents himself, approaches them predisposed to see in them just what he wants to see.   I am lucky to find a copy of Artusi's two dialogues and of his treatise on counterpoint in my friend's library; for none of the summaries of the controversy, not even those of Ambros and Emil Vogel, tell the whole story so clearly that a student of it can afford to neglect the original documents.   Surely one has only to read these without any *parti pris* to realize the true state of affairs.   The Italian generation of about 1585 to 1615 must have been as racked by controversy as our own is.   Then, as now, an old art was fighting for its life against a new one.   Human nature being eternally the same, we may be pretty sure that what is happening around us now was also happening then; the controversies were not as public as they are now, but a vast amount of controversy there must have been; Muzio Effrem's attack on Marco da Gagliano was probably only one of many affairs of the kind. Then, as now, there were confident declarations on the part of the innovators that a new dispensation had dawned; then, as now, the lovers of the older art could not see that most of the new men were producing anything as rich in expression and as masterly in technique as the old art that they so despised. Then, as now, there was a good deal of eager and voluble dilettantism, at which the solidly schooled classicists of the period could only smile indulgently. They, in their turn, knowing the perfection of the art that it had taken centuries to develop, would often be nettled at the lack of understanding of it displayed by some of the younger spirits, whom they rightly regarded as little more than semi-amateurs.

What could a sound musician of the old school do but curl a contemptuous lip when he heard Caccini declare that he had learned more about music from the discussions about the drama of the Greeks in Count Bardi's house than he had learned in more than thirty years from the study of counterpoint? Out of these discussions and out of the experiments of dilettanti in the new genre something significant might some day come; but it had certainly not come as yet. The conservatives knew *their* art inside out; most of the innovators were thoroughly at home in neither the theory nor the practice of theirs. They could not have the theory for the simple reason that as yet they had not the practice; for a complete and workable musical theory always follows an epoch of rich achievement. Even when G. B. Doni, a good many years later, set himself to justify the Florentine ideal and commend the practitioners of it, he could not put forward a rationale of the technical principles of the new style. "What the new style was in the utmost need of on the theoretical side," says Ambros, "—a properly developed theory of harmony, of structure, of modulation, of accompaniment—of all this neither Doni nor anyone else had the least conception. Not till long afterwards, when the practitioners had discovered all these things, did theory enter as usual, testing, searching, getting down to foundations, and win from the practice that now lay ready to its hand the rules that in turn could govern and lead practice. As with all reforms that come about, not peacefully by way of gradual transformation, but through a sudden declaration of war on firmly-founded and seemingly immovable conditions, the activity of the Florentines was at first mostly negative, their manner polemical; but what they were going to put in the place of what they destroyed, this meanwhile only hovered before them in the vaguest outlines; the one positive thing about it was merely the aspiration towards a new birth of music in the antique [i. e., the Greek] sense, and, where possible, in antique forms. . . ."

Too much attention has been concentrated both by historians and by students on the efforts of Peri, Caccini and Monteverdi (the Monteverdi, that is, of the *Orfeo* of 1607, for the later Monteverdi, as we see him in *L'Incoronazione di Poppea* towards the end of his life, more than thirty years later, is a different man, with different artistic aims from his own earlier ones and from those of the first Florentines), and too little on the changes that were going on in the madrigal and other polyphonic forms during this period. Even yet not one twentieth part of the madrigals of Marenzio, Gesualdo and Monteverdi are accessible in

modern reprints, and a still smaller proportion of the
work of Cyprian de Rore, Willaert, the two Gabrieli,
and other composers of the time who had been nib-
bling, at this point or that, at the old tissue of polyphonic music. But even from such material as we
yet have to go upon it is evident that Italian musical
circles of the period must have known many a sharp
controversy between the musicians of the old school
and those of the new. The former had at any rate a
working theory of their own, and they clung tightly
to it. This theory, that had been built up with immense difficulty over a long course of years, was being
strengthened and added to, during the very period of
the birth of the new ideals, by such men as Zacconi,
Zarlino, Cerretto, and Artusi. They can be forgiven,
knowing their business as well as they did, for feeling
a little contemptuous of the dilettanti. The theorists
and teachers formed, apparently, a sort of close cor-
poration; we gather that only the best among their
pupils were initiated into all the profundities of the
science of counterpoint, and such of the masters as
published books on the subject were regarded with a
certain amount of suspicion by their more prudent colleagues; "not for a thousand ducats," said Costanza
Porta to his pupils when he saw the first part of Zacconi's *Prattica di Musica* in a shop in Padua in 1595,
"not for a thousand ducats would I have made public
all the secrets that this Frate has done." The less
broad-minded among them must have regarded music
less as an art than as a science, or at any rate as an art
that should not try to escape from the leading-strings
of science—which attitude, indeed, has been that of
the pedant in all ages. And, as Ambros notes, the
fact that most of them were ecclesiastics would account

in part for their conservatism; the clerical mind has never been well disposed towards innovators in music. Further, the popularity of the new methods in thoroughly worldly circles would be a reason for the clerics feeling a certain amount of professional jealousy of these methods. None of the innovators—not even Monteverdi—permitted himself the same licence in religious as in secular music; and it was natural that the ecclesiastical professional mind should feel a vague irritation not merely at the infringements of musical rule, but at this spectacle of music shaking itself more and more free from the control of the Church.

Artusi was not only an ecclesiastic and a hide-bound theoretician, but, seemingly, a dogmatist easily irritated by whatever countered his own ways of thinking —though it must be confessed that the ordinary musical controversy of that epoch was as acid as that of any later day. Anyhow, a strain of acerbity runs through his *Ragiomenti*. The incurable, inaccessible pedantry of his mind is shown by his whole manner of dealing with Monteverdi. The whole point of some of Monteverdi's departures from the "rules" was that the musical expression of the moment came spontaneously out of the words; Monteverdi's brother, who was entrusted by the composer with the task of replying to Artusi at a later date, particularly insisted on this, and a century or so later Padre Martini, when analysing a couple of Monteverdi's madrigals, was careful to impress on the young student the fact that what would not be permissible in church music might be justified in secular music, as here, by the emotion at the back of the words. Artusi has been censured for quoting the offending Monteverdi passages without the words; he has even been accused of deliberate bad faith in doing so. But it is probable that it never occurred to him to take the words into consideration. Counterpoint was counterpoint, he would no doubt say, and that was an end of the matter; what was bad from the point of view of music pure and simple could not be made good by being associated with this word or that. Rules were rules, and there was nothing more to be said about it. These rules, for an Artusi, were fixed for all time. He appeals, as, in their simplicity, the objectors to new effects have done from his time to the present, to the ear. He could not realize that his own ear had ceased to be a natural and independent organ and become a mere lackey of his theory. He admits that there is much that is good in these new madrigals, but there is too much that is novel in them. "The texture is not ungrateful," he says, "but he introduces new rules, new modes, new kinds of phrases, that however are harsh and unpleasing to the ear, and could not be otherwise; for if the good rules are broken, rules founded partly on experience, the mother of all things, partly on nature, and partly on demonstration, we must believe that these novelties are deformities of the nature and of the propriety of true harmony, and far removed from the true end of music, which is to give delight."

The theorists made a sharp distinction between consonance and dissonance. Monteverdi does not recognize this distinction; therefore Monteverdi is a barbarian.

*
* *

Some of Artusi's objections are so trifling, even on theoretical grounds, that even in their own day, surely, no importance could have been attached to them by the ordinary music-lover; they are merely the niggling fault-finding of the pedagogue.   At a later date (for he attacked Monteverdi again in 1606 and 1608, and with more rancour than ever) he picked a quarrel with him over the three-part songs, *Damigella tutta bella, O Rosetta* and *Clori Amorosa,* which, he said, bore the same time signatures, though the rhythms were different. If the signature was right for the first two, it was necessarily wrong for the third.   "Let Monteverdi say what he will, he has shown that he knows nothing of the proportions."   Monteverdi is further accused of introducing measures of three "whites" into a madrigal that is marked C; he is, in fact, incapable of distinguishing between three in a bar and four in a bar. One can hardly believe that anyone took pedantic remarks of this kind seriously; I rather imagine that everyone smiled quietly at the childish temper of the cantankerous pedant.   M. Henry Prunières thinks that "the intentions of Monteverdi in the *Scherzi musicali* [the volume in which the songs just mentioned appeared in 1607] remained obscure for many auditors who were disconcerted by the pieces 'without any ruled measure,' but that were to be sung according to the value of longs and breves, in the French manner." But as M. Prunières himself points out, in the same sentence, that the *Scherzi musicali* had "a great success," as is attested by the "considerable number" of the editions that were issued of them, we may perhaps surmise that the average singer or listener of the day experienced no great difficulty with them.   Certainly no one but an Artusi would have ventured to say that Monteverdi showed himself ignorant of the difference between three and four.

Another of Artusi's points was that it was impossible to say which mode the *Cruda amarilla* madrigal was in. Was it the seventh or the tenth? At the beginning, the middle and the end are found the cadences of both modes. Monteverdi's reply was that the madrigal was plainly in the seventh (the Mixolydian) mode, since, "as is generally known," the mode of a work is defined by the first and last chords. Once more, can we imagine Artusi being taken seriously by Monteverdi's contemporaries in a criticism of this kind? Even supposing the criticism to be theoretically justified, would any hearer of the time refuse to admire the music on that account? What would be thought of any academic pedant of to-day who told us that the first movement of Elgar's first symphony is not worth our consideration because no one has yet been able to tell us what key it begins in? (I mean the movement proper, not the preamble.)

Artusi falls foul of a couple of well-known bars from *Cruda amarilla;* just look, he says, at this rough, uncouth passage; after a pause the bass enters with a diminished fifth against the upper voice! Other composers have used the same interval, but not in this way—never after a pause, only after a sixth or some other consonance. Let it not be said that a pause can count as a consonance! The ear only perceives what it actually hears. Masters like Cyprian de Rore, in the madrigals *Non gemme, non fin' oro,* and Morales in his *Magnificat quinti toni,* at the words *Sicut locutus est,* have shown us the only right way to use the diminished fifth.

The truth is that, as Ambros says, the "diminished fifth" is really an unprepared dominant seventh, and the chord an incomplete $\frac{6}{5}$. Artusi's objection here was subconsciously the same as his objection to the unprepared ninth, followed by a seventh, in another part of *Cruda amarilla.*

Monteverdi's general reply to Artusi was that the latter had failed to see that the unusual harmonies were motived by and justified by the words. He was aiming at emotional effects that could not be got in any other way. The really interesting thing about his replies, however, is the implication that everyone—except fossils like Artusi—knew that both the spirit and the language of music were changing. Monteverdi marks off the *Seconda Pratica* (the new style) from the *Prima Pratica* of the older masters and theorists. He promised to write a book on the *Seconda Pratica,* but apparently if he ever began it he did not find time to finish it. His way of referring to the old and the new styles shows that he was addressing an audience to which the distinction was quite clear; that is to say, we must rid ourselves of the old notion that he alone was springing a novelty upon the world, and a novelty so startling that his contemporaries could not assimilate it. He implies that he himself is only one among many. There may perhaps, he says, be some people who, believing that there are no other rules of art than those laid down by Zarlino, are surprised at the *Seconda Pratica;* they may rest assured, however, that as far as consonance and dissonance are concerned, a new view from the customary one is justified, which vindicates the modern way of composing with a freer appeal to the ear and the reason. He disclaims for himself the honour of being the discoverer of the *Seconda Pratica.* The honour really belongs to his predecessor, Cyprian de Rore. Artusi has done his (Monteverdi's) madrigals an injustice by

quoting the music without the words. A similar procedure would do equal injustice, he says, to Cyprian,
especially in the case of the madrigals *Dalle belle con-
trade, Se ben il duol, Et se pur mi mantien' amor,
Poichè m'invit' amore, Crudel acerba* and *Un altra
volta*. There are in these many violations of the old
rules; he himself, in fact, is only carrying the principles of Cyprian further. The rules, indeed, are
often flouted by composers whom Artusi has cited as
models, *musici eccellenti*—for example, Marenzio in
such madrigals as *E sò come in un punto, Cosi nel mio
parlar, Dura legge,* and *S'io parto*. "It is always better to invent new things than to go on repeating old
ones."

Artusi can give no answer but another pig-headed
appeal to the rules. The man was beyond argument;
he was a pedant of the first water, and must have cut a
ridiculous figure in the eyes of the musical world of his
time. How little weight he carried is shown by the
quiet contempt of the only reply that Monteverdi at
first permitted himself—the publication of the offending madrigals *after* Artusi's attack on them.
(They had previously circulated in manuscript.) As
Emil Vogel says, an artist who could do this must have
been pretty sure of himself and of the public judgment.
There is another piece of evidence of how the affair
looked to contemporaries. In one of his later dia-
tribes Artusi attacked Ercole Bottrigari along with
Monteverdi. Bottrigari, who was then seventy-two
years old, protested against Artusi's cavalier treatment
of the greatest composer of the day, and shows us
clearly enough what a great many of the musicians
of the time thought of the irritable and intolerant old
pedant; Monteverdi, he says, is "a man who knows

much and can do much; he will defend himself with spirit and good sense, and will crush the baseless audacity and arrogance of this man [Artusi], who expects everybody to bow down to his opinion, while he himself is to be at liberty to do what he likes."

We may be tolerably sure that the generation of 1600 did not take the good Artusi with anything like the seriousness that the present age has done. We must rid ourselves of the grotesque notion that Monteverdi was a solitary pioneer whom the whole of musical Italy was hounding down, Artusi being the accredited leader of that ignorant mob. The truth is that Monteverdi was only one innovator among many, that the innovations were very much to the taste of the average music-lover of the period, and that Artusi was merely an arrogant and obstinate pedagogue of no particular importance even in his own day. Monteverdi does not take him quite seriously even as a pedagogue; he advises him to read Zarlino for information on the subject of the mixed modes. And more than once in the reply of 1607 Monteverdi shows that he was confident he had the public with him as against the pedantic Artusi. This is especially evident from the concluding words of the reply: "When an art [i. e. this new manner of composing] is welcomed by the world with open arms . . . my brother [the reader will remember that it is Giulio Cesare Monteverdi who is speaking for the composer] cannot believe, and will never believe, that it is the world that is wrong, but that his opponent is. And so be happy!" [*E porre cotal modo di comporre, vien dal mondo abbraciato, in maniera tale che uso con giusta ragione si può chiamare, perciò non può credere, ne credera mai, quando anco le ragioni sue, non fossero bone, per sostentamento della verità di cotal uso che il mondo s'inganni, ma si bene l'oppositore e vivete felici"*]. It is continuously evident from the Artusi dialogue that the pedant was attacking not so much Monteverdi himself as the movement for which Monteverdi stood; there is reference after reference to a body of musicians and music-lovers of a new way of thinking—*gli autori o inventori di esse.*

It only remains to be added, perhaps, that even Artusi, before many years were out, recognized that he had been in the wrong. So, at any rate, we assume from a letter of Monteverdi's of 1633, in which he says that a former antagonist changed in the end (Artusi had died in 1613) from blame to praise of him, and had begun to like and esteem him.

Burney long ago said the common-sense word on the affair: "Monteverdi defended himself in prefaces and letters prefixed to his works; but his best defence was the revolution he brought about in counterpoint; *for his licences pleasing the public ear, were soon adopted not only by dilettanti, but professors.*"

*

* *

Artusi, in fact, was living in a changing world in which it was rapidly becoming impossible for the rigid theorist to take his bearings. We must do him justice. We always have to remember, in considering the reactions of the conservative mind against the innovators of its time, that the conservatives must have seen a great deal of sheer incompetence around them. Just as to-day we have Stravinsky, a man of genius who sometimes gets out of his depth, and the imitators of

Stravinsky, whose feeble follies tend to bring the master also into disrepute, so in the early years of the seventeenth century there must have been, besides the half-dozen sane masters whom we know, and whose work has survived because it is sane, innumerable amateurs, bunglers, dilettanti, experimenters, who angered the old-fashioned experts by their self-assured incompetence.   That the innovators had the usual sublime self-confidence of their type, the same sweeping contempt for those who differed from them, the same conviction that they were making a new heaven and a new earth, may be gathered from various passages in Artusi's first dialogue.   One of the interlocutors, Vario, describes the effects of the "moderns" as "impertinences," and asks how they can justify them. Luca replies that these gentry do not regard them as impertinences, but as a new style, in fact, the only proper way to compose (*e vogliono che questo sia il vero modo di componere, affirmando che questa novità a novo ordine di comporre sia per fare molti effetti, che non fà, ne farà, la musica ordinaria*).

It is the old story—the arrogance and intolerance of the self-conscious innovators goading the "classicists" into revolt not only against what is foolish in the new music but what is rational in it.   We know that towards the end of the sixteenth century the facility for making new harmonic effects on keyed instruments was leading to a corruption of the pure polyphonic style; it is quite probable that Gesualdo picked out some of his effects on the clavier and then transferred them to voices.   And what Gesualdo did with a vast amount of talent must have been attempted by scores of experimenters without talent.   The strict old theorists probably regarded these people with the same contempt that is to-day poured on the head of the amateur who composes at the piano. If Artusi had had a little more sense he would have been able to discriminate between the dilettanti and the men of genius who were reaching out not only to new effects but to a new language of music. But, like the true pedant, he could not see the distinction; and he evidently tried to persuade himself that Monteverdi was one of the dilettanti who got new ideas about dissonance by experimenting on instruments, which, as he puts it, has been shown by Aristoxenus to be a grievous error. These misguided people trust wholly to their ear, instead of going by reason! Evidently they had not read Boethius, Book I, chapter ix, and Book V, chapter i, and Ptolemy, Book I, chapter i!

Artusi's objections, then, are purely theoretic. That alone is sufficient to indicate that they were not shared by the ordinary musician or the plain man; for neither of these ever makes the mistake of judging æsthetic values by the "rules" of theory. Indeed, the plain man knows nothing about these; he could not tell you when and where and how a composer has innovated; he knows only whether the effect seems to him to be good or bad. And that the ordinary musician and the plain man of that period were greatly taken by Monteverdi's madrigals, and quite indifferent to whether the theorists approved of them at every point or not, is shown not only by the number of editions that were issued of his works, but by this very attack of Artusi's; for obviously Artusi picked him out for attack precisely because of his great vogue.

It is sometimes said that Beethoven was one of the geniuses who failed to win recognition in his own day. Only the other day I read an article in which were

given copious extracts from the English critical reviews of the early part of the nineteenth century, de-
signed to show how sadly wrong "the critics" were
over him. But nothing is surer than that almost
from his boyhood Beethoven was looked upon by those
who came in contact with him as possessing a genius
out of the common. When still a young man, as he
himself tells us in one of his letters, the publishers were
fighting each other for the privilege of bringing out his
works. In later days he was universally regarded as
the greatest composer of the epoch. That he was a
popular "draw" is shown by the fact that whenever a
charity concert had to be given in Vienna—for the
wounded soldiers, or some object of that kind—his co-
operation was sure to be sought, and a new work obtained from him if possible. And in the very article
that is meant to prove the imbecility of the contemporary critics we get evidence enough of Beethoven's
high standing among the musicians of the time. A
London critic of 1823 may have some objections to
make to the Diabelli Variations; but he finishes up by
saying that "the air itself is very pleasing, and derives
additional interest from having been selected as a
theme by the greatest musical genius of the century."
In 1824 another critic can say that Beethoven's "latest
productions" are "little relished in London"; but he
adds that they are "much admired by the young artists
of Vienna." In the Austrian city, it seems, the Ninth
Symphony is regarded as "the *ne plus ultra* of this master's orchestral works"; this is "the unanimous opinion of the first-rate professors of the capital."
"Happy Albion," on another occasion, is congratulated
on the purchase of the collected edition (Haslinger's)
of Beethoven's works; "when posterity shall have

formed a due estimate of the merits of Beethoven, it will be necessary to journey to thy shore in order to survey with astonishment the numerous creations of genius of this sublime master, united in one handsome and masterly collection." If to be deluged in your lifetime with eulogies of this sort is to be universally misunderstood, there are few composers of to-day who would not pray for a similar misunderstanding of them.

X

In recent years the great object of sympathy, among recently dead composers, has been Hugo Wolf. The legend is already well established that it was left to the decade that followed his premature death to atone for the scandalous neglect of his contemporaries. Only the other day a newspaper correspondent, combating my view that history records no case of a great musical genius being so far ahead of his time that his contemporaries could not do him justice, confronted me with Hugo Wolf. "One can confidently assert," he said, "that practically nothing but nonsense was written about him in his own day." History, however, does not support this confident assertion. Excellent and appreciative articles on Wolf's music were written during his lifetime by several people, including Emil Kauffmann, Josef Schalk, Michael Haberlandt, Edmund Hellmer, Karl Hallwachs, Paul Müller, Karl Grunsky, and O. E. Nodnagel. It may be said that these were mostly members of the Wolf circle. Precisely; but they had become members of the Wolf circle through their enthusiasm for his music. And if it be asked why Wolf's music made so little general headway during his lifetime, the answer is that comparatively few people could, in the circumstances of the case, have any acquaintance with it. Few of the German singers who knew anything about the songs cared to sing them; we all know what singers are. The songs were difficult, and the average singer, not seeing sufficient opportunities for applause in them, could hardly be induced even to study them. The ac-

companiments are often so difficult that even to-day
the ordinary amateur can make little of them. While
skilled interpreters of the songs were thus few, it was
yet only through public performance that the mass of
the public could hope to become acquainted with them,
for the simple reason that Wolf himself, with his
hopelessly unpractical idealism, forbade their publication in separate form. The general public, as everyone knows, cannot be induced to buy volumes of songs
unless they are so put together as to suit the special
needs of the purchaser. The amateur soprano would
like this song, but she does not want that, because it
does not appeal to her, because it is too difficult for
her, because it is not within her range, or for half a
dozen other reasons; and she refuses to buy a volume
containing a number of songs for which she will never
have any use. The contralto, the tenor, and the bass
share the same amiable foible. Wolf refused to let
the publishers issue his songs separately, or in any key
but the original; and it is therefore not surprising that
there were not queues outside the music shops clamouring for the Mörike volume, with its 53 songs, the
Eichendorff volume, with its 20 songs, the Goethe
volume, with its 51 songs, the Spanish Song Book,
with its 44 songs, and the two Italian Song Books,
with their 22 and 24 songs respectively. A composer
who elects to put himself before the world in this fashion can hardly wonder if his vogue spreads slowly.

Wolf, again, like Wagner, had been imprudent.
He had done what no composer ought to do—become
a musical critic. He had made for himself powerful
enemies, especially in Vienna, where his disparagement
of Brahms had given great offence in influential and
journalistic circles. Yet in spite of everything his

music made headway wherever it was heard. The legend that it was incomprehensible, that it aroused nothing but opposition, has no more historical justification than the corresponding Wagner legend. Wolf, poor and friendless as he was at the commencement, and trying as his manners were, soon found a number of people who listened respectfully and admiringly to him; and these people, realizing the difficulty, in the peculiar circumstances of the case, of working through the ordinary singer and the ordinary concert, arranged for the performance of the songs at meetings of the Wagner Societies that were at that time scattered all over Germany and Austria; sometimes a "Hugo Wolf Evening" would be given. After a little while a Hugo Wolf Society was founded, solely for the spreading of a knowledge of his songs and for maintaining the composer in comfort. Invariably the songs were greeted with enthusiasm; Wolf, in his letters, speaks again and again of their gratifying reception; and I can find in his correspondence no more than in Wagner's any evidence that he felt the general musical public to be against him, or incapable of understanding him.

XI

THE object of the writers who tell us that every great composer has been misunderstood and vilified in his own day is, of course, to make us who practise criticism to-day more careful what we say about those contemporaries of ours about whom controversy rages most fiercely. If it could be proved, even in a single instance, that a great man has had to wait for posterity to see his greatness, it would certainly make us think twice before we committed ourselves to out-and-out disparagement of any composer of our own period. But is there a single instance?

I cannot find one. At first sight, Bach may appear to be a case in point; as everyone knows, it was not till the second half of the nineteenth century that men began to see him for the colossus he was. But that was partly because a new Europe came into being in the years immediately following his death—a Europe spiritually remote from everything that went to make up the mentality of Bach—and partly because the great bulk of his work was not accessible to that generation.

On the first point, we must remember not only that Bach came at the end of a certain period of musical evolution, after which a change of orientation in men's minds was inevitable, but that he and everything he stood for were, in a sense, *passés* even in his own day. Even while he was alive he was the great provincial of music. That is his paradox—that this modest German provincial should be the most universal of musicians. He was provincial even among a race that, so far as music was concerned, was itself the despised provincial of Europe. The most cursory examination of the musical literature of the eighteenth century will show how little Germany counted in the estimation of the artists of other countries. This attitude towards Germany, indeed, persisted well on into the nineteenth century. There was never a more intelligent dilettante than Stendhal; but even he had no notion of the relative values of the Italian, French, and German music of the day.

Stendhal had at any rate heard of one or two German composers—Mozart, for instance, whom he regarded as almost a competitor of Cimarosa, Paisiello, and a host of Italian opera composers whose very names are almost forgotten to-day. But the French and Italian writers of a generation or two before that seem, for the most part, to be unaware even of the existence of German music. Rousseau is typical of them. He quarrels with his compatriots over the question of whether Italian or French music is the better, but apparently knows nothing of German. He brings out his *Dictionary of Music* more than a decade after the death of Bach, and nowhere gives any hint of knowledge that he or Handel had ever lived. The average Frenchman or Italian of that day would as soon have thought of looking to Germany for his music as to Russia.

In that provincial country the most provincial of all the bigger men was Bach. Even among his compatriots he was generally prized as organist and clavecinist rather than as composer. He passed his life in the service of petty princelings and town councils. Leipzig, the largest town he ever inhabited, was a provincial town. Dresden was the capital, and no doubt prided itself on its Italian opera, and looked down pityingly on the old-fashioned religious music of the ordinary German cantor. But the strange thing is that, provincial as Leipzig must have been, it looks even more provincial when we approach it through Bach.

To see the truth of this statement, let anyone reconstruct for himself, as best he can, the Leipzig of Bach and the Leipzig of Goethe. What impression of Leipzig does Bach's record give us? That of a stuffy little town unduly addicted to religious practices of a depressing character. We are conscious of the official musician held down by rectors and consistories very much as a Scottish musician might have been in the late seventeenth century. It is apparently among people of this sort, plus a handful of dirty and rowdy little schoolboys, that the Leipzig cantor passes his time, getting up in the shivery hours of the morning to conduct interminable church services, listening to tiresome sermons, teaching the boys Latin, coaching them painfully and enduring their awful squawking in the next Sunday's cantata, and always grinding out official music.

Bach, as the Eton boy said in his essay on him, was an habitual parent; his hours at home must have been filled with all the dullness of domesticity. Seemingly he had no friends of any particular artistic or literary or musical eminence or even taste. For a German musician of his day he was well read; but his reading had no great range. A prosier life, a prosier town, it is impossible for us to conceive.

Some fifteen years after Bach's death the young Goethe (then in his seventeenth year or so) settled in Leipzig for a time; and the Leipzig he shows us is not recognizable as Bach's Leipzig. It is a gay city—"a little Paris," Goethe calls it; no one can see any gaiety in the Leipzig of Bach. It is full of lively young people, interested in art and literature and life in general; the only young people we can think of in connexion with Bach's Leipzig are the urchins of the St. Thomas school. In Goethe's Leipzig there are girls—there usually were, in fact, wherever Goethe went; Bach and his work and his associates bring with them no suggestion of anything young, least of all of young women. Bach's Leipzig seems to spend most of its time in church. Goethe's story hints that religion in Leipzig was more honoured in the breach than in the observance. He shows us a town that was the meeting-place of races from East and West and North and South—a little cosmopolis, rich, gay, well mannered. There were many descendants of the Huguenots in the town, and these gave a French tone to its culture. Goethe was soon made to feel ashamed of his Frankfort manners, his Frankfort accent, his Frankfort clothes; he felt like a provincial come to the capital. His life in Leipzig was a round of dinners, suppers, theatres, wine-shops, dances, drives, and drawing-rooms. After he had left the town he remembered it as a place where, if you were not careful, you "burnt yourself out too quickly."

It is improbable that Leipzig had altered greatly in the fifteen or sixteen years between Bach's death and Goethe's visit; the truth must be that in Bach's time, too, there were young men and maidens in Leipzig, and riotous students, and a good deal of hard drinking and dancing, and all the rest of it. But his business was with none of these things. He belonged to a past generation. His own son, years after his death, spoke patronizingly of him as "the old pig-tail." He must have seemed an incurable old fogy to the young musical people of his own day—one who maundered about in musical forms of which almost everybody was getting thoroughly tired. The really "modern" thing was the Italian opera.

Bach, in fact, was not even a man of his own day; he belonged, mentally, socially, temperamentally, to a much older Germany. It was no wonder, then, that the decade or two that followed his death showed no particular interest in him and his dead world.

Everyone knows the story, to which I have already referred, of Mozart making his first acquaintance with the Bach motets. We owe the story to Rochlitz, who was present on that occasion, and who tells us that "Mozart knew Bach more by hearsay than from his works." This was in 1789—thirty-nine years after Bach's death, and only two years before the death of Mozart.

*

*   *

But that epoch could hardly have known Bach even if it had wanted to, for the simple reason that his work was not accessible. Hardly any of it was published. Most of it was church music, and in the second half of the eighteenth century, as Schweitzer points out, the cantors who would have been willing to give the cantatas from the manuscript copies mostly found themselves without choirs (for the times had changed), and had to face the opposition of the clergy, who regarded the texts of the cantatas as theologically out-of-date. The big choirs were not in the churches, but outside them; and for these choral masses Handel's works, which were then coming into favour, were more suitable than Bach's—again, in part, by reason of their texts. But "even if anyone, in despite of the epoch," says Schweitzer, "had wished to give Bach's works, he could hardly have done so, for the simple reason that they were nowhere to be had. The possessors of the five yearly series of cantatas were Emmanuel and Friedemann, who had divided the treasure between them. Those in Friedemann's hands were soon dispersed. Emmanuel took more care of his." They could not be published, however, on the ground of expense. "The piano and organ works were hardly more widely diffused. Of those that had been engraved, there had always been so few copies, that they were scarcely better known than those which, in Bach's lifetime, circulated only in manuscript. It is hardly credible how little was known of Bach by those who spoke admiringly of him."

How little was known of him may be gathered from the case of Burney and Samuel Wesley. The latter was probably the first musician in England to perceive the greatness of Bach—"our Sebastian," as he used to call him in his letters, "our Demi-God," "the greatest master in the world," "our matchless Man, if Man he can be called," in short, "THE MAN." Wesley wrote to Burney in 1808 in protest against the latter's remarks on Bach in his *History* and in the journals of his tour. Burney, who was then an old man of eighty-two, made the confession that "I shall feel exceedingly gratified in hearing his elaborate and erudite compositions performed by you (for I never yet *heard* any one of them), and can tell you that I have a very curious and beautiful copy of his Fugues, which was presented to me many years since by his son Emmanuel, and which I shall have much pleasure in showing you." Wesley called upon his "venerable friend," and on trying to play from the "very curious and beautiful copy" found it "so full of scripture faults" that he could hardly get through one of the fugues that he knew most thoroughly. Burney, however, was delighted, "and the very first part of his critique expressed his wonder how such abstruse harmony and such perfect and enchanting melody could have been so marvellously united." But the manuscript contained only the *first* twenty-four of the Preludes and Fugues; and Burney, who had written a large history of music, was "aghast" to learn, fifty-eight years after Bach's death, that there were twenty-four more. It was not until 1829, when Mendelssohn gave the *Matthew Passion* in Berlin, that the German musical world awoke to a sense of the greatness of the composer. It was not until the middle of the nineteenth century that the Bachgesellschaft began the slow publication of the works as a whole—a task that lasted till 1900.

How was it possible, then, for Bach to win, before the second half of the nineteenth century, his rightful place in musical history? In a sense, of course, it is quite true to say that his full greatness was not recognized for a century or so after his death; but we can hardly blame people for not seeing the greatness of a man whose work they had no opportunity of knowing.

XII

It has been suggested lately that Gesualdo, Prince of Venosa, is an instance of a composer having to wait a long time—in this case three centuries—for appreciation. The casual reader can perhaps be forgiven for coming to this conclusion, for probably all he knows about Gesualdo is the angry disparagement of him in Burney's *History*. He contrasts this with the interest that is being shown in Gesualdo in many quarters to-day, and the praise that is lavished on him, and assumes that here is a case of a truly great genius having to wait for a long period of musical evolution before a generation comes that can justify his innovations. But if we draw a line through the Gesualdo criticism from the sixteenth century to the present day, we soon see that there is no real foundation for this assumption.

Few verdicts of the past have been so often quoted as that of Burney on Gesualdo, to the effect that his music shows little "except unprincipled modulation, and the perpetual embarrassments and inexperience of an amateur in the arrangement and filling up of the parts." This was virtually the opinion of Kiesewetter also (in the early nineteenth century), for whom Gesualdo was merely "a distinguished dilettante." No one who now looks at the madrigals through his own eyes will agree with either of these verdicts. Gesualdo was well grounded in contrapuntal technique, and his harmonies and modulations do not strike us to-day as being in the least "unprincipled." But in correcting the errors of Burney and Kiesewetter, modern criticism seems to me inclined to fly to the other extreme. Burney obviously counts for next to nothing. He was an industrious historian but a poor critic; his harmonic sense seems to have been especially limited. He appears to have studied Gesualdo as conscientiously as he could; but the latter's harmony was plainly abhorrent to him temperamentally. Kiesewetter seems to have done little, if any, original research in the matter, but to have mainly contented himself with the two or three madrigals quoted in Burney, Hawkins and Martini.

The tone of the latest criticism of Gesualdo is mostly very different from this. It is apt, I think, to go almost as far in the direction of over-praise as Burney and Kiesewetter went in over-disparagement. This is as easily explicable as it is pardonable. One of the things a critic has to guard against is excessive enthusiasm over what he regards as his own special discoveries; he catches sight, or fancies he does, of something or somebody before other people do, and because the discovery is his own he is, quite understandably, inclined to over-value it. Dr. Hugo Leichtentritt, it seems to me, has not been free from this error. When annotating the fourth volume of the new edition of Ambros's *History,* he found, or thought he found, Ambros blind to the significance of Gesualdo's new harmonies; and he tells us that the harmonies are perfectly logical to the modern ear, but that it has taken three hundred years of evolution of the harmonic sense to make them seem so; only, he says, after Chopin and Wagner and Liszt and Wolf and Strauss are we in a position to grasp the chromaticism of Marenzio and Gesualdo. The conclusions the ordinary student would be justified in drawing from Dr.

Leichtentritt's remarks are that Gesualdo was a genius unrecognized till to-day, and that what has happened in his case might very well happen in others—that it may be reserved for the next century, or the one after that, to appreciate the genius of some composer of to-day who is not regarded as a genius by the bulk of his contemporaries.

But both conclusions seem to me to be unjustified; criticism (by which I mean not merely professional criticism but instructed musical opinion in general) has nothing on its conscience with regard to Gesualdo, apart from Burney. That the latter's view was not even the view of his own century is shown by the appreciative remarks of Hawkins, for whom "the distinguishing excellencies of the compositions of this admirable author are fine contrivance, original harmony, and the sweetest modulation conceivable." In Gesualdo's own day and in the generation or two that followed him he was greatly admired. It has been said that these praises are to be set to the account of the prince rather than of the composer; there can be no doubt that his social power would make critics cautious of attacking him, and his murder of his wife and her lover had shown him to be a man of spirit and action. We find one of the hangers-on of his court, Muzio Effrem, fulminating wildly against Marco da Gagliano for *his* departures from the rules, while praising Gesualdo for his. But even after allowing for all this it is clear that Gesualdo was praised as he was by his own generation because musicians found his music remarkable. He was recognized for what he was, an original thinker, a daring harmonist, and a pioneer of pathetic expression. He was evidently studied in the seventeenth century. Hawkins relates that

Geminiani "has been often heard to declare that he laid the foundation of his studies in the works of the Prencipe di Venosa." Archangelo Spagna, in 1706, says that in the discussions that took place "in the preceding century" at an *Accademia* that used to meet once a month at the house of Abbatini (1605–1677), it was recognized that dramatic recitative was the outcome of the madrigals of Gesualdo and Monteverdi —a perfectly just observation, for, to us of to-day, Gesualdo's final historical significance is perhaps less as a madrigalist than as a forerunner of dramatic expression and of solo song. (Whole passages from some of his madrigals could be sung as solo songs with an instrumental accompaniment.)

Padre Martini, in his *Saggio di Contraprunto* (1774–5), sums him up very fairly along with his leading contemporaries in the same genre: "Gesualdo's style will perhaps appear a little rough to some people to-day; but his real richness in the finesses of the art and his powerful expression of the words of the madrigals outweigh the touch of *morbidezza,* the sentimentality, that generally pleases the hearers."

In all this there is nothing whatever to support the theory that it has taken three hundred years for the world to reach a point from which it can see Gesualdo as he really was. In the early and middle nineteenth century, Winterfeld (1834) and Fétis can be set against Kiesewetter. Fétis, in 1837, speaks of Gesualdo's "original genius"; he pronounces Burney's criticism "severe and unjust," and explains it by Burney's inability to appreciate Gesualdo's originality of idea; he expressly declares that the harmony, though not modal, is justified by the nature of the thought. And Fétis's verdict will be, I think, the ultimate verdict

of history—that Gesualdo surpasses his greater contemporaries in pathetic expression, but in no other respect. Winterfeld's judgment also is balanced, but
by no means unsympathetic. Nor, in my opinion, is
Ambros as far wrong as Dr. Leichtentritt seems to
think. Ambros quotes a remarkable harmonic passage from Gesualdo, and asks: "But how does it help
the composer to have captured this wonder-beast?
There fails him the right understanding of this construction." To which Dr. Leichtentritt replies that
he cannot see how Gesualdo can be said to miss this
understanding, as "the employment of these altered
chords is absolutely correct according to the rules of
the new harmony." But, with all resepct, this is to
miss the whole point of Ambros's criticism. Ambros
was as well able as any of us to appreciate this particular harmonic sequence; indeed, he speaks admiringly
of its "great effect." The whole point of his criticism,
as I see it, is that a composer may be a remarkable
harmonic innovator, but not see all through and all
round his new effects, so that, instead of their being
woven into the very tissue of his style as a whole, they
remain embroidered, as it were, upon it. This, I
think, is largely true of Gesualdo; he has two different
styles, one for ordinary purposes, one for purposes of
pathos and word-painting. Ambros sees as clearly
as Dr. Leichtentritt that Gesualdo's modulations are
not only remarkable for their own time, but perfectly
logical in ours; but, as I read him, he claims that
these things come and go and excite wonder in themselves without making us feel that Gesualdo had the
easy mastery of his new style that Palestrina or Byrd
had of the older one. "Gesualdo reminds us . . . of
a naïve savage, who rapturously feasts on a delicious

fruit that has dropped from a tree on his path, but troubles no further about the tree itself, much less of a rational cultivation of this, so that he may bring his master more of such fruits."

An image must never be taken too literally, and this of Ambros is a shade too decisive; but the truth underlying it seems to me unquestionable. It applies equally well to many another eager innovator; it is the fate of these people in general not to be able to innovate with equal success over the whole field of their work, so that their style becomes a medley of new and old. As Ambros shows, and as Keiner also notes, the harmonist in Gesualdo does not find it easy always to square matters with the contrapuntist. But Ambros calls him a genius all the same. All in all, Ambros's judgment of Gesualdo is as sound and sane as any that has yet appeared.

Criticism, then, as I have said, has practically nothing to reproach itself for with regard to Gesualdo. He has always been seen by those who have studied him (except Burney) steadily and whole. *His* case certainly will not support the theory that there are geniuses so far ahead of their own or the next century that many generations have to go by before they can be rightly judged.

XIII

WHAT is the object of the people who reprint these fragments from the musical criticism of the past, if not to discredit, in some degree, the musical criticism of the present? Almost everybody feels that some pet composer of his own among the living is not getting quite the recognition he deserves; and so he attempts to derive consolation for himself, and support for his own opinion, by recalling cases in which critics have been wrong about this or that composer of the past. Mr. Calvocoressi, it is true, hedges his quotations about with reservations. "Of course," he writes, "no sensible human being would think that the fact that protest against a contemporary composer's music runs on the same lines as protest previously uttered against works which have since proved great is one to build upon for controversial purposes; it may, however, be used as a reminder." But a reminder of what? If the reminder is not intended as a warning, why is it given? The plain truth is that these citations from the past *are* intended as horrible warnings to the critic of to-day. Mr. Calvocoressi's own use of such citations shows this. He brings them down to yesterday; two of them are from French writers on *Pelléas and Mélisande* at its first production; another is from some remarks of Mr. Frederick Corder's on Schönberg in 1915. One of the French writers in question said: "I heard sounds in uninterrupted sequence, without finding a trace of design, of form, of a motive, of an accent"; the other said: "The ear is helpless, one feels irritated and bored." But surely these critics were largely justified in saying what they did. What hearer who listens dispassionately to *Pelléas and Mélisande* to-day does not feel irritated or bored at a good deal of it? The beauties of the work are unquestionable; but are there not many pages in it in which we feel that Debussy is merely underlining Maeterlinck's text without making an organic musical tissue of his own?

From an article in the *Musical Quarterly* of July, 1915, Mr. Calvocoressi quotes Mr. Frederick Corder as having described Schönberg's music as "unmeaning bunches of notes . . . clotted nonsense." The phrase "unmeaning bunches of notes," by the way, was actually applied by Mr. Corder to Bela Bartok, but I do not suppose he would demur at its being applied to Schönberg also. What I have to complain about is not the amount of truth or untruth there may be in the opinions expressed in these and other quotations, but the illegitimate use Mr. Calvocoressi makes of them. The implied inference from them is that anyone who talks in this way about a living composer is in danger of some day being pilloried along with Artusi and the others who failed to see the significance of their great contemporaries. If the quotation from Mr. Corder is not intended by Mr. Calvocoressi to carry this implication I cannot see the object of it at all. Mr. Calvocoressi, in the very act of warning us that *we* cannot anticipate the verdict of posterity, virtually claims for himself the ability to anticipate that verdict. He is obviously assuming that when the values of the twentieth century come to be settled, say a hundred years hence, these expressions of Mr. Corder's will seem as absurd as Artusi's criticism of Monteverdi does to us now. If he is not, then there is no point in Mr. Calvocoressi's citation of the remark. But surely it is not beside the mark to ask Mr. Calvocoressi *when* this confutation of Mr. Corder by posterity is likely to begin? For there are no signs of it yet. We need not take Mr. Corder's actual phrasing too literally; Mr. Corder has always expressed himself with a picturesqueness of idiom that would do credit to any of the "journalists" whom he so despises. The essential fact is that Mr. Corder, in 1915, did not think the later Schönberg was the great composer he was claimed by some of his partisans to be. Mr. Corder had chiefly in his mind, as is evident from his article as a whole, the *Three Piano Pieces* that make up Schönberg's op. 11. These were published about 1911. Mr. Corder, as he says, "derided them in the musical journals" at that time, giving quotations from them. "Everybody," he says, "went into fits of laughter over the absurdity, but I found, to my surprise, that no one would believe that they were genuine samples; people thought that I was pulling their leg and had invented the whole thing as a skit. How much greater, then, was my surprise when a critic told the public that I was a mere pedant and 'academic,' and that these silly things were masterpieces of art! And a well-known pianist actually performed them in public, amid the irrepressible sniggering of musicians but the profoundest interest of the bulk of his audience!"

Well, we all know those *Three Piano Pieces,* and I think that if the musicians of Europe and America were polled on the matter, ninety-nine per cent. of them would say that Mr. Corder was right; they would not necessarily approve of his phrasing of his opinion, but they would think, with him, that the music is of no account as music, however interesting it may be to the theorist as one of the earliest specimens of atonality. It was only the other day that Malipiero, who is himself by way of being a "modernist," politely derided it, pointing out that we had only to strip one of the *Pieces* of its harmonic sophistications to get a commonplace Mendelssohn *Song Without Words*. The world has had thirteen years in which to make up its mind about these *Pieces*. They no longer have any novelty for anybody; they contain no surprise now; they cause no shock. They have been tried fairly *as music,* and have been found wanting. If we are to be told that posterity will reverse that judgment, we may rejoin that surely thirteen years, as things go now, is quite long enough for the illumination to have come upon the world if it is ever going to come. Can anyone point to another single work in the whole history of music that conveyed nothing whatever to the average intelligent musician for so long a period, and then turned out to be of great significance? Which conclusion, then, seems the more reasonable—that these tiny *Pieces* of Schönberg are of such a profundity, so future-piercing a quality, that a new race of musicians will have to be born before the beauty and the force of them become apparent, or simply that they are of no account as music? And if the latter, what is the use of printing Mr. Corder's remark among a collection of past errors of judgment, as if the mere fact of describing a work by a prominent contemporary as nonsense wrote the critic down a fool? Strange as it may sound, critics *are* sometimes right in saying that a contemporary composer has missed the mark in this work or that. Mr. Calvocoressi seems to assume—unconsciously, of course, for I am sure he would deny that he does it consciously—that a composer of reputation never goes so far wrong as to justify critical disparagement of him. If this is not what is at the back of Mr. Calvocoressi's mind I am utterly at a loss to account for his quoting, among the typical blunders of judgment in the past, this from "Fétis on Mozart": "I examined the autograph manuscript of the work. Mozart actually wrote this irregular chord. Let us not say, with Haydn, that he had his reasons for doing so; errors of this kind offend our reason, our senses, and our taste." Mr. Calvocoressi gives the date of the quotation—1839. Fétis is referring, I think, to that introduction to the C major quartet about which I have already written. I cannot quite see how Fétis's remark, whether it be right or wrong, can be regarded as "contemporary" criticism of a work published more than fifty years before. As I have tried to show, people were still worrying about, and arguing over, that dubious passage after half a century because it still seemed to them unworthy of Mozart. If this music still "tried the ear," as Mr. Calvocoressi says, "ran contrary to the hearers' customs and tenets, and did not make sense for them," if Sir Henry Hadow, sixty-five years later still than Fétis, and five generations after Mozart, is still constrained to call the passage "an enigma," it cannot be said that this is a case of the music being too new for its judges. The fair assumption is that there must be something wrong with the music. Mr. Calvocoressi, departing from his usual cautious practice, has apparently not inquired into the circumstances of the matter; it is enough for him to discover that a Fétis has found fault with a Mozart for him to decide, without further inquiry, that it must be the critic who is wrong, and to lay it down that Fétis's criticism is "a reminder" to critics generally to be more careful.

*

*   *

I feel myself compelled to disagree with Mr. Calvocoressi on another point.   He quotes this from myself: "Why do historians go on repeating one after another the false judgment of some contemporary critic or other, instead of trying to find out what the mass of plain sensible hearers thought of the new work? If historians would only take that trouble, they would find that nine great works out of ten have been seen from the commencement to be great."   Mr. Calvocoressi seeks to dispose of this fallacy, as he calls it, with a quotation from Mr. Arnold Bennett's *Literary Taste and How to Form It:*

"The fame of classical authors is entirely independent of the majority.   It is originally made, and it is maintained, by a passionate few.   Even when a first-class author has acquired immense success during his lifetime, the majority have never appreciated him so sincerely as they have appreciated second-rate men. In the case of an author who has emerged into glory after his death the happy sequel has been due solely to the obstinate perseverance of the few.   They kept on savouring and talking about him, and generally behaved with such eager zeal that at last the majority placidly agreed that he was a genius."

Mr. Bennett is speaking of literature, not of music, and the two cases are not precisely the same.   But even in the case of literature I doubt the justice of

Mr. Bennett's claim that "the fame of classical authors" is "originally made . . . by a passionate few," and that "the majority" have nothing to do with it. One seems to remember that Shakespeare was extremely popular with Elizabethan audiences—not with the "passionate few," but with the crowd; so popular, even at an early stage of his career, as to arouse the jealousy of rival dramatists such as Greene. The pirating of his plays is evidence of his attraction for the public. Of Cervantes I read: "There was no doubt or hesitation in the public mind as to *Don Quixote*." Hitherto Cervantes "had been nothing more than an unsuccessful dramatic author." *Don Quixote* was greeted everywhere "with acclamations of joyous enthusiasm." In the year of its publication four editions were brought out, in Madrid, in Valencia, and in Lisbon—"the best of all proofs of its immediate appreciation." The work "flew all over the country, and in a very short time was translated into English, French and Italian. Its success was beyond doubt." The passionate few seem in this case, at least, to have been the passionate many. Was it the passionate few in ancient Athens, or the general public, that picked out Æschylus, Euripides and Sophocles as the best of their time? It is not impossible, of course, that we have lost plays as good as theirs, or even better; but at any rate the Athenians did think a great deal of the three dramatists whom we think so great. I fancy that a careful examination of literary history would supply us with a large number of reasons for doubting the full truth of Mr. Bennett's generalization.

But with regard to music the generalization will not bear a moment's examination. A "passionate few" implies an unpassionate many. It is the spectacle of the passionate many, however, with which musical history provides us. The records are conclusive that such men as Josquin, di Lasso, Palestrina, Monteverdi, Byrd, Marenzio, Schütz and Dowland were popular favourites in the sixteenth and seventeenth centuries. Monteverdi's third book of madrigals, first published in 1592, when the composer was only twenty-five years of age, but had already made his reputation, ran through eight editions in twenty-nine years—an enormous number if we consider the smallness of the population in those days and the extent to which music circulated in manuscript. I need hardly extend the list from the seventeenth century to the present day. It is surely evident that no composer *could* have got this contemporary reputation unless he had appealed not to the passionate few but to the passionate many. For music is what books are not—a matter mainly of public performance, which in turn is a matter of finance. Concert givers and opera impresarios do not waste much time on composers who do not fill the house. A Mozart, for instance, would not be in such demand for a new opera unless it were already known that his music would draw the crowd; a Beethoven would not have the publishers running after him as they did if his music appealed only to a few, however passionate the few might be. And Wagner, as we have seen, needed no passionate few to force him, in the course of years, on a world that was reluctant to hear him. It was not the passionate few who lined the streets, as Angelo Neumann describes them doing, at the first performance of the *Ring* in Berlin.

How, indeed, could or can the few "make" a composer? Music, let me repeat, is an art that people enjoy in masses. They pay their money to be interested and pleased, and if they are not interested and pleased, nothing will make them go through the same experience again. Professional criticism is powerless either to make or mar a reputation; if people like a man's music, not all the unfavourable criticism in the world will keep them away from it; if they do not like it, not all the favourable criticism in the world will send them to it after one or two unrefreshing experiences of it. Indeed, the plain man reads very little musical criticism; and as the critics invariably disagree with each other, "criticism" cannot claim either the credit of making an audience for a new composer or the discredit of keeping audiences away from him.

*

*   *

Why is all this fuss made about one kind of error that "criticism" has been guilty of in the past, and nothing at all said about the other kind, which, when all is said, probably does the more harm? The histories and biographies ring with denunciations of an Artusi or a Hanslick for his depreciation of a Monteverdi or a Wagner; but we hear nothing of the critics who blundered even more grievously than any of these legendary examples of the absurdity of criticism ever did, but blundered in the other direction. For one first-rate work that has been underpraised, a hundred second-rate works have been overpraised; particularly is this true of to-day. Yet so completely lacking are we in any standard, any ideal, of criticism that the very people among us who habitually overpraise mediocrity take it upon themselves to warn the

critics who try to look impartially at contemporary
music of the danger that *their* judgments may be upset
by the court of appeal of the future! Surely it is as
positive a sign of critical infirmity to write eulogis-
tically of a Pratella as to write dyslogistically of a
Wagner, for, after all, a *Tristan* is a so much bigger
thing than the ordinary opera and the ordinary listener
of its day that a man may be excused for being baffled
by it at a first hearing, while the once "futurist"
Pratella is so obviously below the average of his day
both in invention and technique that only a dilettante in
criticism could for a moment take such a dilettante
composer seriously. Surely there is less discredit in
failing to see at a glance all there is in a work like the
Ninth Symphony than in failing to see at a glance that
a Malipiero, thoughtful musician as he is, is, not, and
probably will never be, a composer of the front rank.
An Anglo-French critic could write thus of Malipiero
in 1918: ". . . there is to-day in Italy a young man
of thirty-six whom . . . I regard as one of the most
remarkable composers of his generation, a young man
from whom may be expected not merely interesting
works but works of the first order." . . . "Francisco
Malipiero will ere long be recognized as one of the
leading composers of the present time. It is pleasing to me to reflect that I shall have been among the
first to greet him as an outstanding figure of a new
Italy, and to perceive in his works the touching and
profound revelations of a great artist." Malipiero
is now over forty, and has produced a large quantity
of music; yet who will say that in any circle of competent musicians in Europe or America he is regarded
as "a great artist," whose "revelations" are "touching
and profound," whose works are "not merely interest-

ing but works of the first order"? Does any competent person really believe that a hundred years from
now Malipiero will be recognized as of the company
of the "great," that his music will then be talked of
as men talk of the music of Bach and Beethoven and
Wagner and Palestrina and Chopin and Mozart and
the score or so of other composers whose work alone
is recognized as of the "first order"?

Surely if we are to learn from the criticism of the
past something that will help us, even negatively, in
our criticism of the music of to-day, we must take as
warnings—or, as Mr. Calvocoressi would say, "reminders"—not only the underpraise of genius but the
overpraise of talent and of mediocrity. And if we
could see a past epoch in something like its totality,
see it at a distance great enough for us to get the
proportions and the focus right, not being confused,
as the men of the period were, by one's too great
nearness to this or that feature of it, not having our
judgments twisted, as theirs so often were and ours
are apt to be, by personal prepossession or personal
prejudice, by the *esprit de corps* of the school, by the
self-protective instinct of the clan, by the collective
vanity of the claque and the clique, by the emotional
glow of the Mutual Admiration Society, would not
this help us to get some kind of an idea of the things
we must try to avoid in our judgment of our own
contemporaries? To be thoroughly serviceable to us,
such an epoch of the past would have to be as like
as possible in essentials to our own.

XIV

THERE is only one such period in musical history—that centring round 1600, and extending roughly to twenty-five or thirty years on each side of that date. From the middle of the seventeenth century onwards the line of development of music has been unbroken. In vocal and in instrumental music alike, one generation has continued the work of another, adding to its predecessor's vocabulary, enlarging its predecessor's forms, developing its predecessor's resources, but never turning its back on the past. But in the period that, for convenience' sake, we call that of 1600, a distinct and self-conscious break was made with the past. Many people felt that the polyphonic and modal systems it had taken so many centuries to develop to their perfection had reached the limit not only of their capacity but of their usefulness, and were now a hindrance to the freedom of growth of music. That, *mutatis mutandis,* is the situation again to-day. There is a general feeling that we have come to the end of a long road, and that new paths must be opened out. Vocabulary, forms, ideas, are all in the melting-pot.

One curious feature of the case is that the present revolters, while they carry, unknown to themselves, the same banner as the revolters of 1600, carry it upside down. The complaint of the extremists of to-day is that music has become too "literary" and must be made more "objective"; instead, that is to say, of turning literary concepts into sound, music should be concerned with sound and nothing but sound, with the building of sound-shapes pure and simple. Occasionally this passion for the "objective" takes curious and even laughable forms. Not only is the voice used, as it legitimately enough may be, purely as a musical instrument, instead of as the carrier of an "extramusical" literary idea, but attempts are made to discredit "poetic" music by writing songs to nonsense verses. Among Stravinsky's partisan followers the *mot d'ordre* went round from headquarters some time ago that *Le Sacre du Printemps,* which is really programme music, in that it was written to a ballet, and, as is shown by the titles given to the movements in the score, has no meaning apart from the underlying "literary" idea, was to be regarded henceforth as "objective" music only, a vital stage in the "emancipation of sound" *qua* sound. A little later, I am told, Stravinsky's *Pieces for String Quartet* were dutifully put forward as pure "objective" music, the descriptive titles that were affixed to them at their first production being suppressed. Like all revolts, this against "literary" music is largely justified; there is never smoke without fire. Since Wagner and Liszt, music has come to rely too much on literary or pictorial suggestion, not merely for its inspiration but for its form; and musicians do right to insist that the art should sail under its own colours. The question, of course, is a far more complicated one than the extreme partisans of the "objective" imagine. Ever since man began to write music at all he has written "poetic" music, and one may be sure that he will go on writing it, whatever the partisan theorists may have to say. All we have a right to insist on is that the composer shall make his music and his poetic idea one and indivisible —not that the music shall be self-subsisting apart from the words or the programme, for that would obviously make an end of the song, the opera, the Mass, the dramatic overture, the ballet, and the symphonic poem, but that he shall completely *musicalize* the poetic idea, not make up for a deficiency in musical logic by calling in the aid of literary logic. But when all the absurdities of partisan over-statement have been put on one side, there remains a sound core of truth and reason in the demand that modern music shall now cease to lean so much as it has done during the last thirty years or so on literary suggestion, and shall rely more on its own inner logic. Music of this kind, needless to say, would be anything but a novelty in the world; it has always existed; a Byrd fantasia or a Bach fugue or a Scarlatti sonata is a simple example of it. But we should all be glad to see a new development of what is called purely objective music, if only for the reason that we are weary of the perpetual exploitation of certain standardized emotional moods and certain formulæ of expression that have tyrannized over music since the triumph of romanticism.

*

* *

The revolt of 1600 was the same revolt, with a difference. What faces the young composer of to-day who wants to beat out a new logic of "pure" music is the enormous accumulation of "poetic" devices in the music of the last hundred years. What faced the new composer of 1600 was the enormous accumulation of purely musical devices during the two preceding centuries. To-day we ask for a music that shall be nothing but music, the pure combination and setting-off against each other of sound and sound. But it was precisely against this that the men of 1600 revolted, and that in the name of poetry. To-day the innovators want to eliminate words and all that words stand for; in 1600 the innovators fought for the rights of words and what they stand for. To-day the cry is for "music" and nothing but "music." In 1600 the cry was that music had become too completely "music." The Mass, the madrigal, the motet were simply the cunning interweaving of sounds. Polyphony had become the tyrant of words. It worked out its woof and its patterns in almost complete disregard of every consideration but those of pure music; it separated and dismembered and prolonged the words to suit the fling of the musical phrase, till they became almost unrecognizable; they became completely unrecognizable when four or five or six voices sang different words at the same time, and when one rhythm was made to overlap another, with each voice insisting on its own melodic and verbal accentuation. The cry of to-day is that music, as an art of sound, ought to appeal solely to the ear, not to the intellect. The complaint of 1600 was that polyphonic music *did* appeal solely to the ear, and cheated the intellect of its rights, that is to say, of the perception of the meaning of the words and of the appropriateness of the music to the sentiment of the moment. Caccini called counterpoint "a laceration of the poetry"; his own order of merit in music (following Plato) was first the words, then the rhythm [of the words], and last the sound; (*Quella maniera cotanto lodata da Platone ed altri filosofi, che affermarano la musica altro non essere che la favella e il ritmo ed il suono per ultimo, e non per lo contrario*), counterpoint being unable to make the marvellous effects on the intellect that are described by the ancient writers (*quei mirabili effetti che ammirono gli scrittori, e che non potevano farsi per il contrappunto nelle moderne musiche*). The "reform" did not, as is too often supposed, begin with Caccini and Peri. It had been stirring for more than a generation within the polyphonic music itself; the harmonic innovations of Monteverdi, Gesualdo and others were primarily motived by the desire to "paint" this or that significant word.

In that epoch, as in this, the more ardent of the reformers had a supreme contempt for the classics. There was even, as there is now, an element of nationalism and race hatred in the desire for change. To-day the reaction is against the great German tradition, which is alleged to have killed or suppressed the true national spirit in England and elsewhere; we have even been assured, with apparently perfect gravity, that sonata form is a specifically German product, the equivalent in music of the rather complicated structure of the German language. At the end of the sixteenth century there was a similar reaction in Italy against the Netherlanders, who were, in music, what the Germans were to the modern musical world. The great art of counterpoint had come, in the main, from the Netherlands. The Low Countries had sent one after another of its sons to settle in Italy, where they monopolized the best posts, as the Germans did for so long in nineteenth-century England. When the revolt came not only was there an outcry against the Italianate Netherlanders, such as Willaert, Cyprian de Rore, Josquin, Mouton, etc., and a good deal of derision even of the harsh Netherlandish names, especially those of Obrecht and Okeghem, but polyphony itself was regarded in some quarters as an alien imposition upon the native music, as in a sense it was, for it submerged for a long time the simpler native forms, and once the true Italian spirit managed to reassert itself Italian vocal music became and remained the rather superficial, sensous thing we now know. G. B. Doni belongs to a rather later date than the first Florentine reformers—his *De praestantia musicae veteris* was published in 1647; but he was in close touch with them and their descendants, and is the accepted spokesman of the new party, along with Pietro della Valle, whose *Discorso della musica dell'età nostra* belongs to 1640. Both men had a charming scorn for the music of the period before the "reform." The war on counterpoint had, as Ambros points out, its analogue in the war of Filarete, Vasari and other on Gothic, which also was "ultramontane" in origin. Counterpoint, says Doni, "was born in the rudest of epochs, among a people [the Netherlanders] destitute of any kind of letters or culture, their very names being a proof of this—Hebrecht, Ogheghen." (Doni, it will be seen, even had a difficulty in inducing his cultured Italian pen to spell the abhorred barbarian names correctly.) He extended a rather contemptuous patronage to the Palestrina style, as did Pietro della Valle, and no doubt many others. Anyone who admired this style was a "reactionary," just as, in some circles, anyone who now admires Beethoven or Brahms is a "reactionary." "And I admire that famous music of Palestrina," says della Valle, "which pleases you so much, and that was the excuse for the Council of Trent not banishing music from the church, on which account these works are now prized not for use, but to be preserved in a museum, like beautiful

antiques." So far had the new generation travelled
from the ideals of the old.

*
*   *

Then, as now, the new ferment brought out all
kinds of eager dilettanti, of vain composers, of opin-
ionative critics. Typical of them was Kapsberger, a
German musician settled in Rome, who styled himself,
as any young man of our own day might do, "composer in the most modern style." His superficial
facility brought him a good many admirers. Then,
as now, there were Mutual Admiration Societies that
combined extreme rigour of judgment of anybody outside their own magic circles with extreme toleration of
everyone inside them. Pietro della Valle, for instance,
turns upon his fellow "modernist" Kapsberger a much
more indulgent eye than he does upon any of the
"reactionaries" who follow Palestrina—though Kapsberger, too, dabbled in counterpoint in a way of his
own. Mediocrity as he was, he was as certain of his
mission as a reformer as any modernist of our own
time could be of his. Palestrina's religious music, he
told the Pope of the day, "sounds well enough, but
handles the [Latin] words in a raw fashion, and one
ought not to listen to music of this kind in so cultivated a century as this and in the most august city in
the world," i. e., Rome. Into the breach left by the
mental deficiency of Palestrina, Kapsberger obligingly
stepped; he would show Pope and public what religious
music really ought to be. Unfortunately for him, the
singers of the papal choir, among whom the old tradition still survived, at first refused to sing the music

of the conceited dilettante, and then, when they were compelled to do so, sang it so badly that it failed completely. But he had his following, his claqueurs. He was of a type to be found in plenty in the music of to-day—a musician of moderate endowments, with a comprehensive contempt for his forerunners, and a touching belief in his own "modernism."

The "reform" of music and the later practice of it were in large part the affair of dilettanti and of composers of the second rank. The harmonically accompanied solo song was an easy genre to work in for anyone with a smattering of musical knowledge. The older and more thoroughly schooled musicians mostly stood aloof from the new movement, as their successors do in somewhat similar circumstances to-day. They had a great art, a great system of technique, of their own, which it would be folly to abandon in order to try experiments in a new and much more limited genre. As Dr. Hugo Leichtentritt points out, the Florentine manner was instantly adopted in Venice and elsewhere. But in Venice the experts in the older style left the newer style alone. "Neither Giovanni Gabrieli, Merulo, Croce, nor the foreign masters who had studied in Venice, such as Hassler and Sweelinck, paid the least attention to monody, although they all saw the triumphal course of the new art. It was the younger, unknown North Italian composers, who had less to risk, who followed in the tracks of the Florentines." The situation is precisely paralleled to-day.

But gradually a change came over monody itself. The early monodists had done their best to drive out something like three-fourths of what constitutes developed music. It was pretty soon realized that no one could get very far along the declamatory or arioso lines of the first operas and the *Nuove musiche;* nor could the earlier men possibly do very much with so limited an outlook and an endowment as theirs. One of the laws of "progress" in music seems to be that it comes about, at first, largely through the activity of men of the second rank—a law we find operating among us to-day. The men of the first rank have, in the first place, a great deal to express, and in the second place know instinctively that it can be expressed only in a language that is already, as the result of a long evolution, copious and flexible, a language that is to them second nature. The dilettante or the composer of the second rank has much less scruple about trying experiments. What he has to say is a very small thing, and the task of discovering a new way to say it does not seem to him a hopeless one. In our day any musician of intelligence would shrink from the task of trying to make a completely new symphonic structure of the size and scope of the old; he would know that to build on that scale one has to take over, in music as in architecture, the accumulated knowledge and skill and much of the material of preceding generations. But in a smaller composition one feels more at liberty to try a new idiom and new devices; and so the first works in a new genre are small in scale as well as limited in invention. Carl von Winterfeld truly says that the first efforts of the Florentines in the new genre were hardly more than a childish lisping. And Hugo Goldschmidt is right in pointing out that had it been in the power of the "theorizing fanatics of the Camerata" to impose their practice upon music generally, there would have been no such development as that which has resulted in modern music. The Florentines could do little more than open the gate into a new field; to cultivate more than a tiny corner of the field was beyond their powers. The new movement came to very little until the musicians of the older school began to take part in it, enriching it with devices drawn from the practice of the past. "It was not the representatives of progress," says Goldschmidt, ". . . but the men who were at once devoted to the older art and had their eyes turned to the new, who were called to lead it onward." History, we may be sure, will repeat itself. We have the right to ask no more of the most enterprising innovators to-day than that they shall suggest new paths for music. They cannot hope to get very far along the paths themselves; if musical history teaches us one thing more positively than another, it is that the works of pioneers have for posterity an antiquarian rather than an æsthetic value; the new art will not come to very much until it is fertilized by the old.

*

*   *

This is what happened in the early years of the seventeenth century. It is significant that Florence itself carried the new style no further than its first beginnings; the style only began to consolidate and extend itself when it was taken up by cities, such as Rome and Venice, that were concerned more with musical practice and less with literary theory, and could infuse something of the older life into the as yet feeble veins of the new music. "The backward-looking [i. e., to the ancient Greek drama] doctrinaire spirit of the Camerata," says Goldschmidt, "was hard and intolerant; therein precisely lay its strength. But now the

eye no longer looked backward to the nebulous, re-
treating distances of the antique tragedy; men's powers
strove forward to goals that could be reached, free
of the scruples of a self-imposed constraint, bent on
employing in the service of the opera all the resources
of the rich musical apparatus of the past. The
tabooed counterpoint accommodates itself to the new
task, the choral portions make use of the older technique, and from the madrigal form win life and a
command of style. Recitative escapes from the childish, petty limitations of a speech-recitation that is
purely theoretical. Its melodic turns (that even
Caccini and Peri cannot avoid), although rejected in
theory, are taken up at once by Marco da Gagliano,
develop into broader, stronger and more pleasing
ideas, and finally pass into definite, well-organized
forms; secco recitative, arioso recitative, aria and en-
semble separate themselves one from the other."

The new spirit, in fact, seems at once, by its very
violence, to have called into being a counterpoise from
the older art. Adriano Banchieri was himself anything but a "reactionary," either in theory or in practice. In 1607 he brought out his *Prudenza giovenile*
—a music drama in the new monodic manner; he describes it, indeed, in the title as "a new comedy in the
recitative manner for voices and instruments . . .
composed in the modern style." The fourth edition
of the work appeared in 1628 under the new title of
La Saviezza giovenile, and in the preface to this,
Banchieri inveighs against the limitations of the "new
style" and the arrogances of its partisans. There is
no praise to-day, he says, except for "representative
[i. e., Florentine] music"; whoever remains attached
to the good rules and to counterpoint is struck off the

roll of musicians and registered among the antiquaries. The "representative drama" has stiffened into a set of formulæ, and *this* is called the "modern style." It is so modern that cultivated musicians do not bother about it. He, for his part, will blend the new with the old: "observe, good reader, that here you find the old style combined with the new, as with so many judicious composers to-day." We get a similar hint of the reaction of the more solid musicians of the time against the superficialities and dilettantisms and formulæ of the "modern" style in the preface to Domenico Mazzocchi's *Dialoghi e Sonetti* (1638): "I confess frankly," he says, "that it has always pleased and always will please me to go by the trodden roads; but now and then, by raising oneself a little from the common things, it may be permissible to seek out some rarity, to take delight at least in the variations of the strings, or of the genera, or of the modes." The "high school of study" in music is for him the madrigal—a counter-revolutionary statement to make at that time, as Goldschmidt points out, in view of the war that the monodists had declared on the old contrapuntal technique. In his opera *La Catena d'Adone* (1626) we meet with one of the first thorough blendings of the "modern" *stilo recitativo* with the older polyphonic technique. By this time it had been perceived that recitative in itself was too dry for long endurance; it had to become more melodic if that "tedium" of which Mazzocchi speaks in his preface were to be avoided.

Music, in fact, had almost from the beginnings of the "reform" been asserting its rights against those who were trying to restrict its function to that of being a mere handmaid of poetry. Too strong to be resisted was this unconscious impulse of music to proceed by way of forms and a technique of its own. It brought back in time something like the old choral structure, and it evolved the aria. And these changes came about as soon as the writing of music drama passed from the hands of the dilettanti and the theorists into those of the skilled musicians. There is in all this a lesson for us of to-day. We may be sure that the music of the twentieth century cannot live any more by theory than the music of the seventeenth century could. Music is itself, one and indivisible; it will not submit to be deprived of this or that mode of expression, this or that resource of technique, by composers who happen to have no use for them because they have no sense of them. To tell us that music "ought" to be "objective" is to imitate the theorists of 1600, who told their contemporaries that music "ought" to be "representative." In a very little while it became evident that though the new theory had some truth in it, it had not the whole truth. Insistence on it to the letter would have meant the sterilization of the art. The instincts of both composers and the public revolted against this sterilization; and what was really vital in the new style was saved by blending it with what was still fertile in the old. If musical history can teach the critic anything, it is that a similar process will have to be gone through during the next generation. The more extreme innovators would throw too much of the past away. Their successors will have to retrieve some of it if their own art is to endure.

Russian music of the last half-century, indeed, sup-

plies us with corroborative evidence of this. The
"Five," in their early days, revolted against symphonic
"working-out" very much as the Florentine monodists
did against counterpoint. The explanation was the
same in each case: the men despised an art in which
they themselves were not particularly proficient; it
was the tailless monkey trying to induce the rest of
the tribe to abolish tails. The Russians, in truth,
had a very imperfect idea of what "working-out"
meant, and of the differences between the working-out
of a Beethoven and that of the ordinary academic
symphonist. They would play German symphonies
in piano duet form, and would say, when the working-
out began, "Now we come to the mathematics."
Their own music has convicted them of having been
almost completely lacking in that sense of logic in
music that controls the working-out of an organic
mind like Beethoven's. They could not "develop"
their music: all they could do was to string tune to
tune. The world has grown a little tired of their
picturesque helplessness in construction; their instrumental art, for all its colour and its charm, is, like
that of Caccini and Peri, essentially childish, or at any
rate childlike. And what happened to the Florentine
music happened again to the Russian; it was not until
Russian composers assimilated the methods of the
older "mathematical" art that they succeeded in building large orchestral structures that could make any
pretence of holding together. The trail of amateur-
ishness, of dilettantism, is over a great deal of the
work of these genuinely gifted men, as it was over that
of the monodic reformers.

The ardent spirits of the generation of about 1600

to 1620 thought that they had made a new heaven and a new earth in music. They did not quite succeed in driving out the older music from the churches, but they very nearly did so, and in any case they were sure that the Palestrina style was now merely a curious antique, fit only for the museums. It would no doubt astonish them painfully if they could return to earth now and see what has happened—how the work of Palestrina and his fellows is as vital as ever, and indeed a fountain from which the music of to-day, after a further three centuries of evolution, can drink and renew its youth; while *their* work is merely a historical curiosity. Even the music dramas of Monteverdi, passionate as their life is, have to be approached and appreciated through the historical quite as much as through the æsthetic imagination; and it is not in that way that we approach and appreciate Palestrina and Morales and Vittoria and Byrd and Weelkes and Wilbye.

*

* *

Perhaps we may see, in the further course of Italian music during the earlier part of the seventeenth century, certain other similarities with the state of affairs to-day. Then, as now, it seemed to many composers that they were extending the resources of music by multiplying the effects of harmony. The two things are not necessarily the same. It is possible to have a new harmony without getting, in the full sense of the term, a new music; that is to say, the works that may be theoretically most interesting may also be, from the musical point of view, of little artistic value in the long run. There was a great amount of harmonic restlessness among the writers of accompanied solo music in the first quarter of the seventeenth century, and there can be little doubt that the harmonic audacities of certain of these composers attracted to them an attention, and won for them a reputation, that posterity judges to have been beyond their deserts. As in the case of Gesualdo, or indeed in the case of Mozart, we have to distinguish between theoretical harmonic correctness and æsthetic value. We can give the chords and progressions of the introduction to Mozart's C major quartet any technical names we like, but that will not make a first-class piece of music of it. Gesualdo's harmonies and his resolutions of them may be, as Dr. Hugo Leichtentritt says, perfectly correct according to the latest twentieth century practice; but this does not always and of itself make the madrigal in which they appear a piece of first-class music. And while it is quite true that many of the harmonies to be found in the monodic chamber music of the first half of the seventeenth century are such as composers might indulge in to-day, that fact of itself does not absolve the music from the charge of a lack of vital interest. The point is not whether a Benedetti or a Saraceni now and then effects a modulation or employs a cadence that anticipates, say, one of Chopin's, but whether he can bend it to his imaginative purposes in the way that Chopin can, and fix it in a phrase that is permanently beautiful or significant.

Benedetti is very fond of using a B flat in the melody against a B natural in the bass (or a C sharp against a C natural), as thus (I quote from the examples given by Dr. Leichtentritt in his chapter on *Der monodische Kammerstil in Italien bis gegen 1650,* in his new edition of Ambros:

Domenico Belli indulges in audacities of his own:

Claudio Saraceni specializes in harmonies and modulations that must have seemed very "advanced" to the musicians of his own day:

ahi las . . . . so,

Music of this kind, coming when it did, is a historical phenomenon worthy of the attention of criticism. Note that it all comes from composers who, *as* composers, have virtually no artistic standing in the eyes of the modern world, however interesting they may be historically. Some of the experimenters in the new harmony must have been more or less dilettanti. It is often from this type of half-musician and second-class musician that the most audacious experiments come. There is not the restraint upon their diffuse imagination and unprecise thinking that there is upon a composer of a higher rank, whose mental processes are controlled by a subconscious logic that keeps him from taking a step of which he cannot see the further consequences. Dr. Leichtentritt points out that the things most characteristic of the Florentine innovators "are of quite minor significance for the later monody. Their art was too exclusive to have much influence outside its own circle." The early Florentines, he goes on to say, are "much more reckless and headstrong in their harmony than Monteverdi is—so much so that now and then the whole apparatus of the most progressive harmonic theory of the twentieth century has to be called upon to explain their chordal successions. . . . It would be very easy, at the first sight of their incongruous basses and melodies, to account for them as clumsy experiments, and to dispose of them with the phrase, 'the childhood of art.' But after Marenzio, Gesualdo and Monteverdi this will no longer do. It is the business of the inquirer to seek for a rational solution of these knotty harmonic problems; and a solution can be found. Men like Caccini, Peri, Gagliano, Benedetti and Belli deserve, by reason of their treatment of 'speech-song' and of harmony, to be regarded as thoroughly original artists, worthy of being taken seriously, more especially as their kind of art was buried with them, and only in the twentieth century are similar notes sounded once more."

This is a point on which Dr. Leichtentritt had already insisted in his discussion of sixteenth century chromaticism, and especially that of Gesualdo and Marenzio. "With the eye of genius," he says, "Gesualdo had perceived what it has taken us centuries to reach. He knows already that all the chromatic tones (even all the conceivable chords) can be added to any major or minor scale whatever; which is the quintessence of modern harmonic theory. When, for example, we find in a modern work a C major cadence with an F sharp major in it, or when Chopin flashes A major into an E flat minor cadence (op. 10, No. 5), we are inclined to laud this as an achievement of the nineteenth century. As a matter of fact, it had to be won afresh in the nineteenth century. In an epoch when this principle was still regarded as caprice, extravagance, almost as a senseless dissipation of force, the right attitude towards Gesualdo's bold and yet quite lucid chord-linking could not be found. . . . According to the twentieth century conception of harmony, Gesualdo undoubtedly ranks among the greatest harmonic masters. His harmony sounds fresh and new even beside that of Chopin, Wagner, Liszt, Strauss and Reger." And Dr. Leichtentritt compares this new harmony of the period to a stream that, immediately after its rising, disappears underground, whence it does not emerge till after something like three centuries.

We get, then, the interesting fact that composers of the second or third rank can innovate to such an extent that neither their own nor the immediately succeeding generations can make any rational use of their innovations. The inference is that innovation, of a kind, is one of the easiest things in the world. Anyone who has had much to do with the manuscripts of amateurs must have been struck with the "audacities" —sometimes very happy audacities—that they display; one meets again and again with turns that an accredited composer of the day would never dream of using. It has apparently been so in every age. It was certainly so in the first decades of the seventeenth century. The harmonic audacities of Saraceni and his like must have sounded extraordinary in the ears of their contemporaries. But this venturesomeness was rarely accompanied by anything approaching genius. And it is easily to be seen why this was so. The genius instinctively feels that he cannot express himself freely if he has to make a new language; so he accepts the language current in his time, modifying and extending it cautiously as he requires, but never setting himself the problem of making a quite new vocabulary and grammar for himself. A composer has only so much intellectual energy at his disposal, and if he dissipates any of it in consciously making a new language he has so much the less left over for his musical thinking; he is like a builder trying also to make his own bricks.

The greatest geniuses, then, have always been rather conservative, and, indeed, have always come at the end of a long period of development, never at the beginning of one. It is generally the men of the second or third order who experiment, and in no case do they use their medium with the ease and variety and force with which the geniuses use theirs. Gesualdo's texture cannot compare with that of any of his great contemporaries in these respects. Remarkable as many of his harmonic progressions are, we often feel that he is their servant rather than their master— which is the gist of that criticism of him for which Dr. Leichtentritt finds fault with Ambros. He was a little too conscious of his fine effects, perhaps because he had reached them by experiments on the lute or the clavier (we know that there was a good deal of this kind of instrumental searching for new harmonic effects in those days) ; and his habit of at once repeating his fine effect in another key, after the fashion of Liszt, is a sign of his servitude to it; like Liszt, he does not quite know what he ought to do next, so he does the same thing again.

*

* *

Genius of a kind, or at any rate a decided talent, cannot be denied to Gesualdo; but it is impossible to see more than average talent in the work of most of the monodists of the first generation after 1600. When the men of greater talent got to work, they simplified the texture of their music; a Carissimi could not or would not work in the experimental harmonic idiom of a Saraceni. May we not be sure that some-

thing of the kind will happen again? The minor
men of to-day are experimenting with all the ardour
of their predecessors of the sixteenth and seventeenth
centuries. They are producing, like these, more harmonies than they quite know what to do with. There
is a certain type of critical innocence among us—sometimes merging into critical charlatanism—that hails
this or that weaver of new harmonies as a Heaven-sent
genius merely *because* his texture is unlike that of
any of his predecessors. But if history teaches us
anything, it is that few great or enduring works are
likely to be written in conditions such as these. Criticism is safe in taking a bold line with works of this
kind. It must distinguish carefully between the technical (using the word in its fullest sense) and the
æsthetic aspects of the work; and it must remember
that it is only in virtue of their æsthetic qualities that
musical works survive. The critics of the early seventeenth century can be forgiven for not having always
been able to make the distinction; but the failure to
make it cannot be forgiven to the critic of to-day.
These men of the seventeenth century were so en-
chanted with the new thing that had come into music
—the expressive illustration and accentuation of
words—that they were unable to do justice to the
polyphonic music of the great days. They sought for
only one thing in music; if they found that, the music
was very good; if they did not find it, the music was
either bad or less good. One is constantly struck, in
reading the critical literature of the period, by the
insensitiveness of these composers and writers to what
is so great a delight to us to-day, and had, of course,
been of equal delight to the men who made the music
—the exquisite texture of the polyphonic music, the

marvels of its rhythm. What swept out of the minds
of these critics, in particular, the sense of the rhythm-
ical value of the old music was their conviction that
music *must* be imperfect in which words were obscured
by several voices saying and doing different things at
the same time. For them, this one defect was sufficient to outweigh all the excellences; and music that
was free from this defect, that gave due effect to the
words, and that ministered in its rather easy and obvious
expressiveness to the need of the time for emotional
expansion, was valued by them beyond its real worth.
In the work of the later monodists there were piquant
new harmonies to fascinate them, and to blind them
to the essentially second-rate quality of the work in
which these piquancies appeared.

These men had few data to go upon that would
help them to distinguish between technical and æsthetic
values, or, indeed, to realize that such a distinction
needed to be made. The musical world was younger
then; musicians could not have the long and broad
view upon the past that we have. They thought that
change must necessarily be for the better, and that
when one form of the art superseded another the first
was finally done with. They could know nothing of
the cycles of the art, of the temporary submergence of
a form or a spirit and its later reappearance. But
with us the case is different. The centuries are laid
out before us for our dissection. We, alone among
the generations, are privileged to see ourselves in an
earlier period and it in us. The men of 1600 passed
through a decisive stage in the development of music
without having, as we have, the good fortune to be
able to compare their situation with that of an earlier
time. Music always goes about its business rather

despotically; it can only live by killing; it can bring certain impulses and aspirations to perfection only by suppressing others for a time. This is what happened in the fourteenth, fifteenth and sixteenth centuries in Italy; purely Italian song had seemed to be well set on the line of its own development when Northern polyphony thrust it into the background. In two or three centuries, vocal polyphony had reached its climax of perfection; and then the ineradicable Italian impulse to emotional song, that had been merely driven underground, reappeared and fought a successful war against the ageing giant that had so long oppressed it. It seems to be a natural law that music cannot develop at the same pace in each field simultaneously; the centuries, like individuals, have to simplify their problems by isolating them. The course of evolution is always towards a balance of forces—a merely temporary balance, as it turns out; the problem is to find a form of art in which melody, harmony and rhythm are blended in ideal proportions. This state of affairs comes about at the end of a long period, and it comes about by music instinctively rejecting for the moment whatever is likely to prevent the realization of that perfect balance. But the balance is no sooner obtained than it tends to become lost again. One of the suppressed impulses begins to assert itself, and, with the abundant life and blind egoism of all young things, pursues its own development regardless of everything else.

This was what happened at the close of the sixteenth century. The long-suppressed Italian inclination towards monody and the sensuous had been trying to assert itself for a considerable time before 1600. It had always found, even during the glorious polyphonic epoch, a certain amount of expression in popular and amateur song. There are signs of it again in many of the madrigals of the latter years of the century, that seem to be trying their best to be emotional solo songs with a vocal accompaniment. And, as bearing on the question of the reassertion of the native Italian bent towards the sensuous in music, we have to recall to our memory what is generally forgotten, and, indeed, to many students not known—that it had been the practice for something like three-quarters of a century before 1600 to sing madrigals with the "divisions" (i.e., melodic embellishments and variations) that are familiar to us in the eighteenth century opera. The practice may have had its origin in the vanity of the singers, and is, in fact, much older than the sixteenth century madrigal; but that it was accepted by the composers of the day—who, to our modern thinking, should have been as annoyed at this maltreatment of their music as Brahms would have been if the tenors were in the habit of singing *Wie bist du, meine Königin* with variations of their own—is shown by the number of madrigals that were published in the "decorated" style, along with the original, while the composers were still living. The monodic coloratura of Caccini and his fellows is merely a continuation of this madrigal coloratura of the preceding generations.

What we are accustomed, then, to regard as a sudden upheaval about 1600 was merely the coming into the light of day and into full consciousness of itself of an Italian impulse towards a simplicity of song that had been long kept under by the massive artifice of counterpoint, with its subtle interweaving of rhythms and its consequent suppression of the individual for the benefit of the mass. What especially interests us

in the new development is what the men who took part
in it could not perceive or be expected to perceive—
that they did not know how to use their new-found
freedom.   It was not long before the silent, inexorable
logic of things made it clear that this was a condition
of unstable equilibrium that could not be permitted
to last.   Almost from the very beginning, as I have
already pointed out, the composers who had any
music worth speaking of in them began to draw upon
the resources of the older art to help out the defi-
ciencies of the new.   Very gradually the spirit of
music gathered the dispersed elements up into a new
synthesis.   The instinct for form took hold of the
rambling fancies of the monodists and beat out, in
time, the aria, the operatic chorus, and the simpler
instrumental structures.   In the course of less than
a century two new balances of forces were reached,
two forms, to use a convenient term that need not be
taken too literally, in a condition of stable equilibrium,
in which once more men had no longer to take thought
about making the substance and the grammar of their
art, but, secure in the possession of these, could de-
vote their whole energies to expressing themselves
within the form.   There came, on the one hand, the
Italian opera—the result of a synthesis of many elements—and on the other the new harmonic counterpoint.   The great masters, Bach and Handel, accepted
the new synthesis as unquestioningly as Palestrina
did the synthesis of his own time; the Handel opera
and the Bach instrumental or choral polyphony
show the art of music settling down once again, after
more than a century of struggle and adjustment, into
the condition of a machine each part of which not
only does its own work but co-operates smoothly with

all the others. And similar movements went on in the later days in both vocal and instrumental music, an element of disturbance being introduced here or there into the perfectly functioning machine and putting it slightly out of order, until in time another machine was evolved that once more represented a sound working compromise—the symphony of Beethoven, the music drama of Wagner, the song of Hugo Wolf.

XV

WITH musical history thus spread out before our feet, we of to-day can see what the men of 1600 could not possibly see. We are conscious of laws of musical evolution of which they could have no conception, for they had no complete previous cycle of adjustment and disturbance and readjustment that might have enabled them to see their own epoch as an inevitable and recurrent phase of the art. There is no excuse for us if we fail to extract from the phenomena of the sixteenth and seventeenth centuries the lessons they carry, the laws they illustrate.

One of these laws is that no genius of the first rank uses anything like the full theoretically possible resources of his time. It is sheer ignorance on the part of modern journalism to call a contemporary composer a reactionary because he refuses to avail himself of all these theoretic new resources. He is obeying a sound instinct; he knows that if he is to express himself with perfect freedom he must not diverge into the speculative. Sir Charles Stanford has pointed out how Wagner, in the introduction to the third act of *Tristan* (bars 6 to 10), "experimented with the whole-tone scale, and drew his pen through it, as was to be expected from a composer whose every work proves the writer to have had the pure scale inbred in him." Wagner would no doubt be fully conscious that interesting discoveries might be made by plunging into this unexplored jungle; but he must also have felt that to plunge into a jungle was not the best way to get quickly from one high road to another.

We see the same unwillingness to do more than touch the fringe of experiment in the great masters of the sixteenth century. Practically all of them turned, now and then, an inquisitive eye on the chromaticism that was as new and as alluring to the sixteenth century as atonality or polytonality can be to this; but they touched it, when they touched it at all, only with the tips of their fingers. They knew all about it, but felt that they had no particular use for it. When they do employ it, it is generally in a rather self-conscious and sometimes half-joking way, to "paint" a sentiment or a word. Thus Palestrina, in his motet *Peccantem me quotidie,* indulges in one of his very rare uses of chromatic notes to express the confusion of "conturbat" in the words "timor mortis conturbat me." Byrd uses chromatics for a kind of musical pun at the words "Some strange chromatic notes do you devise," in his *Come, woeful Orpheus* (in the 1611 volume of *Psalmes, Songs and Sonnets*). The English madrigalists used chromatics with considerable boldness— sometimes not quite successfully from the æsthetic point of view; but even with them, chromaticism is a flavouring, not a staple diet. Orlando di Lasso experimented with it in his early days, but later saw, presumably, the general impracticability of such experiments. In his youthful motet *Alme Deus* he puns like Byrd, using the "new style" chromata to point the words "canoque simul dulce *novumque melos.*"

That the attention of the whole musical world of the time was directed to these experiments is shown by the importance attached to the famous motet of Cyprian de Rore, *Calami sonum ferentes* (1555). So profound was the impression made on the consciousness of the sixteenth century by this remarkable work, opening, as it seemed to do, doors into a wonderful future, that when other madrigalists made similar chromatic ventures they would describe the piece as "ad imitatione di C. R." By a slight effort of the historical imagination we can place ourselves at the point of view of the sixteenth-century musician, and realize that the prospects of atonality or quarter-tones cannot be more exciting to us than the prospects of chromaticism were to them. Yet the great masters did ninety-nine hundredths of their work in sublime disregard of what was felt at the time to be the new spirit. And it is easy to see why this was so. We can imagine a Palestrina saying to himself: "Yes, this is extremely interesting, and some day something may come of it. But at present it is not for me. If my musical faculty is to function freely, I must be content with the normal language of music; I must not try to build with materials of which I do not fully understand the use, and which, indeed, I shall have, in part, to make as I go along." And we may be pretty certain what would have happened had there been musical journalism in those days. Palestrina would have been derided as a conservative, a reactionary. Extravagant praise would have been poured out on the experimenters in chromaticism, and, feeling it to be "in the air," and fearing to be stigmatized as old-fashioned, the feebler heads among the younger men would have launched out into extravagances of which they themselves could see neither the first reason nor the ultimate end, but that would at least have earned for them the praise of being thoroughly "progressive." Progress there certainly would come in time from these experiments, in the sense that a new language would be made for music. But little great music—music, that is to say, recognized as great by posterity—could have come out of it at the time. The theoretical future might be with the experimenters; the practical future was with the immovable "conservatives," who, masters of a material and a technique that they thoroughly understood, built fabrics that all the revolutions of time cannot shake from their foundations. The phenomenon is not a chance one. It obeys a law; and we may be sure that the law is operative to-day. Criticism need have no fear of stultifying itself in the eyes of future generations if it tests contemporary musical activity in the light of this law.

*

*   *

A study of 1600 as a type-period reveals, I think, another law that will help us. It is this: that it is futile to speak of "pioneers" in the music of to-day, for no one knows what the future course of music will be. If an explosion takes place in a dark building, and everyone runs about blindly seeking a way out, it is ridiculous to regard them as "pioneers." Most of those who try to rush out will perish; and those who find the way out do so by accident. We could rightly regard any party of the present as the "progressive" party only if we knew definitely what the future of music is to be; for obviously a pioneer is not a progressive pioneer if he takes himself and his followers into a *cul de sac*. The history of seventeenth-century music proves conclusively that the ultimate outcome of a revolt is something quite different from what the revolters anticipated, because forces soon come into play of which they could have had no foreknowledge. The Florentines thought they had slain and buried counterpoint; it arose from the tomb more vigorous than ever. They thought they were creating a music drama like that of the ancient Greeks; what came out of it was something vastly different—the opera. The chamber monodists no doubt thought that their venturesome harmonies would be the foundation for a new harmonic system; their wiser successors put the ventures aside as being, for the moment, impracticable. Which of the new resources of to-day will become an organic part of the music of the next twenty years it is utterly impossible for any man to say; but, judging from the past, comparatively few of them will be found to be immediately serviceable. We must constantly remember that while there is a certain inevitableness about musical development, a certain unconscious "urge" of forces towards a goal, there is nothing approaching complete inevitability in these matters, as I have tried to show in the case of Wagner and the music drama. Whether the unconscious forces shall realize themselves depends on the coming of some man of rare genius. We can say, with a good deal of truth, that the Beethoven symphony is the logical outcome of the symphony of Mozart and Haydn; but all the same, it would never have come had not just that one man happened to have born just then.

The future is veiled from all of us; our power to draw conclusions from the factors before us is vitiated by the fact that the seminal, original geniuses bring into the problem a factor that is unforeseeable and incalculable; who, for instance, could have deduced from instrumental music as it was in 1825 the inevitable coming of a Chopin, or, from the French music of 1800–1870, the inevitable coming of a Debussy? But though none of us can see what the music of the immediate future will be, we can, I think, guided by the past, see in part what it will not be. It will not be very much like what a few "progressives" would fain make it, any more than the Italian opera and cantata of the later seventeenth century were like the music drama of the Florentines. And, again reasoning from the past, we may be sure that the next commanding genius will be as negligent of the more extreme theoretical new resources that the last few years have placed at the composer's disposal as Palestrina was of chromaticism. Gounod long ago said that the next great man in music would be great in virtue of his simplicity. That, indeed, seems to be a historical law; the great man attains his freedom by submitting to an apparent restriction of it.

*

* *

We may then take it for granted, I think, that none of the new works of to-day that fail to justify themselves at once, *æsthetically,* to the average musical sense of the period will be of much significance for the future, no matter how fertile they may be in suggestions of new technical resources—suggestions which the future may or may not choose to take up. We can hold fast to the unshakable principles that no composer of genius has failed to be recognized as such in his own day, and that while the average musical consciousness is quick to respond to any vital originality of thought, it is inclined to be critical of the pseudo-originality that consists merely in being different from the rest. This type has abounded in every age. Burney, in the Journal of his German tour, gives us a glimpse of the type in the person of a Portuguese composer whom he met in Vienna. He first heard of him through the Duke of Braganza. "His royal highness gave me an account of a Portuguese Abbé, whom Lord Stormont and M. L'Augier had before mentioned as a person of a very singular character; a kind of Rousseau, but still more original. He is of the most difficult access; refuses every offer of service in the way of money and presents, though he has nothing but his mass to subsist on, which produces him just fifteen pence a day. He is determined to be independent, and hates to be talked of by the world, and almost to talk to anyone in it. The Duke of Braganza, however, thought he had just interest sufficient to make him and me acquainted; and as another select musical party was forming on my account, for Friday, to dine with Lord Stormont, the duke promised to do all in his power to bring this extraordinary Abate with him. His musical opinions are as singular as his character. He plays very well on the large Spanish guittar, though in a very peculiar style; with little melody, but, with respect to harmony and modulation, in the most pleasing and original manner. He is a professed enemy to the system of Rameau, and thinks the *Basse Fondamentale* the most absurd of all inventions; as it destroys all fancy, connexion and continuity, by perpetually tending to a *final close* and termination of whatever is begun; falling a fifth, or rising a fourth, cuts everything off short, or makes the ear, which is accustomed to a fundamental base, uneasy till a passage is finished."

A few days later, Burney met the composer. "The

musical party, which dined to-day at Lord Stormont's, was select, and in the highest degree entertaining and pleasing. It consisted of the Prince Poniatowski, the Duke of Braganza, the Portuguese minister, Count and Countess Thun, M. L'Augier, the Chevalier, Madame and Mademoiselle Gluck, the Abate Costa, etc. This Abate is the extraordinary musician that I mentioned before, who, disdaining to follow the steps of others, has struck out a new road, both as composer and performer, which it is wholly impossible to describe; all I can say of his productions is, that in them melody is less attended to than harmony and uncommon modulation; and that the time is always difficult to make out, from the great number of ligatures and fractions; however, his music, when well executed, which happens but seldom, has a very singular and pleasing effect; but it is certainly too much the work of art to afford great delight to any ears but those of the learned."

I search the pages of history in vain for any other record of the Abate Costa and his original music. One recognizes the type at once, from its frequency in the musical world of to-day—the speculative dilettante who takes his own line, "disdaining to follow the steps of others," in whose music "melody is less attended to than harmony and uncommon modulation," and who, no doubt, is theoretically in the line of "progress," but who rarely succeeds in writing anything that other people can feel to be worth hearing twice. It may be, of course, that the Abate Costa was a great original genius whose music was beyond the powers of comprehension of his own generation, and who must look to a more enlightened age for recognition. But the law of parsimony will again help us. Since there is not another case in musical history of a composer so much in advance of his time that none of his contemporaries were equal to the task of valuing him correctly, it is extremely unlikely that this is a case of the kind. It is infinitely more probable that Costa was an example of the "originality" that does not matter, either to its own day or to any later one. His misfortune was that he lived in the days when musical journalism was not. Had he been alive to-day he would assuredly have had an admiring article on him in one of the musical periodicals, with copious illustrations from his manuscripts, showing how very different his music was from that of anyone else; he would have been hailed as one of the founders of the new and better order of things, and his eulogist would have publicly congratulated himself on being the first to call attention to so remarkable a genius.

We need not be deterred from saying categorically that this or that "original" composer of to-day will be, so far as the general musical public is concerned, completely forgotten twenty years hence, by any of those "reminders" that Mr. Calvocoressi would revive for us from the past. Every age has a very fair sense of which are the men who matter and which are the men who do not. If the age makes a mistake at all, it is in the direction not of failure to recognize the truly vital minds but to over-estimate the minds of only partial vitality, such as a Telemann or a Spohr. Of a thousand men who are writing music in any country in any given decade, not more than half a dozen are likely to receive much attention from posterity; and the critic who says that the vast majority of the new and original works of to-day will be forgotten in a

few years need not fear being proved to be wrong a
century or so hence.

*
*　　*

Every period of violent change calls out a large
amount of merely excited music-making, that, in the
last resort, represents no positive achievement, but is
merely a cry of impotence and despair, a firing in the
air in the hope of hitting a target that is not clearly
seen.　Ours is not the first epoch to witness a phenomenon of this kind; it recurs whenever men have
a dim sense that a new goal is to be reached and an
ardent desire to reach it, without quite knowing how
it is to be reached, or, indeed, precisely what the goal
is.　In this respect our own age is very like that
period in the fourteenth century when, intoxicated by
the vision of what might be done by combining sounds,
but having as yet no clear idea of the rules by which
they could be combined, men rushed blindly into a
sort of catch-as-catch-can discant, the singers impro-
vising upon the canto fermo as they went along.　The
effect on the ear must have been dubious enough sometimes when the serious musicians tried to make a
workable counterpoint by taking two or three familiar
melodies, clamping them together, and then filing away
at this point and that until the tunes showed a certain
accommodation to each other.　But it must have been
infinitely more painful when the singers took matters
into their own hands and tried to rush the position by
a wild frontal attack.　The sober musicians of the
time put their fingers in their ears while this charivari
was going on.　Johannes Cotton had said of the

singers of an earlier epoch that he could only compare them with "drunken men, who indeed get home,
but themselves do not know how they did it, or by
what route they went." The passage reads like a
description of some of the more absurd attempts at
atonality or polytonality in the music of our own day
—the music of the innocents whose notion of polytonality is to write half a dozen tunes for half a
dozen instruments and to play them together, trust-
ing to Providence to bless the result. We can say
nothing about these simple people that was not said
of their ancestors, the improvisatory discanters, six
centuries ago by old Jean de Muris. "Supposing that
our rules are good, how can the singers have the assurance to discant [extempore] or to compose a discant, when they know nothing of harmony, have no
idea that some combinations of tone sound better
than others, do not know which to use and which to
avoid, where they are to come, and all the other points
of genuine art? When things come out right with
them it is pure accident. Their voices [parts] wander
round the tenor without any system; they trust to
God for them to agree; they throw their notes out
and trust to luck, as it were a stone hurled by an
unskilled hand, and that hits its mark only once in a
hundred times. . . ." Then comes a passage that I
cannot forbear to quote in Burney's skittish translation: the Latin, he says, "is so obsolete and monkish,
that it seems as if it would fall more naturally into English of the sixteenth century than into that of the present
times." "But alas! in these our dayes, some do stryve
to glosse over theyr lack of skyll with silly sayenges.
This, cry they, is the *newe* method of discantynge,
these be the newe concordes." (One remembers some

of the catchwords of to-day—"juxtaposition of tonal values," and so on—and Moriz Rosenthal's description of some of the wilder speculators among the modern composers, "They know nothing, and capitalize their ignorance.") "Howbeit they grievously offend thereby both the hearing and the understanding of suche as be skylled to judge of theyr defects; for where we look for delight, they do induce sadness. O incongruous sayenge! O wretched glosse! irrational excuse! O monstrous abuse! most rude and bestial ignoraunce! to take an asse for a man, a goat for a lyon, a sheepe for a fishe, a snake for a salmone! For in suche sorte do they confound concordes with discordes, as ye shall in no wise discerne the one from the other. O! if the good old maysters of former tyme did hear suche *discanters,* what wolde they say or do? Out of doubte they wolde thus chyde them and say, This discant, whereof ye now make use, ye do not take it from *me;* ye do in no wyse frame your songe to be concordaunt with me; wherefore do ye thrust yourselves in? ye do not agree with me; ye are an adversary, and a scandal unto me. O that ye wolde be dumb! This is not *concordynge,* but most doatynge and delyrious *discordynge.*" John of Salisbury had said much the same thing in the twelfth century about the singers who, by way of making a new art, defaced the melodic outline with embellishments of their own: "they want to dazzle the stupid hearers, who fancy they hear in all this not human song but the song of the sirens."

It was a good thing for Jean de Muris and his fellows, as for Palestrina, that there was no musical journalism in *their* day; otherwise they would certainly have been accused of being reactionaries, dull fellows unable to keep pace with the advanced spirits of the time.   In the fifteenth century, Franchinus Gaforius gives us a specimen—at which he holds up his hands in horror—of the kind of music that was made when the singers added catch-as-catch-can discants of their own to a melody:

Ambros, no doubt rightly, correlates this wild improvisation with the general extravagance of the life of the time.   We may see, perhaps, in the madder "polytonal" music of to-day a reflection of the confusion that has come into most of our standards of life and thought during the last few years.

*

*   *

I have said that had there been journalism in Jean de Muris's day he would have been vilified as a reactionary. In some respects, it is true, he was one, and I have no doubt that in the controversies of the time he was abused in the regulation fashion. I recur to him because he may serve to point the moral already furnished us by Lobe, with whom, perhaps, he has a good many resemblances. A consideration of the two cases will show us how the same critical problems, the same critical types, reappear in generation after generation, and so will help us to a rule for our own praxis, if only a negative one. Happening to run this morning through the pages of Dr. Robert Hirschfeld's treatise on de Muris, I found that in 1884 Hirschfeld was looking at the eternal question of progressive and conservative, classic and romantic, very much as I have been doing lately. The fourteenth century saw perhaps the first conflict between the classics and the romantic in music. It may seem, to our modern eyes, to have been waged largely over technical and theoretical rather than æsthetic matters, but at the root of the theoretical innovations was an æsthetic impulse. An *ars nova* and an *ars antiqua* were drawn up in battle array against each other, and no doubt the usual compliments were bandied about. De Muris was on the classical side. As Dr. Hirschfeld says, he was too unyieldingly conservative; he could not see the element of good there was in the "moderns" and their departures from the ancient practice. And the reason was that, like Lobe and like so many others in every age, he recoiled further than he need have done because the other party, in its juvenile assurance, advanced too far. The moderns would fain have made too clean a sweep of the older art, that seemed to them to be in their way. As I have tried to correlate these ancient conflicts with that going on around us to-day, so Hirschfeld correlated them with those of his own period—i. e., the time when triumphant Wagnerism was bringing all sorts of unhealthy things in its wake. "It is a common phenomenon," he says, "and one to which our own age is not a stranger, that the people who are continually looking towards the future in art are only too prone to overlook the ground at their feet, and to spill out too much hatred and contumely on their predecessors and those who still associate themselves with these. *They* preach the true gospel; whoever does not go with them is incompetent, uncultivated; until there is nothing left for the sober-minded people, in face of this kind of talk, but to hold to their ideals and convictions with the utmost tenacity. Just so was it in the time of de Muris. He was one of the older men, he tells us, 'whom the modern youth cry down as *rudes.'* " The "moderns," then as now, were roughly contemptuous of everyone who disagreed with them. "Some of the moderns (*aliqui moderni*)'" says de Muris, "call those singers raw, crazy, silly and ignorant who take no notice of the *ars nova,* or who sing in the ancient, not the modern, way; and as a consequence they style the old art also crude and irrational, and the new art rational and subtle."

There were cliques then as there are now, and the moderns would have nothing to do with the admirers of the ancients. "It is wrong," says de Muris indignantly, "that anyone should be banished from the fatherland without any definite and just reason, and, innocent as he is, be excommunicated from the band of the faithful. I will not deny that the moderns also have composed many good and beautiful things; but the ancients should not, on that account, be depreciated and boycotted by the singers. One good thing no more excludes another than one virtue excludes another." And Hirschfeld develops the theme, which has also been the theme of the foregoing pages, that "the reforming efforts of prominent artists, that really have many a fruitful seed in them, are misunderstood and misconstrued by the artists' partisans, who pursue the new directions with a blind passion. The new excites; and the people who cannot grasp the true significance of it look to extravagance for strength, to the incomprehensible for depth, to excitement of the senses for beauty. . . . So it comes about that progressive ideas, that spring solely from a practical need and pursue a practical end, become, through the irrational behaviour of blind zealots, surrounded by an impenetrable crust of wordy and sterile speculation. The future alone can show whether there is strength enough in the seed to break through the obstructing husk and cast it aside. . . . The younger contemporaries of de Muris were probably too much inclined to errors of this kind, and indulged in many aberrations in their art. . . . By their lack of moderation and the extravagance of their compositions and their performances they must, at any rate at first, have hindered rather than helped the *ars nova,* which was

being cultivated by worthy and gifted men. . . . And
so de Muris fights only against the encroachments of
those musicians who saw in the *ars nova* just an arena
for their own unbridled fantasy. And there must
have been many of these. No one who reads carefully de Muris's suggestive descriptions of his time
can fail to be struck by the similarity between the
æsthetic impulse of that epoch and the position of the
art to-day [1884]. Music was already very popular,
and anyone who could discant a little thought he had a
right to make his voice heard in the council of musicians. . . . People outbid each other in reformatory
projects; they rushed forward without any definite
goal. One new idea chased another, and the preten-
sions of the art changed so rapidly that the 'new' of
the moment only too soon outlived itself, as we might
say. . . . The composers prided themselves on making their works very complicated, looked scornfully on
the period that preceded them, and vaunted their own
new art, which was more 'difficult' than that of their
predecessors. Jean de Muris's shrewd comment on
it all was: 'Quod autem ulterius dicitur quod ars
moderna *difficilior* est quam antiqua dicendum quod
non sequitor ex hoc, quod sit *perfectior*. Non enim
quod difficilius est, perfectior est.' "

Plus ça change, plus c'est la même chose! In
every age of drastic readjustment of musical forces we
come across the same phenomenon of the classically-
minded men being driven into a sort of ultra-
conservatism (for de Muris was even reactionary in
some respects, fulminating against already accepted
things as "novelties") not so much by the innovations
of the one or two really vital composers as by the absurdities, the extravagances, the arrogances, of the

crowd of little men who see in every new movement a chance to assert and advertise themselves. Unfortunately for the later reputation of the critics, these little people are soon forgotten, only the bigger men being remembered; and the poor critic goes down to posterity as the opponent of these latter, whereas it was the former whose stupidities and incompetence stiffened his critical back. Lobe, as I have said, obviously shows that what makes him unduly suspicious of Schumann and Wagner is not so much the work of these composers themselves as the work of the numerous minor men of the period whose names are now completely forgotten. De Muris often seems to be aiming directly at his progressive contemporary, Philippe de Vitry, whereas it is clear from his treatise that what must have angered him most was the large number of inferior musicians who, we may conjecture, were very much to de Vitry what the Wagnerian small fry were to Wagner, or the Stravinskian small fry are to Stravinsky. If we could know the whole truth, we might even find, perhaps, that poor Artusi was almost as much sinned against as sinning. His later recognition of Monteverdi's genius shows that he was not permanently impervious to the spirit of the age when it expressed itself rationally and convincingly. Probably what goaded Artusi into protest was a long spell of suffering under the inanities of the minor composers of the time, who, like their successors of the present day, could handle the new idiom just about well enough to make themselves and it ridiculous. He speaks of "the moderns" who indulged in experiments at the clavier—that easiest of all ways, in this day as in that, of hitting upon novel combinations—and then prided themselves on having discovered something new, something, however, of which they could make no rational use. Neither Artusi nor Lobe could be expected to see that the first business of the critic, in a time of change, is to distinguish between the seminal forces and the impotencies among the innovators; but we, with the lesson of the past before us, must make that distinction.

XVI

SHALL I be accused of begging the question? Shall I be asked how, till the veil of the future be rolled away, anyone can be sure which of the new composers will be vital for the later history of music and which will not? If so, I would reply that nothing is easier. I have shown in the foregoing pages that there is not a single case in musical history of a great composer being so far ahead of the average musical thinking of his day as to be unintelligible to it. There is no likelihood, then, of such a composer being among us to-day. Anyone who tells us that some work of Schönberg on which we have vainly expended hour after hour of study over a course of several years will some day be recognized by the world as a work of genius, may be invited to cite some evidence from the past that such an event is *a priori* likely. I repeat that there is not a single work in the whole history of music with which humanity has had that experience. Differences of temperament, of appetite, there will always be, as there always have been. It is to these differences, not, as people are inclined to think, to differences in intellectual calibre, that musical "camps" owe their origin. It may flatter the vanity of a critic to persuade himself that the reason other people do not fall, with him, at the feet of this or that composer is that their poor brains are incapable of keeping pace with the latest developments of music— that is to say, incapable of keeping pace with *his* swift athletic mind. But the truth is not that the composer's music is to them as a message in Chinese would be to one ignorant of that delectable language, but simply that, understanding the message quite well, they do not like it or do not think much of it. The people who disliked Wagner in 1870 or 1880 mostly did so not because his music was intellectually beyond them, but because, having got into them, it set up unpleasant emotional or moral reactions. It was not a matter of the novelty of the sensation but of the disagreeableness of it; there are anti-Wagnerians in plenty to-day, musicians to whom *Tristan* is musically no more complex, no more difficult, than *Don Giovanni* is, but who see nothing in it but a long erotic convulsion, and who turn away from it for their soul's health. "The whole man thinks" is as true in music as in ordinary psychology; music sets up different reactions in each of us according to our physical and moral chemistry. But the extremes of musical temperament in a population cancel each other out, and we are left, as I have argued already, with a body of plain, sensible, instructed music-lovers whose taste is fairly catholic. Mr. Arnold Bennett would no doubt call these people the passionate few. I should prefer to call them the intelligent average.

This intelligent average is quite capable of dealing, in any age, with any æsthetic problem of contemporary music. I lay stress on the word "æsthetic." I mean that the average intelligent musical man, although he may not be competent to sustain a discussion on the theoretical aspects of a new musical development, is perfectly competent to decide upon the æsthetic value of this or that work. No composer has ever been, or ever will be, so far in advance of his time that the average intelligent musical man cannot follow him, at all events by making an effort.

And when musicians as a whole honestly and consistently make that effort in a given case, and find themselves, in the end, neither liking nor disliking the work—as one may like or dislike *Tristan* or *Le Poème de l'Extase*—but simply unable to see anything in it either to like or dislike, something that means nothing whatever to them—as with some of the Schönberg works—they are justified in saying that the fault is not in them but in the music, that the composer has either not seen clearly the thing he wanted to say or has not succeeded in saying it clearly (if, indeed, the two processes can be differentiated). There is no reason whatever why they should turn over to posterity the job of distinguishing between the works of to-day that really matter æsthetically and those that do not. Every other age has succeeded in doing this, to the extent of its knowledge—an important qualification, for, of course, no age can be expected to discriminate nicely between the values of two factors when one of the factors is not known to it. I would cite once more, as an illustration of this, the case of the great popularity of Hasse and Telemann, whose music was known to everyone in Germany, as against the smaller popularity of Bach, whose music was known only to a few. Broadly speaking, in every age and every country the best works in their genre have been picked out contemporaneously as the best. We must take the long view, not allowing ourselves to be distracted by little things close to our eyes and so to lose our sense of the proportions of the whole. We are trying, as it were, to make a graphic chart of the public appreciation of music throughout the centuries; we must therefore ignore the tiny fluctuations that do not affect the great curve. We find

Mozart, for instance, complaining that Vienna did not take to his operas as Prague did. There were local circumstances—intrigues, jealousies, and so on—to account for this. Ignoring all trifling indentations of this kind in the curve, the main line of this shows us that every age has had a clear perception not only of its best composers in each genre but of the best works of each. It is impossible, I think, to point to a single work that was ranked lowly in its own day by intelligent people who had proper opportunities of becoming acquainted with it that turned out to be a masterpiece in the eyes of a later generation. Many a man, many a work, has been dignified with the title of genius by his or its contemporaries and been degraded to the rank of talent by a later day; but I know of no case in history of the opposite process.

Music, indeed, no matter how new it may be, can be good or bad only in virtue of the qualities that are already familiar to the ordinary instructed musician in the works of his own and preceding epochs. If any generation could have been forgiven for going wrong in its judgments it would be that of the early years of the seventeenth century in Italy. The "drama in music" that was then being experimented with was something more novel than anything that any generation has had to face since; yet the average sensible man of the day saw quite clearly that Marco da Gagliano, Monteverdi and Cavalli were the superiors in this new field. We need have no fear that posterity will take a different view from ours of the relative importance of the innovators of our own day. We can see that Stravinsky stands head and shoulders above all his imitators and hangers-on; and we can hazard our soul's salvation on the wager that, even though a good deal of his work should become for future ages only what much of Monteverdi's is for ours—evidences of an interesting stage in musical development rather than creations eternally valuable as art—posterity will confirm our judgment that *Le Sacre du Printemps* or *L'Histoire du Soldat* is to similar efforts of the day in the same genre as Monteverdi's *Orfeo* was to the average dilettante essay of the time in the new Florentine "drama with music."

XVII

THE critic's first duty, then, is to separate the vital man of a new movement from the rest, and then quietly ignore the rest. They make a great noise in the world now, but they will mean nothing to posterity, and therefore are of no importance to the critic of to-day. I hasten to guard myself against a possible, indeed, a too probable, misunderstanding. The doings of the minor musicians from day to day are as well worth recording, from the journalistic point of view, as the doings of any other human insects—minor politicians, minor novelists, and so on. But the critic's, as distinct from the reporter's, aim should be always to see things *sub specie aeternitatis*, to trace connecting lines of force, to see the history of music as an organic whole. In this organic whole the minor men play no part. They are mere flies upon the wheel; who can suppose that the history of eighteenth century music would have been any different had the Abels and Anfossis and Gassmanns and Kozeluchs and Voglers and all the rest of them never been born? They may have given a certain amount of legitimate pleasure to their hearers, but for the history of music they are insignificant; and an eighteenth century student of musical evolution would only have had his standards, his sense of proportion, perverted by taking very much notice of them. It is against this perversion of his standards that the critic of to-day has to guard, for the lesson of the past is that by taking the crowd of minor composers too seriously he runs the risk of missing something at least of the significance of the major men.

We have seen this happen in the case of Lobe; irritated by the extravagances and arrogancies of the young "moderns" of his day, he unconsciously visited upon the heads of Schumann and Wagner some of the sins of their weaker brethren.   In 1884, again, we find a thoughtful musician like Hirschfeld perturbed over the extravagances and arrogancies of the later Wagnerian partisans.   Had men like Hirschfeld been able to take a calm long view of the critical problem as it arises in every age they would have seen that since the smaller Wagnerian echoes would very soon become inaudible it was unnecessary to waste much time listening to them even then.   There is nothing in the musical life and the musical journalism of to-day that cannot be paralleled in the life and the journalism of thirty or forty or fifty years ago.   It seems hardly credible to-day that such men as Cyrill Kistler and Felix Draeseke and Alexander Ritter and August Bungert and Heinrich Zöllner should ever have been thought worthy of entering, even by a side wind, into a discussion of Wagner and Wagnerism; but we have only to turn up the literature of the time to see that these now forgotten worthies took the same place in the thought of critics and journalists with an imperfect sense of proportion as —— or —— or —— (I refrain from mentioning the composers' names, so as not to hurt any susceptibilities) does in the thought of the present-day successors of those critics and journalists. Will it be believed that Bungert was taken so seriously by many of his admirers, who saw in him a continuer of Wagner's work (as if the work of any tremendous and original personality *could* be "continued," like a train that is taken by Driver Smith as far as Birmingham, and then handed over to Driver Jones to take to Crewe!), that it was actually proposed to build a special theatre on the Rhine (on the model of Bayreuth) for the performance of his Homeric tetralogy?

The library in which I am burrowing is rich in records of the critical follies of the past. I have only to run my eye over some representative writings of the Wagner and post-Wagner period to realize how great is the resemblance between that day and this, and how necessary it is for the critic to-day, if he would win a clear view of the vital factors in musical development, to make a ring fence round the really big man and keep the minor men out of it. A work of some little imitator of Stravinsky is given to-day. It is praised grossly beyond its merits by one party, who accuse those who disparage it of being blind to the significant developments of the age. I turn up an old article (1899 or so) of Dr. Arthur Seidl's on "The Heinrich Zöllner Case." It deals with the production of a *Faust* opera by Zöllner, that was apparently hailed in certain quarters as yet another "continuation" of Wagner. Dr. Seidl poured out his ridicule freely upon it, and was no doubt duly reviled by the "progressives" for doing so. But Dr. Seidl was right, and the progressives were wrong; Wagner's work was done once for all by Wagner, and the Zöllners and Kistlers and Bungerts could add nothing vital to it. Stravinsky's work is being done to-day by Stravinsky, and being done by him precisely because he *is* Stravinsky; and no one who is not Stravinsky can come any nearer to doing his work, or "continuing" it, than the post-Wagnerian opera composers could come to "continuing" the work of Wagner.

*
*   *

I go so far to say that the critic should look backward much oftener than he should look forward.
Some critics—descendants, no doubt, of Sister Anne
—make a great point of standing on the watch-tower
and always looking forward. They delude themselves; for it is not within the power of any critic to
foresee the future of music or to help music to "progress," for the simple reason that "progress," so far as
the word has any meaning at all in music, depends on
the coming of two or three dynamic personalities at the
most in each generation. Nothing is easier than to
win a cheap reputation for progressiveness by chasing
along in the tracks of each new composer and hailing
him, on the mere ground of his difference from his
predecessors, as an advance upon them. We may say
of the work of critics of this kind what Walter
Bagehot, one of the profoundest of modern critical
minds, said (applying a phrase of one of the Cole-
ridges) of the verse of Béranger: "Nothing can re-
deem it from the reproach of wanting *back* thought."
Back thought is really much more difficult than, if not
so superficially showy and noisy as, forward thought.
For the latter you need only an optimistic imagination
and a glib pen; equipped with these, you can shape
the future to your own fancy, and cheerily distribute
certificates to or issue warrants against the composers
of the day for their compliance, or their failure to
comply, with your forecast of the future. For back
thought you need more solid knowledge, some train-

ing in reasoning, and a desire to understand rather than a passion for prophesying. The less we concern ourselves with the future the better; the only thing we can be sure of in connexion with it is that it will correspond no more with our forecasts of it than the music of the late seventeenth century did with the forecasts of the men of 1600. Our humbler concern is with the present; and we must try to understand this as well as we can by the aid of the past. And one of the lessons that back thought will teach us is that no pioneer ever enters the Promised Land. Bagehot, in his *Physics and Politics,* has expressed this truth also with his usual robust sense. Inquiring how a new style in literature comes in, he says that "the true explanation is . . . something like this. One considerable writer gets a sort of start, because what he writes is somewhat more—only a very little more very often, as I believe—congenial to the minds around him than any other sort. This writer is very often not the one whom posterity remembers, not the one who carries the style of the age farthest towards its ideal type, and gives it its charm and perfection. It was not Addison who began the essay-writing of Queen Anne's time, but Steele; it was the vigorous forward man who struck out the rough notion, though it was the wise and meditative man who improved upon it and elaborated it, and whom posterity reads."

We have to learn that in music, as in literature, "the vigorous forward man" has fulfilled his function when he has "struck out the rough notion," and that he "is very often not the one whom posterity remembers." The first step towards a genuine science of

musical criticism would be a thorough, impartial study
of the typical "vigorous forward minds," and especially
of the most typical of all, Monteverdi. A great deal
has been written upon him in recent years, but I cannot
feel that any of the studies we have of him is quite
satisfactory, not even the admirable one of M. Henry
Prunières. The real study of Monteverdi would have
to be carried out in a mood of passionless detachment.
The modern biographers are too facile in their sympathy to be perfectly critical. They are advocates
rather than judges, and they speak too much to their
self-given brief. It is a very likeable, even a touching, trait in human nature that impels a modern critic
to paint the portrait of a Monteverdi with more insistence on the lights than on the shadows; but the
method does not make for sound portraiture. We
of to-day see Monteverdi as the great, restless
genius who was for ever adventuring beyond the
established confines of the music of his day; and our
enthusiasm for the spirit of adventure is apt to make
us insufficiently critical of the quality of the spoils
brought back by the adventurer. How much of
Monteverdi's music can be called really first-class?
Less, perhaps, than we care to admit. Every page of
his that has survived for us is of absorbing and enduring interest to the student; and we feel a peculiar
warmth of affection for the bold, restless spirit that
anticipated so many of the methods that later periods
were to bring to perfection. But there are two things
we have to bear in mind. One is that Monteverdi
probably gets the credit now for innovations that were
more or less "in the air" in his days. He certainly
handled unprepared discords with a new freedom; but

when we are invited to regard his treatment of the seventh as something unprecedented in the music of the time, we do well to remember that the seventh was then no longer regarded by musicians in general with the old horror. The text-books of to-day still tell us that in sixteenth century counterpoint the melodic intervals of the major sixth and the major and minor seventh were strictly forbidden. But that the sixteenth century itself was more flexible in its notions than the modern text-books would imply is shown by such a discussion of intervals as that in Banchieri's *Cartella: overe Regole utilissimi a quelli che desiderano imparare il Canto Figurato* (Venice, 1601).

Banchieri describes intervals as being of three kinds, ordinary, extraordinary and forbidden. The first kind comprises the fourth, fifth, octave, third and minor sixth. The third kind comprises the tritone and the false fifth (i. e. the augmented fourth and the diminished fifth). The "extraordinary" intervals are the seventh and the major sixth; these intervals, says Banchieri, are sometimes motived by the "extravagance" of the words ("Gli straordinarii (quali i musici alle volte pongono per stravaganza di parole) sono di settima, e sesta maggiore"). And he tells the singer how he can strike correctly a major sixth or a seventh *sciolto* (i. e. without any intermediate notes) —by *imagining* the inner notes. The historians recognize that Monteverdi used unprepared discords as he did in order to "paint" the words of a madrigal —indeed, it is on these grounds that he himself justifies them; but it is not generally recognized that the passion for "painting" words had laid hold also upon the ordinary composer of the time, and that, as we see from Banchieri, this desire for colour had destroyed the old academic awe of the major sixth and the seventh as melodic intervals.

*
* *

But even after all credit has been given to Monteverdi for his innovations, there remains the second point to be considered—the actual value of his music, not as a collection of innovations, but *as music*. Can anyone lay his hand upon his heart and swear that, all in all, Monteverdi's music has the vitality for us of to-day that that of his "conservative" contemporaries has? Towards a great deal of it have we not to extend the tolerance that the student of beginnings always has to extend to the work of the primitives? We smile at the naïveté of Kuhnau's programme music. Is not a great deal of Monteverdi equally naïve? It is impossible to read through his *Combattimento di Tancredi e Clorinda* without admiring at every turn the forward-reaching mind that could anticipate so many of the ideals and the effects of later music; but will anyone say that, purely as a work of art, the *Combattimento* is as alive to-day as a madrigal by Wilbye or a Mass by Palestrina? The *Orfeo* is visibly a tentative work; and even the earlier madrigals, for all the colour, the passion, and the energy of them, do not always bear the application to them of the criteria of excellence that we can apply to less adventurous works of the period. We have to distinguish, in fact, between what is of permanent value to us *as artists* in Monteverdi's work, and what is interesting to us as students of a new development in music. The critics of his day would have been on safer ground had they dealt with him not as theorists but as artists. It is folly to attempt to check the expansive impulses of music, and indeed, the world has probably learned too much during the past three centuries ever to venture again to condemn a new utterance because it flouts an old theory or discards an old technique. I have conjectured that it would have been difficult for the Italian musical world of Monteverdi's day to make the right distinction between the innovation value of his work and its æsthetic value—that that age had not behind it the historical experience to teach it that an expansion of technical methods does not necessarily mean the creation of music capable of enduring by its own inner strength. But after all, I do not see that this should have been utterly beyond the capacity of the time. The mass of musicians evidently took their ear as the test; the passionate expression of Gesualdo and Monteverdi appealed to them for its own sake, and they evidently cared little whether the "laws" were observed or broken. It surely ought to have been possible for them to have made an attempt also to separate what was likely to be of permanent value in Monteverdi's music from what could only be regarded as the first fumblings after a new style.

Perhaps these attempts were made, and made successfully. We have no written record of them, but it is hardly credible that sound and thoughtful musicians did not value many pages of Monteverdi just for what they were worth—as interesting and perhaps pregnant experiments, but not, *qua* music, comparable to the "classical" art of the day. Such an anticipation of the opinion of posterity is not inconceivable. I gather, from a paper on "Criticism of the Living" (read be-

fore a meeting of the Musical Association), a summary
of which I have just been able to run through, that
Dr. George Dyson, for whose opinion on such a subject
I have the greatest respect, thinks otherwise. He
rightly stresses the importance of historical perspective
in our judgment of a past epoch, and seems to hold
that since such a perspective must necessarily be lacking
to us for our own period, it is only by a happy accident,
if at all, that any of us can divine "which of the conflicting tendencies of our age will be embraced by its successors." "For a contemporary it is difficult or impossible," says Dr. Dyson, "to determine the relative stat-
ure of an artist, the intrinsic or permanent value of his
contribution to experience. A century ago men had
far from made up their minds as to the respective merits of Mozart, Hummel, Beethoven and Rossini, and
the 19th century was one long record of halting or
ephemeral reputations."

But is there not a fallacy lurking here? What do
we mean when we say that "men" had not made up
their minds as to the respective merits of Mozart and
the others? Do "men" ever all think alike? No
doubt in the early 19th century there were people who
thought Hummel as great as Mozart, and Rossini
greater than Beethoven; just as there were people
in the late 19th century who thought that Bruch was at
least the equal of Brahms. But the question is, what
was the opinion of what I have called the intelligent
average,—the people who knew equally well the work
of each of the rival composers and had a genuine musical culture to back their judgments? The passages
I have already cited from early 19th century criticism
show that, in the opinion of some musicians at any
rate, Beethoven was the greatest composer of the day.

Does the opinion of the mob,—even the musical mob
—that Rossini was the man of the epoch really count
against the judgment of the true musicians? Posterity would hardly be justified in saying that the relative importance of the composers of the early twentieth century was not settled, because Irving Berlin had
a larger public than Ravel. Is there not excellent
ground for thinking that though the general public
went crazy over Rossini, the really musical public put
him surely enough into his true place relatively to Beethoven?

*
* *

For some light on the question I have just run
through the *Thirty Years' Musical Recollections* of
Henry F. Chorley (1862), which cover the third and
fourth decades of the 19th century. On the Italian
opera of that day Chorley speaks with authority. I
find him tilting, like any "modern" of the present day,
against the "conservatives" and "reactionaries," such
as old Lord Mount-Edgcumbe, who shuddered at Rossini's passionate "modernity." "We are now aware,"
says Chorley, "of the glow, the colour, the emotion
thrown into Italian opera by Signor Rossini, as compared with his predecessors; but the purists, thirty-
five years ago, saw none of these things,—none of the
enrichment and enlargement brought into his art by
the master—without any such innovations as imply
destruction. They resigned themselves, with a sort of
fastidious pity, to the enthusiasm of the hour,—as wise
men will do to a passing frenzy—preferred to talk of
the composers and singers whom they thoroughly de-

lighted in when they were young, in the days when Art was Art indeed,—quiet and select, however beautiful, not a delirious orgy, which could only intoxicate those feeble-brained and hot-blooded folk who courted intoxication."

En passant, I find this rather instructive. It would assuredly have been no use putting the question to Chorley in, say, 1840, but we might put it to him with some assurance now if we could find him,—what if the old music-lovers of the school of Paisiello and Cimarosa were after all right, and Chorley and his fellows wrong? These latter thought that Rossini had revolutionized opera. They laid great stress, and, for their epoch, justifiably, on his many innovations. They did not foresee that Rossini's innovations, that were the talk and the delight of opera-going Europe then, would bear so little fruit, would have so little staying power, that not one music-lover in ten thousand today has the slightest idea what they were. The older school, that regarded Rossini and his dazzling innovations as only so much froth on the sea of music, were largely right. Time has justified them. May it not be the same some day with many of the innovations of today? May not the instinct that rejects them be fundamentally sounder than the instinct that accepts them and builds hopes for the future on them? How sadly, humorously ironic Chorley's tirade seems now! The older school, he says, "resigned themselves, with a sort of fastidious pity, to the enthusiasm of the hour, as wise men will do to a passing frenzy"; they regarded the crowds who went mad over Rossini as "feeble-brained and hot-blooded folk who courted intoxication." They seem to have been right. The modern view of the great Rossini public *is* that, whether hot-blooded or not, it was certainly feeble-brained; the "fastidious pity" was justified; the enthusiasm *was* of the hour; and the men who took it to be only a passing frenzy *were* wise men.

*

* *

Chorley was a "modern" of his day so far as Italian opera was concerned: and the fate of that old-time "modernism" may have a lesson for us. But all this is only by the way. My concern with Chorley is rather to use him to show that we cannot speak, without great looseness of language, of "men" thinking this, that, or the other about Mozart and Hummel, or Beethoven and Rossini. For Chorley's following remarks show us that "men" had more than one opinion on these matters. Rossini's operas, he says, "had also to run the gauntlet of criticism totally different in argument and spirit." German music was slowly making its way even in France and England; Mozart, Beethoven and Weber were becoming better known. "Orchestral art was then in the freshness of its youth; and hence the sagacious, the scientific and the sour set their faces against the facile author of the *Barbiere,* as the spoiled idol of fashion, as a mere flimsy tune-spinner, whose seductions . . . must prove transient, palling, unreal." The people, in fact, who were beginning to understand German music slighted Rossini publicly: "there were such things as good and cultivated Englishmen who, on principle, when Signor Rossini entered one music shop, repaired to another."

Poor Chorley! All that he thought it impossible ever to happen to the music of Rossini in general has happened to it: all but an exceedingly small proportion of it has indeed proved "transient, palling, unreal." The "modernist" of his day—as he regarded himself —was hopelessly wrong. His point of view may be gathered from his remark about "one so far in advance of his age as Signor Rossini,"—this, be it observed, in a decade when Beethoven had been dead for some years, and Germany was entering, with Schumann, upon a new period of development.

It looks, then, as if "men," in the full sense of the word, had a very fair idea of the relative importance of Beethoven and Rossini a century or so ago. The whole world did not lose its head over Rossini: "the sagacious, the scientific and the sour" evidently did some quiet thinking of their own. It is customary nowadays to sneer at Chorley as a reactionary, because of his attitude towards Wagner. The epithet would have knocked him speechless with astonishment. In his own eyes he was a progressive: it was Rossini, he thought, who was urging music forward, and the German dullards who were trying to push it back into "the scientific and the sour." He speaks, later on—referring to about 1851 and afterwards—of "the singular and noticeable outbreak in Germany, which for a while bade fair to destroy there all love of what is real and beautiful in art,—the greatness thrust on Herr Wagner,"—another incidental piece of evidence that in the early 'fifties Wagner was regarded in many quarters as the hope of German music. The lesson from it all is twofold. We must not be misled by the enormous vogue of a small composer into supposing that, whatever the general public may have done, the intelligent average musician did not rank him at his true worth in comparison with the great composer of the day. And we must beware of all talk about "progress." To read that Rossini was once regarded in some quarters as "far in advance of his age" is of itself sufficient to make us realize how little being in advance of his age may ultimately matter to a composer if his music does not happen to be first-rate.

*
* *

XVIII

IF we are told, then, that "men" once found it difficult to decide between Mozart and Hummel, Beethoven and Rossini, the appropriate philosophical reflection seems to be that there are men and men. I see no reason to believe that any composer of anything like the first quality ever remained unrecognized by the mass of his intelligent contemporaries; and the evidence all points to the biggest composer receiving the most recognition. The very fact that "men" quarrelled over him is a proof of this: all Europe is not set by the ears except by something or somebody that interests all Europe. That most of the great modern composers have been the subject of contemporary controversy is undeniable. But this is not astonishing: the astonishing thing would be for any one artist of a very pronounced mentality to appeal equally to all tastes. To this day each of us is either a Platonist or an Aristotelian; it is hardly surprising, then, that the average Wagnerian should not be the best of Brahmsians, and *vice versa*. Moreover, in the case of Wagner, as I have tried to show, there were quite exceptional reasons for the obloquy that came to him; and after all, it is generally Wagner that people have in mind when they speak of the inevitably hard lot of the composer of genius.

*
* *

But even about Wagner was so much nonsense talked as is popularly supposed? I have been looking through some of the better-class criticism of him in his own day,—not the mere venom or ignorance or smartness of this or that journalistic hack, who, with no particular knowledge of music, included among his multifarious duties that of musical critic for some newspaper or other, but the considered criticism of the men who really knew something about music. I have come to the conclusion that much of what they said that now seems obstinately anti-Wagnerian was perfectly rational criticism for its day. We talk glibly of the verdict of posterity, as if posterity were the ideal judge. But is it? Is it not too lenient, too easy-going, to be that? Has it not become so familiar with the weaknesses of men of genius that it no longer notices them? Is not posterity, in the main, too sentimental to be perfectly judicial? In the work of every genius there is something against which our æsthetic sense rebels. His contemporaries react violently against his faults because they are so obvious, and because they leave the listeners with a sense of irritation against the artist who cannot himself see what is so obvious, and therefore goes some way to spoiling what might otherwise be a perfect work of art. By a paradox, it is because the same faults are so very obvious that they do not irritate posterity: it has become so used to them by repetition that it is resigned to them.

In the slow movement of Beethoven's fifth symphony there is a passage for the flutes so feeble that the word "inanity" is hardly too strong to apply to it. If it were signed with anyone's name but Beethoven's we should turn away from it with a contemptuous curl of the lip. Coming from him, and coming where it does, we merely pass it by with a tolerant shrug of the shoulders. Homer has nodded, but he remains

Homer. We had rather he had kept awake through the movement, but if he has dozed for fifteen seconds, well, let us pay the great man the courtesy of pretending not to notice it, and of listening with all the more eagerness and reverence to his wise talk when he wakes up. We can do this kind of thing because, for us, a classic is a privileged being. We know the total value of his treasure; and a bit of small change here or a few spurious coins there do not matter. But for his contemporaries no man is a classic, or can be expected to enjoy the immunity of a classic. I do not know whether the critics of 1810 or thereabouts poured their scorn upon this feeble passage in the C minor; but they would have been fully justified in so doing. Had they done so, however, and some delver into the past were to reprint their criticisms today, they would certainly be regarded as having failed to recognize Beethoven's greatness. The assumption would be unwarrantable.

*

* *

I have had the curiosity to read again what John Hullah had to say about Wagner in the early eighteensixties. At first sight Hullah seems obstinately unreceptive: but when we examine his remarks soberly there turns out to be a good deal of truth in them. Like Lobe and so many other people, he was plainly puzzled and irritated by Wagner's prose works, especially *Opera and Drama*; I am strongly inclined to believe that Wagner's verbal exposition of his ideals, instead of making the path easier for his music, made it much harder. The plain man of the mid-nineteenth century could be forgiven for assuming that so lame a thinker, so confused an expositor, and so verbose a writer was more than likely to produce music with all the defects of his prose.   It is difficult for us of today to see *Opera and Drama* as its contemporaries saw it. For us it is not only illuminated but clarified and ennobled by the later music of Wagner's prime; knowing the *Ring* and *Tristan* and the *Meistersinger* as we do, we can understand better the central argument of *Opera and Drama,* recognise the originality and the power of it, separate it from the mass of rubbish in which it is embedded and throw away the rubbish.

But to his contemporaries this was impossible. They had no *Ring* to help them: they could take *Opera and Drama* only for what it was on the face of it.   Is it any wonder that it aroused a good deal of repulsion, that its reading of the past seemed to many people dubious, and Wagner's personal claims to be a trifle arrogant?   With how much of *Opera and Drama* does any of us agree now?   Is it surprising that those who found so much in it to disagree with when it was fresh should have refused to hitch their wagon to the new star until they were quite sure it *was* a star?

Look at Hullah's criticism in the concrete.   He tells us that he had never seen one of Wagner's operas on the stage.   (He could not, under any circumstances, have heard any work later than *Lohengrin.*)   He had tried to attend the Paris production of *Tannhäuser* in March 1861, but did not arrive until the opera had been withdrawn after its third performance.   "But," he says, "I have the same acquaintance with this work that every musician has with nineteen-twentieths of the music with which he is acquainted—that which is derived from study and perusal.   I find in the pieces of which the *Tannhäuser* is composed an entire absence of musical construction and coherence; little melody, and that of the most unoriginal and *mesquin* kind; and harmony only remarkable for its restless, helpless, purposeless modulations. Lulli, the founder of French opera, was complained of, even in the height of his popularity, for the extent to which he carried recitative and *aria parlante*—forms, in good hands, capable of agreeable effect in themselves, and allowing opportunity to the ear to repose from the fatigue engendered by too long continued or too strongly accentuated rhythm. Wagner *out-Lullies* Lulli, and allows the persons of his drama 'of the future' to discourse about the past at a length and in a language which shows a wonderful want of understanding of the *present* patience of any auditory. Were these things found in an ordinary opera, one would simply dismiss it as a very indifferent and very tiresome opera. But they are matters of faith and of principle with the new school. Dullness, ugliness, and want of form are justified by all sorts of analogies which, true or false, are no consolation to those who suffer under them."

Supposing Wagner to have died after *Lohengrin,* would Hullah's criticism of *Tannhäuser* read so *very* stupidly today? It is a little splenetic, and not always wise; but is not a good deal of it rational enough? Is not the melody of *Tannhäuser* sometimes *mesquin*? Is not the opera sometimes very dull? Is not Wagner often long-winded? Do we not have to cut it pretty liberally today to induce our audiences to sit it through? Once more, do we not look with a lenient eye upon the earlier work because the same composer gave us the glorious things of the latter years? And is it reasonable to expect that a generation that did not

know these later works should have anticipated them?
The Wagner of *Tannhäuser* invited a good deal of
sharp criticism. We can hardly blame the critics of
the period for having responded to the invitation.
They were sometimes wrong, but not always so wrong
as a later day is inclined to think.

*

*　*

Contemporary criticism, then, is frequently right
enough in detail. Lobe was not without some basis
for his complaint against the Beethoven of the last
years. Scheibe was not wholly wrong as against Bach.
He charged the great man with being somewhat la-
boured, intricate, over-elaborate. There is some truth
in the charge, as every honest student of Bach is bound
to admit. For us, these occasional touches of over-
luxuriance of vocal ornamentation or—in the chorale
preludes—melodic arabesque or harmonic ingenuity
are hardly worth taking into account when we look at
Bach's stupenduous work as a whole. But in 1737 a
critic could not possibly see the work as a whole, nor
could he see the living Bach as a saint in a stained
glass window; and Scheibe was within his rights in
drawing attention, for the reader of the moment, to
what was undoubtedly a slight defect in the music of
the moment.

It is perhaps because no generation can see its own
art complete and from a distance that, as a rule, the
genuinely critical minds prefer to write about the art
of the past. It does not follow that they are not
interested in the art of their own day: it means only
that the critic, being himself an artist, prefers a subject

he can see right through and all round, and a material to work in that is thoroughly plastic in his hands. Charles Lamb preferred writing about the Elizabethans to writing about the poets of his own day, and was less appreciative of Keats that we could have desired. Marcel Proust says that a list of 19th century authors praised by Saint-Beuve would not have any of the great names at the top; but was this incompetence on Saint-Beuve's part, or the caution engendered in him by long practice in criticism,—an instinct that prompted him not to commit himself finally on any big subject till he could see it complete and from a distance? Mr. Max Beerbohm noted a similar apparent indifference in Swinburne's conversation to the leading figures of his own day: if the poet had heard of Rostand, he had forgotten him, says Mr. Beerbohm. "Indeed, I never heard Swinburne mention a single contemporary writer. His mind ranged and revelled always in the illustrious or obscure past. . . ." "In life, as in (that for him more truly actual thing) literature, it was always the preterit that enthralled him. Of any passing events, or anything the newspapers were full of, never a word from him."

*

*   *

This was an extreme case, perhaps, but Swinburne was not the only critic to feel the peculiar attraction of the preterit. For the critic writes primarily for himself, not for others: his writing is only one of the means by which he helps himself to realise the one passionate desire of his life—to understand; and he knows too well, from his study of the past, that it is impossible for him or anyone to understand fully the art of the present, changing as it does from moment to moment; as well expect the mathematician to solve a geometrical problem half of the factors of which are withheld from him.   One of our young English composers, the other day, naïvely asked the critics why they kept on writing about Bach and Brahms and Wagner, who had long been dead, instead of writing about composers such as himself, who were still alive. He addressed himself to the wrong quarter, however. The proper person to announce the young composer's doings is the journalist; and certainly the young composer of today cannot complain of lack of attention from the journalists: there can be very few young men of the last ten years who have not received more press publicity than fell to the lot of Bach, Beethoven, or Wagner at a similar age.   But to the critic the average new composer is neither a big enough subject nor a subject complete enough.   Some day, in spite even of his littleness, he may be of interest.   Mr. Beerbohm's phrase about "the illustrious *or obscure* past" is significant.   The critic is often extremely interested in the mediocrities of the past, because they throw a light on the geniuses of the time.   There may be fifty dramatists living today who can write a better play than Greene or Peele; but the work of these minor Elizabethans, poor as it is in itself, is of unending interest to the historian or the critic of the drama because it helps him to a better understanding of Shakespeare and the world in which Shakespeare lived. The Smith or Jones of today may be no worse a composer, for his period, than Paer or Steibelt was for his; but the critic may be forgiven for finding the latter more interesting, because he helps to make a certain stage of musical evolution clearer. The day may come when Smith or Jones also will be of real interest to the critic,—not so much for his own work as for the help he affords to the understanding of the great composer of, say, 1950. After all, this is immortality of a sort, and he should be grateful for it.

*

* *

Mr. Augustine Birrell, in a passage in his *Essays on Men, Women and Books* that has just caught my eye, seems to share my view that the true field for true criticism is the past. "The principles of taste," he says, "the art of criticism, are not acquired amidst the hurly-burly of living authors and the hasty judgment thereupon of hasty critics, but by study, careful and reverential, of the immortal dead. In this study the critics are of immense use to us. Dryden, Addison, Gray, Coleridge, Lamb, Hazlitt, Bagehot, Swinburne revealed to us their highest critical powers not while vivisecting a contemporary, but when expounding the anatomy of departed greatness. Teach me rightly to admire Milton and Keats, and I will find my own criticism of living poets. Help me to enjoy, however feebly, Homer and Dante, and I will promise not to lose my head over Pollok's *Course of Time* or Mr. Bailey's *Festus*. Fire my enthusiasm for Henry Vaughan or George Herbert, and I shall be able to distinguish between the muses of Miss Frances Ridley Havergal and Miss Christina Rossetti. Train me to become a citizen of the true Republic of Letters, and I shall not be found on my knees before false gods, or trooping with the vulgar to crown with laurel brazen brows."

I find, for my part, the application of these principles to music easy enough. Teach me rightly to admire Bach and Mozart, and I will find my own criticism of living composers. Help me to enjoy, however feebly, Palestrina and Purcell, and I will promise not to lose my head over Kistler's *Kunihild* or Puccini's *Manon*. Fire my enthusiasm for Wagner or Brahms, and I shall be able to distinguish between the muses of Darius Milhaud and Erik Satie. But I notice that Dr. Dyson throws doubt, by implication, on the correctness of this view. He seems to think that the present age in music lacks what the 19th century had, —distinct ideals and unquestionable standards of taste, summed up generally in Wagner and Brahms, or rather in the enlightened admirers of these. "To those whose lot it was," he says, "to observe the creative power of Wagner or of Brahms at close quarters, there was an atmosphere of character, of achievement, a conviction of permanent worth, which the passage of years rarely failed to enhance. We had not to deal here with comparatively uninstructed enthusiasms, but were in touch with minds whose knowledge covered the whole field of music, and whose sensitiveness was as discriminating with regard to the past as it was active and convinced with regard to the present. Was there today a body of mature opinion that could be compared without obvious incongruity to that which appraised the value of Wagner or Brahms? Was there anywhere today such a circle of unquestioned authority which either possessed or expounded a coherent artistic faith or found in any living composer at once the prime substance and the unfailing justification of its belief?"

*

*   *

But is it necessary to have a contemporary composer of unquestionably the first order to enable us to test the quality of all the others? Will not the great composers of the last generation or two serve for the purpose? Will not the great composers of the past ten or twelve generations serve even better? Is there anything in the art of Christina Rossetti that a student of Shakespeare cannot grasp? Is there likely to be anything in the art of Bartok, Stravinsky or Schönberg that students of the best music of the last four hundred years will find beyond them? To say "Yes" is only to pay a compliment to one's own vanity; it is to mark oneself off as above one's fellows in musical intelligence, to imply that *we*—some dozen or two of us— have an insight into the future that is denied •to ordinary mortals. The climax of this absurdity of conceit has surely been reached recently by Madame Marya Freund. "Schönberg," she says in a contribution to a volume of essays for that composer's fiftieth birthday (13th September 1924), "Schönberg is fifty years old. He is a hundred years old,—for he is many decades ahead of our epoch." There is not a single case in musical history of a composer being a century ahead of his time: the greatest composers have all been perfectly comprehensible to the average instructed music-lover of their day. Is it *a priori* likely that in Schönberg nature has produced a composer so immensely above the musical intelligence of today that the whole world will have to develop another hundred years before it is capable of grasping his message? I will not prophesy like Madame Freund; I will only say that all this is extremely improbable.

Will not the period of 1600 help us with that light on the present situation that Dr. Dyson seems to despair of finding? There ensued then a whole generation in which first-rate composers bore no larger proportion to the general crowd of talents, mediocrities, dilettanti and charlatans than they do today. Need this scarcity of first-rate men and the absence of a generally accepted standard of æsthetic have deterred any good 17th century musician from passing judgment upon the art of the time? The ideals and the methods of music have not changed more today from those of Wagner and Brahms than the Italian ideals and methods of 1600 to 1630 did from those of Palestrina and Marenzio and Byrd. But sound musicians of that epoch who might have judged the new music in terms of that of the two preceding generations would have been right. The opera, the accompanied solo song, the chamber monody, were fully as different, in ideals, in technique, in texture, from the 16th century Mass or madrigal as the *Pacific 231* or the *Pierrot Lunaire* is from *Tristan* or the passacaglia in the fourth symphony of Brahms. But any musical Birrell of the early 17th century who might have said, "Teach me rightly to admire Palestrina and Marenzio, and I shall be able to say where Caccini and Benedetti and the Monteverdi of *The Combat of Tancred and Clorinda* stand," would have been justified. Perhaps posterity will decide also that the present day was not unjustified in testing its newest composers by the general standards of the art of the last four hundred years. Novelty of device or of texture means nothing; in a very few years these things become so familiar that the plain music-lover is surprised to hear that they were once startlingly new (think, for example, of the novel effects with which Rossini and Meyerbeer staggered their contemporaries). The only thing in a musical work that will keep it alive is the amount of good musical thinking there is in it; and if anyone tells us that the thought of any composer of the present day is so far ahead of our time that only a handful of initiates here and there can follow it, and that it will only become generally comprehensible when the whole musical world has risen to his terrific height of intelligence, we can only ask him to give us some evidence from history that so unique a phenomenon is probable.

*
* *

The long view,—the view from the hill—then, is that our own epoch, full as it is of change, hardly differs in essentials from any other, and certainly in no respect whatever from that of the Florentine revolution; and that it offers no insoluble problems to contemporary criticism. There has never been a period yet in which the plain musical sense of the day has not been able to assess living composers pretty well as accurately as the later generations. Such blunders as it makes are in the direction of a temporary overvaluing of secondary men, such as Gade and Spohr; and it is impossible to say, without a careful scrutiny

of the records of the time, how far the capable and
thoughtful musicans of the period shared the popular
delusion about men of this sort. We are told that
when Spohr's German employer refused to let him
come to conduct a work of his in England the aid of
the Foreign Office was invoked. But it is possible for
a Telemann, a Spohr, a Rossini or a Meyerbeer to be
the idol of the general public and yet be quite accurately assessed by the competent musicians of their
day. Lobe, as we have seen, was not duped by Spohr;
and the probability is that the latter's genuinely instructed contemporaries had no more illusions as to the
reasons for his vogue than their successors of today
have as to the reasons for the vogue of *Tosca* or *Sam-
son and Delilah*.

*

* *

It may be said that there is considerable variety of
opinion as to the relative value of contemporary composers. True; but that does not prevent a general
agreement on the main principles. We have no more
right to expect absolute unanimity in the world's judgment of musicians than in the world's judgment of politicians or soldiers. What we have to remember is
that such differences of opinion as there are regarding
contemporary composers are not due to the fact that
they are our contemporaries. We differ over them
not because one critic among us is more "advanced"
than another, that one is "conservative" and the other
"reactionary," but simply because tastes differ. It is
not any tinder that will catch fire from any spark:
there are natural affinities and repulsions to be con-

sidered.   A man responds or fails to respond to certain music by virtue not only of what the music is but of what he is—a point too often overlooked, especially by the victim of an irrational prejudice.   The other day some critic or other informed the world that he preferred Milhaud to Beethoven because Milhaud deals in sensations and Beethoven in moods.   In the same way, I might say that I prefer Sauterne to port, or apples to pears; but so purely personal a preference is hardly worth announcing to the world at large.   Preferences and repulsions of this kind are not limited to the music of one's own day.   There are still anti-Wagnerians and anti-Brahmsians among us. Their repulsion is a matter not of unfamiliarity with the idiom but of temperamental dislike for the personality that expresses itself through it.   There are people among us who rub the whole of Elgar and Strauss off the slate with the assurance of a mediæval monk scratching out a Greek drama to give him room on the parchment for some meditations of his own on the nature of grace.   Dr. Percy Buck confesses that he "cannot read Dickens nor listen to Weber"; and so, he says, "I leave them alone, quite genuinely regretting my disability and envying others who can get a pleasure closed to me."   Had Dr. Buck been a journalist who, after the first performance of *Der Freischütz* or *Oberon,* expressed himself unable to see anything of value in the music, he would probably figure today among Mr. Calvocoressi's list of "reminders" from the past.   Yet the reason for Dr. Buck's low opinion of the *Oberon* overture would have been not that the music was too new for him, that it ran counter to the principles of judgment he had derived from the music of the past, but simply that he was not made for Weber nor Weber for him.

*
* *

The extreme "antis" cancel each other out; they constitute a very small proportion of the musical public. Among the remainder there will still be differences of opinion as to the "placing" of this composer or that: one will rank Stravinsky above Delius, or Ravel above Bartok, and *vice versa*. But I believe that if five hundred of the best and best-informed musical minds of the day,—executants, critics and amateurs—were gathered together (I leave out the composers because they are notoriously bad judges of each other) and asked which were the ten mature composers of the present decade who would be remembered and performed fifty years hence, there would not be three per cent of variation among them. Further, I believe that, with a small percentage of variation, they would agree as to which works of each composer would survive him, and as to the relative future standing of the ten composers; and I believe that posterity would confirm their general verdict.

Am I now claiming for myself that insight into the future that I have denied to be within the possibility of others? I do not think so. I am merely asserting that every age has instinctively picked out its best men (so far as their music was generally accessible) and the best works of the best men; and that no good reason has yet been given for thinking that our own generation is any less intelligent in this respect than the twelve or fifteen generations that have preceded it. Where I deny to any of us the power to pierce the future is not in the matter of musical personalities but in the matter of musical principles. To say that Schönberg's *Pelléas and Mélisande* will survive because we feel that the music of it is good in virtue of the principles that make other music good for us,—whether this music be that of the Mass, the madrigal, the opera, the symphony, the song, the symphonic poem, or what not—or to say that *Pelléas and Mélisande* will perish because the music is not good in this sense, either of these is intelligible and intelligent. But it is neither intelligible nor intelligent to say that *Pelléas and Mélisande* will be regarded as a masterpiece a century from now because only then will humanity as a whole have attained the right eminence from which to see it. That implies not a knowledge of musical values—which remain essentially the same in spite of all changes of form, of vocabulary and of resource—but a prophetic vision of the inevitable course of musical evolution through the next hundred years. Such a vision is impossible to any man, as the history of music teaches us pointedly enough; we can have no conception, for one thing, of the next dynamic personality or two, who will divert the general stream of evolution in their own direction; nor can we have any conception of which among the many new technical resources of today will be found generally useable by the geniuses of the next two decades, and which will be quietly dropped. Vincenzo Galilei would have been greatly astonished had he returned to earth in 1650 and seen the strange building—the Italian opera—that had sprung up upon the foundation he had laid with his Song of Ugolino some sixty or seventy years earlier. Vicentino would have been astonished, had he also returned to earth in 1650, to realize that nothing whatever had come of his attempts to revive the Greek chromatic and enharmonic genera, or of that archicembalo and archiorgano of his invention in which he was so liberal with his sharps and flats. Perhaps the astonishment of Alois Haba, the composer in quarter-tones, may be equally great if he revisits the earth fifty years hence; and the astonishment of some of the professors of polytonality, in that distant time, may be as profound as Caccini's would have been had he re-awakened in 1725 and heard the new counterpoint of Bach. We can be sure of nothing in connection with the future of music except that we can be sure of nothing.

One of the profoundest reflections ever made by a musical historian was that of Ambros upon the eager Florentines who thought they were re-making music in their own image: "they thought they were making the age; but it was the age that made them. . . . The Spirit of Music knew well what it wanted. What tools it made use of did not matter for the realisation of its aims: nothing would remain of these." A hundred years from now, people will know what work it was that the Spirit of Music had in hand in the early 20th century. We cannot possibly know; all we can be sure of is that the great majority of the tools for the work will by then have been thrown upon the rubbish heap as the great majority of those of the period from 1575 to 1625 have been. Nor even if we know by intuition which of our own music will be regarded as good a century hence can we know what the composers of that music will be to the critics of that day. The work of criticism is never finished: in this sense it is true that values are unfixable. We can no more anticipate what the next century will see in our own best music than the man of 1824 could anticipate what we now see in the Ninth Symphony. Some of the points that we think most significant in our music will then be of less significance; but I do not think that posterity will upset our general distribution of contemporary values. In the 19th century, the enthusiasts for the music of the "New German" school laid too much stress on theoretic principles and too little on practice: they over-rated Liszt because his æsthetic theory was fascinating, and were too uncritical of the quality of the music in which that theory was embodied. We may be fairly sure that in another thirty years all the contemporary admirations that come only from sympathy with a new speculative point of view will be subjects for the mortuary: nothing of our judgments will remain but those that deal with the music purely and simply as music; and what is vital in the newest composer of today can be so only in virtue of qualities that are common to the great music of all ages. There have never yet been great composers who were great only for a handful of their contemporaries: the greatest minds are, in the fullest sense of the word, common. "Poets," says Wordsworth, "do not write for poets alone, but for men. Unless therefore we are advocates for that admiration which subsists on ignorance, and that pleasure which arises from hearing what we do not understand, the poet must descend from his supposed height; and, in order to excite rational sympathy, he must express himself as other men express themselves." We shall not go far wrong if we

apply this to the music of those composers of our own
day whose proper audience is alleged to be that of a
century hence.

*
*   *

So I can go back to my work to some extent com-
forted and assured.   The future does not concern me,
except in so far as the past supplies me with one or two
purely negative conclusions with regard to it.   The
critic's concern is not with principles, theories, specula-
tions, prophecies, but only with the present facts of
æsthetic experience; he has to judge new music not by
what it professes to be or hopes to be, but by what it
is; and for this kind of judgment the essential thing is
not forward thought but "back thought."   Our tele-
scopes are useless for the future: they can only help us
by bringing the past nearer to us, and so enabling us to
compare the present incomplete medley with others
that have completed themselves and lie open in every
detail to our inspection.   We must work always with
the past in our minds if we are to maintain a due perspective of the music around us.   The only proportionate view is the long view.   "Let thy thoughts,"
said Sir Thomas Browne, "be of things which have not
entered into the heart of beasts: think of things long
past, and long to come: acquaint thyself with the chor-
agium of the stars, and consider the vast expanse beyond us.   Let intellectual tubes give thee a glance of
things which visive organs reach not."

*
*   *

A NOTE ON THE TYPE IN
WHICH THIS BOOK IS SET

• •

*The type in which this book has been set (on the Lino-
type) is Caslon Old Face, a faithful and authentic re-
production from the original patterns of William
Caslon I. Historically considered, Caslon's old face
types are the most important contribution the English
speaking world has ever made to the art of typography.
No other face has ever attained to so lasting and
general a popularity. Caslon's types were made to
read. Even their apparent imperfections contribute to
this effect being, in fact, the result of a deliberate
artistry which sought above all else for legibility in the
printed page.*

SET UP, ELECTROTYPED AND PRINTED
BY THE VAIL-BALLOU PRESS, INC.,
BINGHAMTON, N. Y. · ESPARTO
PAPER   MANUFACTURED   IN
SCOTLAND AND FURNISHED
BY W. F. ETHERINGTON &
CO., NEW YORK · BOUND
BY THE H. WOLFF ES-
TATE, NEW YORK. ·

WAGNER

AS MAN AND ARTIST

BY ERNEST NEWMAN

Lawrence Gilman in *The New York Tribune:* "Mr. Newman's Wagnerian criticism is unequalled for insight and acumen, is one of those clear-eyed and cool minded historians—psychologist, philosopher and artist in one. A masterpiece of enlivened scholarship and critical insight. Surgical wit, flexibility, sensitiveness and penetration, a blend of irony and human understanding."

A. Donald Douglas in *The Nation:* "The first American appearance of Mr. Newman's *Wagner* should be an occasion for public rejoicing."

Daniel Gregory Mason in *The Literary Review:* "A characteristically brilliant psychological study."

Pitts Sanborn in *The New York Tribune:* "Replete as is every page with fact and thought there is never anything heavy or obscure about the writing. It has vividness, vivacity, impetus, wit, as well as a vast fund of information.

A MUSICAL MOTLEY

BY ERNEST NEWMAN

A new edition, revised and reset, of a delightful volume of musical studies first published in 1919. Some of the chapters are: A Trap for the Critics, The Amateur Composer, The Small Poem in Music, Composers and Obituary Notices, On Instruments and Their Players, The Poets and Orchestral Instruments, On Musical Surgery, Mad Monarchs and Music, Some Musical Parodies, Criticism by Code, Music and the Grotesque, The Confessions of a Musical Critic, The Perennial Bohemian, The Best Hundred Scores, Bach in the Opera House, The Weary Willies of Music, Futurist Staging, On Green Sickness and the Blues, etc.

$5.00